INTERNATIONAL COOKING

INTERNATIONAL COOKING

Robin Howe

PARK LANE PRESS

First published in 1980 by Park Lane Press,
36 Park Street, London WIY 4DE

Editor: Fiona Roxburgh
Art director: Gail Engert
Series designer: Rod Springett Associates
Photographer: Paul Kemp
Props research: Jane Kemp

Text set by SX Composing Ltd, Rayleigh, England
Printed and bound by Dai Nippon Printing Company, Tokyo, Japan

Contents

Notes   6

Introduction   7

Starters and soups   8

Cheese and egg dishes   38

Rice dishes   48

Fish   58

Meat   76

Poultry and game   104

Vegetables and salads   130

Puddings, cakes and pastries   156

Glossary   184

Index   190

Acknowledgments   192

Notes

All spoon measures are level unless otherwise stated.

Egg sizes are specified only where exact quantities are vital to the recipe.

Metric and imperial measurements have been calculated separately. Use one set of measurements only as they are not exact equivalents.

Cooking times may vary depending on the individual oven. Dishes should be placed in the centre of the oven unless otherwise specified.

All flour is plain and all sugar granulated unless otherwise specified.

Spoon measures can be bought in both imperial and metric sizes to give accurate measurement of small quantities.

For further details on the essential ingredients of Western and Eastern cooking there is a glossary on pages 184–189.

Introduction

I am often asked where I get my recipes from. The answer is simple. My life has been one long cook's tour, and as a child I learned an important lesson, to eat what I was given, with the result that there are few, if any, foods that I dislike. Therefore, when I first went abroad it did not occur to me to ask for kippers and porridge but I simply ate what the French gave me. Later I went off to Germany where I attended a domestic-science course. After I married I went to live in Vienna, and then in Budapest, travelling extensively within the region to Czechoslovakia, Yugoslavia and the Balkans. How well we ate in those hectic days, such quantities of food and with what dedication did the peoples of Central Europe cook. We talked at great length about food, happy to divert our attentions from the impending war. When the Second World War came, I went to the West Indies where I learned to enjoy salt fish and ackee, bread fruit and such sweet dishes as matrimony made with fruits. Later I went to Egypt to join my husband. In the Sudan I was invited to eat *ful Sudani* soup and other local dishes. While in Cairo we were fortunate to be paying guests in a Jewish family where the food was a classic mixture of Arabic and Jewish. After the war, we returned to Germany and then went to Turkey where I lost my culinary heart. I learned to appreciate real yogurt and 'sweet water', and the splendid fish from the Black Sea and the Bosporus. From Turkey we went to Syria and the Lebanon, almost a continuation of Turkish food but with a few differences. We went often to Israel whose cooking is a blend of many influences as a result of the influx of Jews from all over the world.

From the Lebanon we went to India where we remained for almost fifteen years, visiting every corner of the subcontinent, including Nepal and Pakistan. Fortunately Burma was then open to visitors and I stayed there receiving tremendous help from all kinds of people. From Burma I went to Bangkok armed with many introductions, including one to a Thai princess who had written a Thai cookbook. I then stayed a while in Singapore and, among the many who taught me about the local Chinese food was the mother of Lee Kuan Yew, the Prime Minister. She loved to cook and to talk about food and gave lessons on Chinese cooking to the wives of foreign diplomats. My cook's tour took me also to Hong Kong and to Malaysia where I went to a domestic-science school to learn about Malay curries and other dishes. In South Korea, I was adopted by the ladies of the university who took me into their homes. 'So seldom', they said, 'had anyone from the West come to see how we eat'. A pity, for they eat well and have sophisticated tastes. Finally, my travels have taken me to Japan, to the Hawaian Islands which will always mean to me the aroma of pineapples, and to the United States.

Now, nearly fifty years later, I have learned that if you want to find a place in the hearts and homes of people everywhere, forget about politics and concentrate on cooking. Talk about food and local cooking – it is the finest passport in the world. In presenting this selection of international recipes, I have chosen not restaurant dishes but those which are made in the ordinary homes of people all over the world; they are neither too complicated nor time-consuming and the ingredients called for are readily available throughout Britain.

Robin Howe

Starters
and soups

Starters

Hors d'oeuvres, or starters as they are more frequently called today, should be easy to digest, stimulating and never clog the appetite or palate. They can be served either hot or cold.

The Russian hors d'oeuvre or *zakuski* was the parent form of this course and in the days of the Tsars the variety must have been fabulous with countless plates of food to whet the appetite, washed down with untold glasses of vodka. *Zakuski* is usually now served as a complete meal rather than as a starter.

The Scandinavian *smorgasbord*, which means literally 'sandwich table', is in reality nothing but a gargantuan display of starters. It is a course which is said to have originated in the days of large country house-parties when guests arrived with gifts of food to contribute to the feast. All the different dishes were arranged on long trestle tables around which the guests would gather, taking their choice in the same way as Scandinavians do today.

The Italians also appreciate greatly elaborate starters or *antipasti* and, like the French, serve them only at the midday meal.

The British are, perhaps, not very imaginative with their starters although there are some splendid first courses, smoked salmon, for example, which is surely the finest starter to a formal meal in the world. At one time the British favoured oysters as a gentle beginning to a meal and many still do despite their high price. The Germans have a repertoire of soused and smoked fish dishes, such as Bismarck herring and *roll-mops*, while the people of the eastern Mediterranean consider starters as a way of life. Many are the hours spent in the Mediterranean and Balkan countries consuming small 'eats' and sipping a translucent white liquor named ouzo.

Starters are also to be found in the Far East, in particular in China where the *dim sum* or small eats are so popular that there are special restaurants for them. The Japanese equivalent are the *sashimi* or *shushi* bars, which are also opening up in London now.

Smoked salmon
Britain

It is generally agreed that the smoked salmon of Scotland, where 'the rivers run true and sweet', is the finest; after that comes the Norwegian, then the Canadian. Ideally it is sliced immediately before it is served; in a restaurant, for example, it should be sliced in front of the customer. Good quality, thinly sliced salmon needs no blandishments, not even a squeeze of lemon or freshly ground pepper. Salmon are at their best in May and June. Serve with thin brown bread and butter.

Smoked salmon butter
Britain

TO SERVE FOUR–SIX

INGREDIENTS
225 g (8 oz) unsalted butter
225 g (8 oz) smoked salmon
juice of 1 lemon

This is a recipe that does not call for the finest Scottish salmon, although the finer the salmon the better the dish. Tinned tuna fish can be prepared in the same way.

Have the butter at room temperature and then cream it. Pound the salmon to a paste. Combine butter and salmon and blend thoroughly. Add the lemon juice, press into a jar – I like to use a small brown stone one – and chill. Serve with crisp toast and wedges of lemon, as for a pâté.

10

Potted shrimps

Britain

TO SERVE FOUR

INGREDIENTS
450 g (1 lb) shrimps
white pepper
freshly grated nutmeg
100 g (4 oz) unsalted butter

These brown shrimps preserved in butter are very much a British speciality. They became popular during the nineteenth century in some of the great London clubs and this led to a worldwide mail-order distribution. Cayenne pepper may be used instead of white pepper and some people like to add a touch of ginger and mace. Other shellfish may be treated in this way.

Preheat the oven to 190°C, 375°F, Gas Mark 5. Shell the shrimps and drop into a small baking dish. Sprinkle lightly with pepper and a good grating of nutmeg. Sprinkle 25 g (1 oz) of the butter, cut into slivers, over the top and bake in the oven for 10 minutes. Take from the oven and let the shrimps cool. Meanwhile melt the rest of the butter and let it cool until it begins to thicken again. Press the shrimps into 4 small jars, or into 1 larger one, and pour over the melted butter, which must come to the top. Put into the refrigerator and leave at least overnight before using: in fact the shrimps will keep for 3–4 weeks in the refrigerator, and perfectly for months if deep frozen.

The correct way to serve potted shrimps is not chilled, but warmed gently until the butter just begins to flow. Turn them out and gently heat in a small pan, then arrange the shrimps with their butter on lettuce leaves. However, if you prefer to serve the shrimps cold, then turn them out and cut into thick chunks. Serve at once with thinly sliced buttered brown bread.

Prawns cooked in port

Camarões com vinho do porto
Portugal

TO SERVE FOUR

INGREDIENTS
50 g (2 oz) butter
225 g (8 oz) onions, thinly sliced
450 g (1 lb) prawns
4 tablespoons dry port
4 eggs
225 ml (8 fl oz) double cream
salt and pepper to taste

For this recipe the prawns should be uncooked, cleaned and de-veined, then cut into halves. As uncooked prawns are not easily come by and you must perforce buy them ready cooked and usually peeled, add them to the pan *after* the port and cook only long enough to heat them, about 3 minutes, then continue with the recipe as described.

Preheat the oven to 160°C, 325°F, Gas Mark 3. Melt the butter in a heavy frying pan, add the onions and fry over a medium heat until they are soft and a golden brown. Add the prawns, stir and gently cook over a moderate heat for 5 minutes, or until they are a good pink. Add the port, stir gently and cook for 4–5 minutes. Meanwhile beat the eggs into the cream, and add salt and pepper. When the prawns are ready, turn them into a baking dish. Pour the egg and cream mixture over the top, mix well but gently and bake in the oven until the custard has set, 30–35 minutes.

Instead of onions, spring onions are often used in this dish and they give a more delicate flavour.

Top: prawns cooked in port
bottom: potted shrimps and 'caviar' niçoise

'Caviar' niçoise

France

TO SERVE FOUR–SIX

INGREDIENTS
8 large anchovy fillets, chopped
350 g (12 oz) olives, stoned and chopped
100 g (4 oz) tuna fish in oil, flaked
50 g (2 oz) butter, softened
3–4 cloves garlic crushed
freshly ground white pepper

This pleasant little dish of tuna fish and anchovies comes from the French Riviera, where anchovy fillets in brine are used, but fillets in oil make a good substitute. If using brined fillets, rinse them under running cold water to take off the salt. Drain the tuna fish before flaking.

Combine the fillets, olives and tuna fish and rub through a mouli-légumes. Add the butter, beat well, flavour with garlic, and then season with freshly ground pepper – no salt as the other ingredients have their full share of this. Turn into a small earthenware jar, chill and serve with French bread.

Oysters on the half shell

Britain

TO SERVE TWO

12 large oysters

Throughout the world there is a rich array of oysters from which to choose, although unhappily they are becoming more and more expensive everywhere. However, from time to time oyster lovers must indulge and the finest way is with large and truly splendid oysters served on the shell. Oysters should be opened just before they are served, but opening them at home is not an easy business unless one has strong hands, an oyster knife and some expertise. However, many years ago the great French chef, Louis Diat, told of a trick he had learned from a Mr Ronald Toner. As he explained: 'He puts the oysters in a fairly hot oven, 200°C, 400°F, Gas Mark 6, for 5–6 minutes, depending on their size, or even 7 minutes for very large ones; then he drops them into ice-cold water. The heat relaxes the muscles and they can be opened as easily as a clam, yet the shell is so heavy that the heat never affects the oysters at all.'

Oysters to be eaten raw are left loose in the lower, deeper half of their shells, placed on a chilled plate and served with cut lemon and freshly ground pepper. In Britain oysters are in season from September to April, i.e. whenever there is an 'r' in the name of the month.

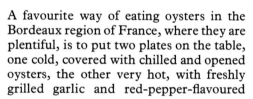

Oysters with sausages

Les huîtres à la bordelaise
France

A favourite way of eating oysters in the Bordeaux region of France, where they are plentiful, is to put two plates on the table, one cold, covered with chilled and opened oysters, the other very hot, with freshly grilled garlic and red-pepper-flavoured sausages, accompanied by a bottle of red or white Bordeaux wine.

It is the custom to eat first a hot sausage and follow it up with a cold oyster, then a good gulp of wine.

Oysters in champagne

USA

TO SERVE TWO

INGREDIENTS
150 ml (¼ pint) champagne
150 ml (¼ pint) clear
  chicken consommé
12 large oysters, opened
25 g (1 oz) butter
salt and freshly ground
  white pepper

Eating oysters must have been a very ancient pastime for archaeologists have discovered that many of early man's habitations are marked by piles of oyster shells.

Oyster eating as a 'sport' was much in vogue in the late 1850s when there was a professional oyster-eater known as Dando who was honoured in *Blackwood's Magazine* with an epitaph in blank verse and became the hero of a tale written by Thackeray. For eight months of the year Dando would 'crawl' from oyster house to oyster house often 'forgetting' to pay for the oysters he consumed, for which neglect he was often brought before the magistrates. But he had an Irish rival who, for a small wager, devoured 200 full-sized Malahides in 19 minutes and 35 seconds with ease. Alas, it was to be his last meal. For this recipe a chafing dish is required.

Pour the champagne into the chafing dish, add the consommé and bring to the boil. The moment it boils, add the liquid from the oysters, let the liquid come once more to the boil, add the oysters and immediately extinguish the flame under the chafing dish. Add the butter, salt and pepper to taste and serve at once, accompanied by the remainder of the champagne.

Oysters Rockefeller

USA

TO SERVE FOUR

INGREDIENTS

450 g (1 lb) raw spinach leaves
6 shallots or spring onions
2 tablespoons chopped parsley
1 stalk celery, chopped
¼ teaspoon dried tarragon
¼ teaspoon dried chervil
dash of Tabasco sauce
salt and cayenne pepper
½ cup fine dry breadcrumbs
3–4 tablespoons Pernod or anisette
50 g (2 oz) butter
coarse salt
2 dozen oysters on the half shell

One might ask, why cook oysters? However, this recipe from the USA is one of the world's most celebrated oyster recipes and is supposed to have originated in a famous New Orleans restaurant called Antoine's. According to the story, a guest to whom it was served remarked, 'This dish is as rich as Rockefeller' – so the dish was at once named Oysters Rockefeller. Recipes for it vary considerably: since the chef at Antoine's was supposed to have kept his original recipe a deep dark secret, others could only guess at the ingredients and method. The number of ingredients that went into that first Oysters Rockefeller was 18; this version economizes with a mere 13 if you count salt and pepper as two. Pernod or Pastis gives an intriguing flavour to many sauces.

Preheat the oven to 200°C, 400°F, Gas Mark 6. Wash and chop the spinach and put it, together with the shallots, parsley and celery, through the finest blade of a mincer twice, or whirl in a liquidizer. Add the dried herbs, Tabasco, and salt and pepper (some cooks prefer black pepper). Add the breadcrumbs and Pernod, mix well, add the butter to the mixture and mix again. This will make a thickish paste.

Prepare 24 tartlet tins. Fill these almost to the top with coarse salt and on top of each place an oyster on the half shell. Put them into the oven for about 5 minutes, or until the edges begin to curl. Take from the oven and put a tablespoonful of the spinach paste over each oyster and return to the oven for about 4 minutes, or until the sauce is melted. Take the oysters from the tins and serve at once on a hot dish.

Left: oysters in champagne
right: oysters Rockefeller

Sushi and sashimi

Japan

These two very Japanese snacks are first cousins and among the oldest known of Japanese foods. Of the two, *sushi* is the older and, to quote the Japanese, 'is prized by rich and poor alike'.

It is hard to call either of these foods a dish since they consist of small, raw, cold pieces of fish and vegetables taken as a snack at noon, or in-between meals. *Sushi* and *sashimi* bars are to be found everywhere in Japan and you either eat at a bar counter, where everything is prepared in front of you, or choose from a selection on a lacquer-ware platter. You can have boxes or baskets of them delivered at your home, or simply take them home with you from the bar.

Sushi and *sashimi* are similar except that the latter is only fish, while among the *sushi* snippets are bits of seaweed, cooked egg, rather like bits of an omelette, as well as prawns, octopus, thinly sliced raw fish and numerous other delicacies. All of these are served with their own sauces, into which you dip the food. Most Westerners blanch at the thought of eating raw fish. But you learn. When I first went to Tokyo I had been warned on no account to miss *sushi* and *sashimi*. I decided I would take my first *sashimi* alone so that, should I not like this pride of Japan, only I and the *sashimi* maker would know. I need not have worried. First I was given a cup of the hot green tea that was served throughout the meal, as is usual in Japan – although some people prefer *sake*, Japanese rice wine. I stared at the counter. There arrayed in front of me were bits of cuttlefish, prawns, clams, bream, scarlet tuna fish looking like strips of raw meat, strips of fish called *toro*, a paler and more oily relative of the tuna, abalone and scallops. I watched the *sashimi* man at his work.

He deftly and skilfully took small portions of vinegared rice from a tub beside him, flipping it between his palms and, in a matter of seconds, forming a little rice shape. The *sashimi* makers of Tokyo are especially famous for the moulding of the rice. The customer indicates what he would like on his rice and this is swiftly placed on the mound, decorated with a leaf or with seaweed and served two at a time on a brightly hued lacquer plate with soya sauce or with strips of ginger. Then and there I became an addict, for the quality and freshness of the foods served are of the highest, and the artistry with which both are served is something to be seen and never forgotten.

I do not suggest that you try to make either of them in your own home, even with frozen fish. But if in Japan, and in these days of cheap air travel and package tours, this is no longer a flight of fancy, do throw away all inhibitions about raw food and boldly attack as soon as possible either or both *sushi* and *sashimi*.

Lucca eyes

Lucca-Augen
Germany

TO SERVE FOUR

INGREDIENTS

225 g (8 oz) minced raw
  beef
2 egg yolks, lightly beaten
½ small onion, chopped
salt and pepper
4 slices white bread,
  1 cm (¼ in) thick
1 small jar caviar
4 oysters

This recipe, a refinement of Beef tartare (*see page 21*), is not named after the ancient Tuscan city of Lucca but after a popular Viennese operatic soprano, Pauline Lucca, who delighted audiences throughout Europe in the middle of the nineteenth century. Not only had she a golden voice but lovely eyes, inspiring the chef of the then famous Kempinski restaurant in Berlin to create this recipe. It is suggested as a prelude to a special breakfast, maybe for the morning after the night before. However, it can be served also as an hors d'oeuvre. Naturally Iranian caviar is to be preferred but a lesser quality one may be

substituted. The meat must be of the tenderest and freshest; the oysters fresh out of their shells.

Knead the meat thoroughly with the egg yolks, add the onion, salt and pepper (and if liked a few drops of Worcestershire sauce). Toast the bread lightly on both sides. Spread each piece of toast with some of the meat, add the caviar in a small half-moon shape and inside the 'half moon' place the oyster. The effect should be that of a 'sparkling' eye.

Smoked cod's roe salad

Taramasalata
Greece

TO SERVE FOUR

INGREDIENTS

225 g (½ lb) soft white
  bread
225 g (½ lb) smoked cod's
  roe
olive oil
lemon juice

Taramasalata used to be made with the pressed dried roe of the grey mullet, but in recent years this has become almost as expensive as caviar. So the Greeks also prepare this favourite salad with smoked cod's roe. The following is one of the simpler and most popular variations.

Soak the bread in warm water until very soft. Dry and squeeze until very dry and crumbly. Crumble the cod's roe finely and

combine the two, mixing well. Gradually add enough olive oil until the mixture is the consistency of a purée, of medium texture, then add enough lemon juice to loosen it.

It is not possible to say exactly how much olive oil or lemon juice is required, but not very much. If possible, use Greek olive oil for an authentic flavour.

Top: Lucca eyes; *bottom:* smoked cod's roe salad

Angels on horseback
Britain

TO SERVE FOUR

INGREDIENTS
butter for frying
8 slices bread
8 rashers streaky bacon
8 oysters
cayenne pepper to taste
lemon juice

According to the French, the British delight in giving *'les plats aux noms imagés'* and this must surely be right. Angels on horseback (*Anges à cheval*) brings a smile to the French face, as does *Diables à cheval* (below). Such dishes at one time were served as savouries at the end of the meal, a habit deplored by the famous French chef, Escoffier. Small Angels on horseback can be served as cocktail snacks.

In old recipes large fresh oysters were called for but this dish can be prepared with smaller or second-grade oysters, or even tinned ones. Large mussels can be prepared in the same fashion. Instead of fried bread, buttered toast may be used.

Preheat the oven to 200°C, 400°F, Gas Mark 6. The bread can be cut into triangles or in rounds and should be about 2 cm (½ in) thick.

Heat enough butter to fry the bread until golden on both sides and crisp. Put aside but keep hot. In the same pan half-fry the bacon. Take from the pan and place one oyster on each piece of bacon, sprinkle lightly with cayenne pepper and lemon juice. Wrap the bacon round the oyster and fasten with a toothpick. Place the prepared rolls on a baking sheet and bake in the oven for 6–7 minutes to cook the bacon completely, or grill the bacon rolls at least 15 cm (6 in) from the heat for about 4 minutes. Overcooking will toughen the oysters. Put the 'angels' on the pieces of fried bread, carefully removing the toothpick without destroying the shape.

Serve hot, garnished with parsley or, better still, with watercress.

Devils on horseback
Britain

TO SERVE FOUR

INGREDIENTS
8 slices bread
butter for frying
8 rashers bacon
8 prunes, soaked and
    stoned

In Victorian days this recipe was prepared with the so-called Carlsbad or French plums stuffed with *foie gras*. Today, instead of *foie gras*, the prunes or plums could be stuffed with a good quality liver pâté, but this is optional. An extra refinement was serving a jug of cream and a pot of English mustard with them.

Fry the bread in the butter until golden brown and crisp. Half-fry the bacon. Place a prune or plum on each slice, roll up tightly and fix them with toothpicks. Either bake in the oven at 220°C, 425°F, Gas Mark 7 for a few minutes to crisp the bacon, as for Angels on horseback (*see* above), or put under the grill. Serve the 'devils' hot on fried bread.

Top: angels on horseback
bottom: devils on horseback

Snails

Escargots
France

TO SERVE FOUR

INGREDIENTS

4 dozen cleaned and
  prepared snails with
  their shells
soft breadcrumbs, soaked
  slightly in olive oil
2 cloves garlic, finely
  chopped
2–3 tablespoons finely
  chopped parsley

Sauce

2–3 tablespoons olive oil
2 tablespoons finely
  chopped parsley
2 tablespoons finely
  chopped mushrooms
2 tablespoons finely
  chopped shallots or
  onions
1 clove garlic, crushed
2 teaspoons flour
275 ml (½ pint) dry white
  wine
salt, pepper, cayenne
  pepper and nutmeg to
  taste
2 egg yolks, lightly beaten

There is a romantic story of the origin of the snail. Venus, the Goddess of Love, at one time descended from her heavenly abode and settled for a while on earth, near Narbonne, with a human lover. She smuggled out with her from the heavens some of Jupiter's favourite food, snails with golden shells and a single wing that enabled them to rise in the air like a helicopter. When Venus finally returned to the heavens above with, I understand, some regret, she left the snails to her lover out of gratitude. To prevent their flying back to the heavens with her, she clipped off their wings and changed their golden shells to a pale fawn. For several centuries afterwards the Catalans, who are supposedly the descendants of the union between Venus and her earthly lover, collected thousands of snails once a year and ceremoniously sacrificed them to the Goddess of Love, their divine ancestress and benefactor.

The size of snails was a matter of great pride to the Romans who organized snail farms called *cochlearia* where snails were fattened with wine until they reached an enormous size. In Liguria, in Italy, there is an annual snail festival in a mountain village with even a snail race. Snails are credited with native intelligence, and a well-developed sense of sight, hearing and smell; and they make interesting pets. Give him a lettuce or cabbage leaf and your snail is blissful. The snail is a gastropod mollusc and there are several edible species in Europe, Asia and Africa.

In Provence, in the most rural parts and throughout Italy, snails are sold in the market still alive. They are kept for a week, purged in a bucket and, after considerable treatment by dedicated cooks, are made ready for the pot. But this is a bothersome procedure and even in France today you can buy your snails all ready for cooking. All that is left to do is to prepare a snail butter or sauce and go ahead. Tinned snails can also be obtained.

Preheat the oven to 220°C, 425°F, Gas Mark 7. To make the sauce, put the olive oil into a saucepan and heat it well. Add the parsley, mushrooms, shallots and the garlic. Cook over a low flame for 5 minutes. Sprinkle in the flour, mix thoroughly, then add the wine, stirring all the time. Add the salt, pepper, cayenne and nutmeg and cook for a further 2–3 minutes, stirring continuously. Take the pan from the heat and stir in the egg yolks, still stirring briskly to prevent curdling – the sauce should have the consistency of a filling. Now add the snails and gently warm them on a low heat. Take from the pan and stuff them into the shells together with the filling.

Arrange the snails on a shallow baking dish, sprinkle with the breadcrumbs, chopped garlic, the second quantity of parsley and a few drops of oil, and bake in the oven for 5–10 minutes, or until the shells are very hot. Serve immediately.

Instead of using a shallow dish, if you have French *cérafeux*, or snail plates, the snails can be baked and served in these. Usually they come in sizes for 6 or 12 snails and most people who like snails can manage the dozen easily.

Russian pancakes

Bliny
USSR

TO SERVE FOUR–SIX

INGREDIENTS
Makes 16–20 pancakes
15 g ($\frac{1}{2}$ oz) fresh or 2 level
  teaspoons dried yeast
150 ml ($\frac{1}{4}$ pint) tepid water
225 g (8 oz) strong flour
  (*see recipe*)
1 heaped teaspoon sugar
$\frac{1}{4}$ teaspoon salt
1 egg yolk
1 tablespoon melted butter
275 ml ($\frac{1}{2}$ pint) milk,
  warmed
1 egg white
extra butter for cooking

My first introduction to *bliny* was in the best possible way, with caviar and soured cream, which gave me the impression that *bliny* were always served in such a way. There are other fillings such as smoked salmon, mashed hard-boiled eggs, sardines, salted salmon or herring, but soured cream is always present. Pancakes, although extremely popular among the Russians, are considered indigestible, and one is advised to start with a bowl of clear soup before indulging in a session of them, and to accompany them with several glasses of vodka. The correct method of serving *bliny* is to stack them in a pile, wrapped in a cloth to keep them warm, and separately offer the filling and a large bowl of soured cream for individual spreading. In Russia they are served as part of the *zakuski*. The Russians usually use buckwheat flour for *bliny*, but a strong white flour with a gluten content of 10–15 per cent can be used instead, or half and half of each. The usual size of a *bliny* is 15 cm (6 in) across. They are made in a small, thick-bottomed pan (an omelette pan is excellent). It is important to eat the *bliny* while hot as they toughen as they become cold.

Dissolve the yeast in the water, mix in half the flour and add the sugar. Cover and leave in a warm place to rise, about 1 hour. When the dough has risen, add salt, egg yolk, butter and remaining flour. Knead the mixture until it is smooth. Gradually add the warm milk, stirring the mixture all the time. Cover and again leave in a warm place to rise. When the dough has risen again, stir it and once more leave in a warm place to rise. Repeat this procedure twice more so that the dough rises and falls three times. Beat the egg white until stiff, add to the dough and leave for 15 minutes.

Grease a small frying pan lightly with butter. When it is hot, pour into it a thin layer of batter. Melt about 15 g ($\frac{1}{2}$ oz) of butter and as the pancake begins to fry sprinkle it sparsely with melted butter and turn it over to fry on the other side. Repeat this until all the pancake batter is used up, keeping the pancakes flat and warm in a cloth while the rest are being cooked.

If you are using equal proportions of white flour and buckwheat flour, make the first dough with white flour plus 1 tablespoon of buckwheat flour. After this has risen continue as above. Buckwheat flour produces a drier pancake.

There are also sweet *bliny* with fillings of puréed fruit, jam or sweetened curd cheese, and of course soured cream.

Pork and veal pâté

Pâté de veau et de porc

France

TO SERVE TWELVE

INGREDIENTS

450 g (1 lb) breast or belly of pork, minced

450 g (1 lb) veal, minced

350 g (12 oz) pork liver, minced

3 eggs, well beaten

225 g (8 oz) onions, finely chopped

2–3 tablespoons flour

salt, pepper, nutmeg to taste

fat for greasing

To a Frenchman pâtés are an indispensable part of his life. *Pâté de foie gras* can be a beginning to a grand dinner; *pâté de veau et de porc* almost always is found in the Frenchman's *picque-nique* basket, while *pâté de maison* is the pride of every French charcutier proving his skill in blending the various meats. There used to be a distinction between a pâté and a terrine: the mixture for both is the same, but when baked in a dish without pastry, it is a terrine; with pastry it becomes a pâté. But today this distinction seems to have been forgotten and both are called pâté.

Although this recipe, which comes from Alsace Lorraine, does not actually recommend it, I prefer always to soak pork liver in milk overnight as this reduces the somewhat strong flavour of the liver. Drain the liver before using.

Preheat the oven to 180°C, 350°F, Gas Mark 4. Combine all the meats, including the liver, mixing them thoroughly. Add the eggs, mix again, then add the onions, flour and seasonings and thoroughly mix again. Rub one large loaf tin, 18 × 23 cm (7 × 9 in), or two smaller ones with fat, lard or butter, it does not matter which, or bacon or pork fat which is even better. Fill the tin right up to the top: remember that meat will shrink in cooking, so pack it well in.

Give the tin a firm bang on the table to distribute the meat evenly. Cover with foil. Put into the oven and bake for $1\frac{1}{4}$–$1\frac{3}{4}$ hours, or until a knife inserted into the pâté comes out dry. Remove the foil after the pâté has been cooking for 1 hour to let the top brown. Take the pâté from the oven

but let it become cold in the tin, and leave for 24 hours in the refrigerator before slicing. Turn out to serve. To avoid cooking too quickly, place the tin in a bain-marie, or in a large baking tin half-filled with boiling water. If wrapped in foil the pâté can be deep frozen when cold.

Minced liver

Gehakte Leber

Israel

TO SERVE FOUR–SIX

INGREDIENTS

450 g (1 lb) chicken or calves' livers

100 g (4 oz) chicken fat

275 g (10 oz) onions, chopped

4 hard-boiled egg yolks

1 clove garlic, crushed

salt and black pepper

This is a well-known Jewish recipe.

Trim the livers, dip them into iced water, pat dry and grill or dry fry until all the blood has dripped off. Put aside. Heat the chicken fat, add the onions, and cook until soft but not brown. Put the onions, liver and egg yolks with the garlic through the finest blade of a mincer. Add the seasonings, the fat from the frying of the onions and mix well. The mixture should be of a loose, spreading consistency, like a liver paste.

Serve on a lettuce leaf with a garnish of tomatoes, or on *matzos*, Jewish unleavened bread, garnished with parsley; or of course serve with toast.

Top: meat, herring and potato pie; *bottom:* little pies or patties

Little pies or patties

Pirozhki
USSR

TO MAKE ABOUT FORTY

INGREDIENTS
200 g (7 oz) soft white
  cheese (*see recipe*)
50 g (2 oz) butter, at room
  temperature
2–3 tablespoons single
  cream
2 eggs
salt and pepper
450 g (1 lb) flaky pastry
extra butter for greasing

These little pies or patties can be served on almost any occasion and in Russia at one time mountains of them would be sent to the table, not all with the same filling, for these are numerous and varied. They can be served hot or cold, with the Russian *zakuski*, with a clear soup and more especially a bortsch (*see page* 26), or with vodka or other drinks, and even at 'five o'clock tea'. In fact, at one time scarcely a meal would pass when they were not served. The pastry they are made with varies. I find flaky pastry the easiest, but a yeast pastry may be used instead. They can be deep fried or baked: my preference is for baked as they are less rich but some people might not agree. As for the fillings, you can simply use chopped hard-boiled eggs, or chopped cooked fish, chicken or cabbage. Flavourings can be added to taste. There is nothing very exact about these little pies. Any dry white cheese may be used, such as Feta.

Rub the cheese through a sieve directly into a mixing bowl. Cut the butter into small pieces, add to the cheese and mix well. Add the cream and beat to a creamy texture. Add 1 whole egg and the whites of 2 more and beat until the eggs are completely blended into the cheese. Add salt and pepper and let the mixture rest while you prepare the pastry.

Beat the remaining egg yolk. Preheat the oven to 220°C, 425°F, Gas Mark 7. Roll out the dough to a sheet about $\frac{1}{2}$ cm ($\frac{1}{8}$ in) thick. Cut into small rounds about 6 cm ($2\frac{1}{4}$ in) and brush each round with some of the beaten egg yolk. Put a small portion of the stuffing in the centre or on the side of each round of pastry and fold over into half-moon or oval shapes, or put the filling in the centre of a round and cover with another round. Press down all round firmly to seal the edges. Rub a flat baking sheet with the butter, add the *pirozhki*, or as many as the baking sheet will take, brush the tops lightly with the remaining egg yolk and bake for 10–15 minutes, until the tops are a golden brown and the pastry has puffed up.

If preferred, *pirozhki* can be fried in deep hot fat until brown. Drain on absorbent kitchen paper before serving.

Meat, herring and potato pie

Forshmak
USSR

TO SERVE SIX–EIGHT

INGREDIENTS
1 225-g (8-oz) salted
  herring
450 g (1 lb) cooked meat
butter
225 g (8 oz) onions, finely
  chopped
450 g (1 lb) cooked potatoes
150 ml (¼ pint) soured
  cream, milk or yogurt
2 eggs, separated
salt and pepper
25 g (1 oz) cheese, grated
fine breadcrumbs

Russian tomato sauce
40 g (1½ oz) butter
1 each small carrot,
  parsnip and onion,
  peeled and diced
25 g (1 oz) flour
425 ml (¾ pint) tomato
  juice
275 ml (½ pint) meat stock
salt and pepper
1 teaspoon sharp tomato
  sauce

To this extremely solid Russian starter is often added some finely chopped fat bacon. For most of us this dish can serve as a main dish but the Russians of old ate well and heartily and the *forshmak* was but one of a vast array of starters.

The best salted herrings, such as the Dutch *maatjesharing*, are preserved in a light brine and packed in boxes.

Soak the herring overnight. Skin, fillet and chop the herring. Dice the meat. Combine these two ingredients and push through a mincer. Preheat the oven to 180°C, 350°F, Gas Mark 4. Heat 50 g (2 oz) of butter. Add the onion and fry until it is soft but not brown. Mash the potatoes. Mix the onions into the potatoes, then combine with the herring and meat mixture. When completely blended, add the soured cream and put it all through the mincer. Beat the egg yolks, add to the mixture with salt and pepper to taste. Whisk the egg whites until stiff and fold into the mixture. Turn this all into a well-buttered, deep oval baking dish, 23 × 18 cm (9 × 7 in), spread it out evenly, sprinkle with cheese and breadcrumbs and dot with slivers of butter. Bake in the oven for about 40 minutes. While it is baking, make the tomato sauce (*see recipe*). When the mixture in the baking dish begins to shrink away from the sides of the dish, pour over it about one-third of the tomato sauce and continue baking until the top is browned. Serve the rest of the sauce separately.

The pie can be served in the dish in which it is cooked or turned out on to a hot oval serving plate and sliced. If liked, a bowl of soured cream or natural yogurt may be served as well. The pie is also good eaten cold.

Russian tomato sauce (*Tomatnyi sous*)
This particular sauce is meant to be served with meat dishes. The tomato juice can be made either from fresh tomatoes put through a liquidizer and strained through a sieve, or from tinned ones rubbed through a sieve. Ketchup makes a good substitute for a sharp tomato sauce.

Melt 25 g (1 oz) of the butter in a pan, add the vegetables and simmer until they begin to change colour. Sprinkle with flour, stir well, then gradually pour in the tomato juice, stirring all the time. Still stirring, cook for a minute or so, then add the stock, again stir and cook gently for about 15 minutes. Just before the sauce is ready, add salt and pepper and the rest of the butter and the tomato sauce. Rub through a sieve before serving (or, as I do, you may prefer the sauce left as it is).

Beef tartare

Germany

TO SERVE FOUR

INGREDIENTS
600 g (1 lb 5 oz) fillet steak
1 teaspoon Continental
  mustard
salt to taste
½ teaspoon sweet paprika
  pepper
1 teaspoon ketchup
juice of 1 orange
1 tablespoon brandy
2 small gherkins
2 small onions
4 anchovy fillets
4 fresh egg yolks
1 teaspoon finely chopped
  parsley

Beef tartare is a dish of minced raw, good-quality beef seasoned with plenty of salt and pepper, reshaped into a steak or 'bun' and served uncooked with a raw egg on top. It is considered a good pick-me-up.

Remove all the fat and sinews from the meat and mince as finely as possible, adding, as you go, the mustard, salt, paprika pepper, ketchup, orange juice and brandy. Chop, but not too finely, the gherkins, 1½ onions and the anchovies. Add these to the minced beef and mix it all thoroughly. Shape on to a plate or wooden platter in the shape of a sandwich loaf. Along the top make 4 wells and into each one put an egg yolk. Thinly slice the remaining onion and garnish the meat with this and the finely chopped parsley. Sliced gherkins, tomatoes and capers can also be used if preferred.

Soups

Soups have played an important role in the kitchens of the world since biblical days and no doubt earlier. The line between soups and stews can be hard to define. Some soups are as thick as a ragoût. Boiled beef started life in the stockpot, with the beef served separately with vegetables and the liquid as a soup. This is still done in France. Soups and stews have travelled hand in hand for centuries and if we follow their close relationship, we also discover an equally close link with puddings. An early English reference describes 'soops' as 'a kind of rich, pleasant broth, made rich with fruits and vegetables and spices'. Gradually this type of 'soop' developed into soft baked puddings such as rice and bread pudding.

Soups can be divided into three main groups or classes:

1 Thin clear soup, consommé or a well-seasoned *bouillon*, and clear broth garnished with thin strips of vegetable *julienne*. Such soups are made with a light meat stock, but there are also clear vegetable soups and herbal consommés.

2 Thin, light, delicate cream soups. These include a cream of asparagus, celery or tomato soup, light *bisques* to which cream is usually added but which are not thickened with a butter and flour *roux*. They are usually strengthened with an egg and cream *liaison*.

3 Thick soups. On the whole these are hearty soups whose general characteristic is that they are often a meal in themselves. They are made with vegetables, chunks of meat, fish, as in chowders, rice, pasta or barley and more often than not made extra thick with a *roux*.

Although soups are not difficult to make, most gourmets consider them the ultimate accomplishment of the cook, whether in the home or the smart restaurant. Much of the culinary wisdom of East and West has gone into their making and many dieticians will tell you that the proper stimulant to start a meal is not a cocktail or even an hors d'oeuvre but a soup. The French and Italians prefer to serve soup in the evenings. Fruit soups can be served either before or after a meal, while the Chinese will offer soup halfway through a meal and continue to serve it throughout, the idea being that it acts as a digestive.

A seventeenth-century German engraving

22

Gazpacho

Spain

TO SERVE FOUR–SIX

INGREDIENTS

450 g (1 lb) ripe tomatoes
1 cucumber, about 450 g
  (1 lb)
1 large onion, about 225 g
  (8 oz)
1 pepper, preferably green,
  about 225 g (8 oz)
3 cloves garlic
salt and pepper
50 g (2 oz) fine fresh
  breadcrumbs
1 tablespoon vinegar
5 tablespoons olive oil
575 ml (1 pint) iced water
225 g (8 oz) ice cubes

What a history this ancient, one-time peasant soup has, and what variations exist. The name *gazpacho* is derived from an Arab expression for soaked bread, and although it is usually referred to as a cold soup, in the province of Cadiz there is a hot *gazpacho* called *ajo blanco con uvas*, a white garlic soup served with grapes and almonds. Some *gazpachos* are not really soups at all and are served as a main course, especially in the south of Spain where in summer it is too hot to eat much in the middle of the day. A *gazpacho* can be served with a light, crisp, dry wine.

Among the many versions of *gazpacho* is one from Seville where the locals have adopted the liquidizer to produce a thick, smooth soup, garnished in its most elegant form with chopped vegetables. My recipe, not from Seville, calls for a mortar and pestle and a sharp knife.

Blanch, peel and remove seeds of the tomatoes. Dice the flesh. Peel the cucumber and the onion and dice both. Halve the pepper, remove the core, seeds and pith

and dice. Pound the garlic in a mortar together with salt, pepper, breadcrumbs and vinegar. When reduced to a paste, gradually add the oil, drop by drop as for making mayonnaise, until a smooth paste is formed. Turn this into a soup tureen or bowl, add the chopped vegetables, stir well, add the iced water and leave until required in a cool place. In some parts of Spain the *gazpacho* is poured into a terracotta bowl and left to settle its flavours, also to gain a little something from the earthy taste of cool clay. Such pots are not difficult to find these days and it is worth using one when making a *gazpacho*. Just before serving, drop the ice cubes into the soup.

Nowadays it has become part of the *gazpacho* mystique to serve small bowls of diced vegetable garnishing with the soup, such as tomatoes, cucumber, peppers, as well as hard-boiled eggs, and even small croûtons. It is important to use olive oil in this soup; no other oil will do, for olive oil never congeals and it blends perfectly with cold dishes.

Vichyssoise soup
France or USA

TO SERVE SIX

INGREDIENTS
900 g (2 lb) leeks
150 g (5 oz) onions
50 g (2 oz) butter
1 litre (1¾ pints) chicken
    stock
salt and white pepper
675 g (1½ lb) old potatoes,
    peeled and chopped
575 ml (1 pint) milk,
    scalded
575 ml (1 pint) single
    cream
275 ml (½ pint) double
    cream
finely chopped chives

This excellent iced soup, although often considered American, is really a refinement of an everyday French leek and potato soup, improved by Louis Diat, the famous French chef who worked for a long time in the United States. Sadly, owing to its popularity, it has become debased: properly it should be made with only the white of leeks and plenty of cream. The soup should be prepared 24 hours in advance of serving and thoroughly chilled. When during the Second World War Vichy came to symbolize the German occupation of France, the soup was temporarily named *crème gauloise* but now has reverted to its old name.

Wash the leeks, slice off all the green tops (these can be used to flavour another soup) and slice the white parts into rings. Peel and chop the onion. Heat the butter, add the leeks and onion and cook gently until soft, but on no account allow them to change colour. Add the chicken stock, salt, pepper and potatoes and cook until these are tender. Rub through a sieve to a purée and return to the pan. Add the milk, stir well into the purée, then add the single cream, still stirring. Bring the mixture slowly to the boil, check for seasoning, adding more salt and pepper if required, take from the heat and cool. Add the double cream, stir well but gently and chill. Serve sprinkled generously with finely chopped chives.

Yogurt and cucumber soup
Tarator
Bulgaria

TO SERVE FOUR–SIX

INGREDIENTS
450 g (1 lb) cucumber
a good pinch of salt
750 ml (1½ pints) natural
    yogurt
750 ml (1½ pints) iced
    water
3–4 cloves garlic, finely
    chopped
12 shelled and chopped
    walnuts
2 tablespoons olive oil

Yogurt has been used by nomads and the peoples of the Balkans for centuries. However, we owe its introduction to the Western world to a Russian, Professor Élie Metchnikoff, who watched Bulgarian peasant women in the fields taking their midday meal of white soup and asked what it was. It was *tarator*, or yogurt soup, they told him, cheap, easy to prepare and it fills you with such energy and health that you live to be over a hundred. The Bulgarian peasants pointed out as proof the many centenarians still alive in their country. *Tarator* can be eaten either as a cold soup or, somewhat thicker, as a salad. The yogurt of the Balkans is thick and ivory in colour, and when spooned from containers comes out like thick clotted cream. If such yogurt is available, or you make this type yourself, this will give you the finest *tarator*. Failing that, buy or make your yogurt as thick as possible. In Iran a similar soup is made with currants or raisins added instead of walnuts and finely chopped mint as a garnish.

Thinly peel and dice the cucumber. Pile in a heap, sprinkle with plenty of salt and put aside for 30 minutes. Beat the yogurt and mix it with the water. Rinse the salt from the cucumber and pat dry. Rub a large bowl generously with garlic, add the cucumber, the rest of the garlic, walnuts and finally the yogurt. Mix well, blend in the oil (do this gently or you will break up the cucumber), divide into bowls and chill. To serve as a salad, omit the iced water.

Apricot soup
Barack leves
Hungary

TO SERVE FOUR

INGREDIENTS
675 g (1½ lb) ripe apricots
150 ml (¼ pint) white wine
575 ml (1 pint) milk
1–2 thin strips lemon rind
1 small bread roll, sliced,
    about 50 g (2 oz)
275 ml (½ pint) dry white
    wine
75 g (3 oz) sugar
2 egg yolks

Before the Second World War I lived in Hungary where I marvelled at the surfeit of apricots and peaches, many of which were fed to the pigs, thus producing a pork tasting of peaches. This soup can be served either before or after the main course.

Ripe peaches may be used instead of fresh apricots.

Cut the apricots into halves and discard the stones. Put half the apricots into a bowl and add the first quantity of wine to marinate them for about 30 minutes. Meanwhile put the remainder of the apricots into a saucepan with the milk, and add the lemon rind and the bread roll. Cook until the apricots are soft, then rub through a sieve, add the second quantity of wine and the sugar and return to the pan. Beat the egg yolks, stir these briskly into the soup, and reheat but do not let it boil. Pour this mixture over the marinating apricots, cool and chill. Serve with whipped cream as a garnish.

Top: vichyssoise and iced avocado soups
bottom: yogurt and cucumber, and apricot soups

Iced avocado soup
USA

INGREDIENTS
2 large ripe avocados
750 ml (1½ pints) chicken
    stock, free from fat
salt and white pepper
pinch chilli pepper
275 ml (½ pint) double or
    single cream
For garnishing
1 avocado, cubed
lightly salted double cream,
    whipped (*see recipe*)

Avocados have been known in Britain since the seventeenth century but only in recent years have they become widespread. They have long been a luxury fruit in the United States, where they are sometimes erroneously called alligator pears. The present name (the Spanish for 'lawyer') is a corruption derived from the Spanish word *aguacate* which in turn is derived from the Aztec word *ahuacatl*. The flesh is yellow, soft and buttery, hence its early nomenclature: midshipman's or subaltern's butter. Its flavour is bland, although some declare it has a nutty taste. There are many varieties of avocados varying in size and in the colour of their skin.

Cut the avocados into halves, removing the stones. Scoop out the flesh and mash this with a silver fork. Combine the avocado pulp with the stock and pour this into the top of a double boiler and cook over hot water. Bring the soup to the boil, stirring from time to time. Add salt, pepper, chilli pepper and cream, stirring this well but gently into the soup. Turn the soup into a tureen or bowl, cool, then leave in a refrigerator until it is chilled. To serve, garnish each bowl of soup with cubes of avocado and just less than a tablespoon of lightly salted whipped cream.

There are variations of this delicious bland soup. Instead of being iced, the soup can be served hot; also it can be put into a flameproof casserole, topped with lightly salted mounds of whipped cream and grilled until the cream is faintly tipped with brown. The Polynesians in Hawaii make an almost identical hot soup, omitting the chilli pepper and, instead, adding a tablespoon of dry sherry.

Bortsch Ukrainian style

Borshch Ukrainskii
USSR

TO SERVE SIX

INGREDIENTS
225 g (8 oz) cooked
  beetroot
350 g (12 oz) potatoes
450 g (1 lb) white cabbage
225 g (8 oz) tomatoes,
  fresh or tinned
2 litres (3½ pints) chicken
  or veal stock
2 tablespoons vinegar
1 bayleaf
salt and pepper
225 g (8 oz) onions
2 rashers fat bacon
about 275 ml (½ pint)
  soured cream

Bortsch, the national soup of Poland and Russia, ranks among the aristocrats of soup, taking equal place with *consommé madrilène* or *pot-au-feu*. This particular recipe comes from the Ukraine where, it is maintained, bortsch was created.

Peel the beetroot and cut into thin, match-like strips. Peel and cube the potatoes. Wash and shred the cabbage. If using fresh tomatoes, peel and mash them or rub through a sieve; if using tinned ones, sieve them. Bring the stock with the vinegar to the boil, add the beetroot and continue cooking until the beetroot is almost white, then add the potatoes and cook for 10 minutes. Add the cabbage and the tomatoes, the bayleaf, salt and pepper to taste. Mince the onions with the fat bacon, add to the pan and continue to cook for 20 minutes. Serve hot. The soured cream is served separately.

Cabbage soup

Shchi
USSR

TO SERVE SIX–EIGHT

INGREDIENTS
2 litres (3½ pints) meat
  stock
225 g (8 oz) onions, finely
  chopped
100 g (4 oz) carrots, finely
  sliced
1–2 stalks celery, chopped
1–2 sprigs Hamburg
  parsley
450 g (1 lb) white cabbage,
  shredded
salt and pepper to taste
1 level tablespoon flour
150 ml (¼ pint) soured
  cream
For garnishing
finely chopped dill and
  parsley to taste

Cabbage soups, popular in all the Slav and Baltic countries, belong to the more ancient forms of soups. There is, for example, an old English recipe for a cabbage soup in a fourteenth-century cookery book, *The Forme of Cury*, published reputedly on the authority of Richard II's highly qualified chef, which reads simply: 'Caboches in pottage. Take caboches and quarter them in gode broth with onyons y-minced and the white of lekes y-slypt and corve (cut) smale, and do thereto safronn and salt and force it with powder douce (allspice).' This is much the same recipe as the cabbage soup of today, and may be even more interesting, but it has rather less exactitude than would be expected from cookery writers today. If Hamburg parsley is not available, use either curly or Continental parsley.

Bring the stock to the boil in a large saucepan, add the onions, carrots, celery and parsley, stir and cook over a moderate heat for 15 minutes. Add the cabbage, stir well again and continue cooking over a moderate heat until all the vegetables are quite tender. Test for seasoning. Take about a cupful of the stock from the pan to mix with the flour into a thin paste and stir this into the soured cream. Pour this mixture slowly into the soup, stirring all the time. Raise the heat slightly and bring the soup to boiling point, stirring continuously. Immediately lower the heat, give one final stir and let the soup simmer for 3 minutes. Just before serving, sprinkle generously with dill and parsley.

If you require an even more filling soup, add peeled and chopped potatoes and tomatoes immediately before adding the cabbage; or, when in season, peeled and coarsely chopped parsnips may be added at the same time as the carrots.

Pumpkin soup

Antigua

TO SERVE FOUR–SIX

INGREDIENTS

1½ kg (3 lb) pumpkin
100 g (4 oz) onions
225 g (8 oz) tomatoes
salt and pepper
fresh thyme and parsley to
  taste
750 ml (1½ pints) milk

Antigua is a small, friendly island claiming to have a near-perfect climate. The cooking is typical of the Caribbean region and this soup could also be attributed to the Bahamas or Jamaica. Pumpkins are very watery gourds with a fair amount of protein, fat and vitamin B.

If fresh thyme and parsley are not available, use dried – but not enough to overpower the rather delicate flavour of the pumpkin in this simple but pleasant soup. Some cooks prefer not to peel the pumpkin before cooking, declaring that it contains much that is nourishing and gives added flavour. However, the peel will not go through the sieve, so peel the pumpkin before sieving.

Preheat the oven to 160°C, 325°F, Gas Mark 3. To prepare the pumpkin for cooking, scoop out all the seeds, peel and cut off the tough outer skin. Cut the flesh into small pieces. Peel and thinly slice the onions and tomatoes. Put these ingredients into a casserole and add salt, pepper, thyme and parsley. Cover and bake in the oven until the pumpkin is soft, about 45 minutes. Take from the oven and rub the mixture through a coarse sieve. Heat the milk in a saucepan to just boiling point and add the pumpkin purée, stirring all the time. Bring to a gentle boil, take from the heat and serve the soup hot, preferably with fried croûtons.

Often the soup is enriched with the addition of 2 well-beaten eggs mixed into 1–2 tablespoons of single cream. For this, the soup must be allowed to cool slightly; add the egg and cream mixture while it is still in the saucepan. Stir well all the time and bring almost but not quite to the boil.

Left: cabbage soup
right: pumpkin soup

Almond soup

Anglo-Indian

TO SERVE FOUR

INGREDIENTS

1 litre (1¾ pints) clear
  chicken stock
50 g (2 oz) ham, in one
  piece
1 stalk celery
1 leaf each mace, bay and
  basil
salt and pepper
100 g (4 oz) ground
  almonds
4 tablespoons dry sherry,
  Marsala or Madeira
75 ml (3 fl oz) double
  cream, whipped
a few slivers of blanched
  almonds

That almond soup is considered one of *the* soups of Anglo-Indian cuisine is proved by the fact that it was served to Queen Elizabeth II in Agra on her tour of India in 1953. It is a soup for which a recipe is found in all nineteenth-century Anglo-Indian cookery books, which were written by earnest English residents.

Put the stock into a large pan together with the ham, celery, mace, bayleaf and basil, salt and pepper, bring gently to the boil, lower the heat and cook gently for 30 minutes. Strain and return to the pan, add the almonds and cook slowly for a further 15 minutes. Add the sherry and stir well. Serve hot, garnished with a spoonful of whipped cream and sprinkled with slivers of toasted almonds.

Peanut soup

Ful Sudani
Sudan

TO SERVE SIX

INGREDIENTS

450 g (1 lb) peanuts,
  shelled weight
1 litre (1¾ pints) milk
1 litre (1¾ pints) clear
  chicken stock
salt and pepper
single cream and butter
  (optional)

I first met this soup when travelling in the Sudan many years ago. It was served at a luncheon in a famous Khartoum club. I liked it then and I have never ceased to list it as one of my favourite soups. It is frequently served also in Egypt, which is not surprising as many of the cooks there are Sudanese.

Roast the nuts in a hot oven until their skins will rub off easily. Leave to cool before rubbing, then put the nuts through the finest blade of a mincer or whirl in a liquidizer. Turn into a mixing bowl, gradually add the milk, stirring all the time, then the stock, and a pinch of salt and pepper. Pour the soup into a large saucepan, slowly bringing it to the boil. Cook for 10 minutes over a moderate heat, stirring frequently. Immediately before serving add a little butter and single cream; how much you add is a matter of taste.

Walnut soup

Sopa de nuez
Mexico

TO SERVE SIX–EIGHT

INGREDIENTS

450 g (1 lb) walnuts,
  shelled weight
40 g (1½ oz) butter
50 g (2 oz) flour
1.7 litres (3 pints) clear
  chicken stock
salt to taste
¼ teaspoon chilli pepper or
  to taste
275 ml (½ pint) single
  cream

Remove as much skin as possible from the walnuts, then reduce them to a powder. This can be done in a liquidizer very easily. Heat the butter, add the flour and stir gently to a *roux*. Gradually add the stock, stirring all the time, then add the salt and chilli pepper to taste and, still stirring, add the crushed walnuts. Lower the heat and cook gently for 20 minutes. Add the cream and stir until the soup is reheated.

This soup can be served hot, garnished with croûtons, or iced and served without a garnish.

From top to bottom: almond, peanut and walnut soups

Black-bean soup
USA

TO SERVE SIX–EIGHT

INGREDIENTS
450 g (1 lb) black beans
2.3 litres (4 pints) water
1 ham bone
2 bayleaves
2–3 sprigs parsley, chopped
2–3 cloves
1–2 stalks celery, chopped
6 peppercorns
1 clove garlic, chopped
25 g (1 oz) butter
175 g (6 oz) onions,
  chopped
½ teaspoon cayenne pepper
½ teaspoon dry mustard
salt to taste
cream (*see recipe*)
dry Madeira or Marsala
  (*see recipe*)
For garnishing
1 lemon, thinly sliced
2 hard-boiled eggs, sliced

This soup, famous in the USA, is traditionally considered there as one of the soups grandmother used to make, yet its origin is in some doubt. Some say it comes from Michigan, others from Kentucky, Cuba, Mexico, or Boston, where it is a favourite winter Sunday dish. Whatever its origin, it is one of the finest soups invented. Black beans, which are a shiny black and roughly the size of haricot beans, are nowadays reasonably easy to find. However, I have found that dark red or brown beans produce an excellent substitute. The colour of black-bean soup is a rich brown.

Soak the beans overnight in cold water. Drain and put into a large pan with the water, ham bone, bayleaves, parsley, cloves, celery, peppercorns and garlic. Bring to the boil, lower the heat and cook gently. Heat the butter and fry the onions until soft but not brown. Add them to the pan, then the cayenne pepper and mustard. Stir well, cover and continue to cook until the beans are very soft, about 3½ hours. If required, add more hot water or better still, stock. Take out and discard the bone and bayleaves and rub the soup through a sieve. Return it to the pan, gently reheat, and test for seasoning. Serve hot, each bowl of soup garnished with a slice of lemon and of hard-boiled egg.

Good as the soup is, there are some additions which do gild the lily, such as adding a cupful of scalded cream, or a glass of dry Madeira or dry Marsala. Cream and wine should be added after reheating and carefully stirred into the soup. A garnish of thinly sliced raw onions, rather earthy but good on a cold night, or boiled long-grain rice can also be added.

29

Lentil soup

Britain

TO SERVE SIX–EIGHT

INGREDIENTS
450 g (1 lb) lentils
2 litres (3½ pints) vegetable
   stock
1 ham bone
1 bayleaf
2 cloves garlic
salt and pepper
275 ml (½ pint) single
   cream or top-of-milk
For garnishing
diced ham, grated cheese,
   or fried sliced onions

According to ancient and learned rabbis, lentils are a food eaten during days of mourning by members of a bereaved family. The round shape of the lentil has been given a symbolic significance for, shaped like a wheel, it consoles mourners who feel they do not suffer alone, that death will roll round to each one in turn, and none can escape from it.

The Romans had such a liking for these leguminous plants that even the most illustrious families – such as Lentulus – took their names from them. Yet it was believed that the moisture in the lentil produced a heaviness of mind and even made men if not lazy then deliberate or reserved; it may have become associated with the Latin *lentus*, meaning 'slow'. So this Roman predilection for lentils was rather odd.

Lentils should be used as fresh as possible as old ones take a long time to cook. If you want the lentils to keep their shape, soak them in cold water for about 1 hour, then cook in the same water. However, for this soup it is not necessary to soak the lentils since they have to be cooked to a mush and then sieved. Failing a ham bone, thick bacon rinds will add sufficient ham flavour to the soup, which is important.

Wash the lentils thoroughly and put into a large saucepan. Add the stock, ham bone, bayleaf and garlic. Bring to a gentle boil, then cook over a low heat for 1–1½ hours until the lentils are a mush, skimming off any excess fat. The cooking time of the soup varies depending on the quality of lentils used. Remove the ham bone and

bayleaf and rub the soup through a sieve. Return it to the pan, add salt and pepper to taste and bring it gently to the boil. Add the cream and bring the soup again gently to the boil, stirring all the while. Serve hot with the chosen garnish.

As far as the garnishes are concerned, you can use one of them, or all three. Diced ham (which can be picked off the ham bone) making 1–2 tablespoonfuls, plus a bowl of grated cheese served separately, and another bowl of dark fried onion rings turn this soup into a main dish.

There are some interesting variations to a lentil soup. For example, in Iran they add about 1 tablespoon of powdered dried mint, mixed with a teaspoon of ground cinnamon and black pepper. This mixture is sprinkled over the soup immediately before serving. The Germans and Austrians like to drop sliced Frankfurter sausages into lentil soup: another variation is to include about 450 g (1 lb) of peeled and cooked tomatoes, adding them just before the cream.

An Armenian version of this soup is popular in the Middle East. There it is known as Esaü soup and is said to have been eaten for the last 3000 years. A large pot is kept on the fire filled with water into which are thrown lentils, any vegetables that are around, chunks of goat or sheep meat, but never of course pork or ham. The mixture is boiled and the potage served, then more lentils, vegetables and meat are added. As the soup diminishes, so it is added to and boiled again and again. A saying goes there that as the soup ages, so, like good wine, it improves.

Yellow-pea soup

Ärter med fläsk
Sweden

TO SERVE FOUR–SIX

INGREDIENTS
350 g (12 oz) yellow dried
    peas
2 litres (3½ pints) water
350 g (12 oz) salted
    shoulder or side of pork
225 g (8 oz) onion, chopped
1 teaspoon dry marjoram
1 teaspoon ground ginger

This is more than just a special and favourite Swedish soup, it is a meal in itself. Years ago when staying with Swedish in-laws it was explained to me that yellow-pea soup was served every Thursday, followed by Swedish pancakes and blueberries. Why the Swedes have been eating yellow-pea soup every Thursday and for how long no one seems to know, but most Swedes think it dates from the Middle Ages when Sweden was a Catholic country. There are family differences in the manner of cooking and serving this soup. In some homes the soup is rubbed through a sieve; in others the peas are left whole but any floating pea skins are skimmed off. However, many

Swedes not only serve the soup without sieving but also leave the floating skins, declaring that half the pleasure of eating this soup is the touch of the rough skins on the tongue.

Clean the peas and soak overnight in boiling water to cover. Next day cook the peas in the same water, cover the pan and bring quickly to boiling point. Add the pork, onion, marjoram and ginger. Cover the pan again and cook slowly until the pork is tender and the peas soft, about 1½ hours, adding more water if necessary. Take out the pork, slice thickly, put aside but keep hot to serve separately with mustard.

Mixed dried-fruit soup

Blandad fruktsoppa
Sweden

TO SERVE SIX

INGREDIENTS
100 g (4 oz) dried apricots
100 g (4 oz) mixed dried
    fruit
1.2 litres (2 pints) cold
    water
100 g (4 oz) sugar
small piece cinnamon stick
1 tablespoon cornflour
juice and rind of ½ a lemon

Soak the fruit in the cold water for 2–3 hours. Turn it with its liquid into a large pan, remembering that dried fruit expands considerably; add the sugar and cinnamon stick and cook slowly until tender. Take out the fruit with a perforated spoon and put into a soup tureen or large bowl. Discard the cinnamon stick. Mix the cornflour with enough water to make a thin-nish paste, stir this into the liquid in the pan, bring to the boil, add the lemon juice and grated rind, stir again, then pour the liquid over the fruit. Stir gently, cool, chill and serve.

In Sweden rusks are served with this soup, which may precede or follow the main course. If prunes are included in the mixed dried fruits, remove the stones before cooking.

Oxtail soup

Ochsenschwanzsuppe
Germany

TO SERVE SIX–EIGHT

INGREDIENTS
900 g (2 lb) oxtail
salt and pepper
350 g (12 oz) onions
225 g (8 oz) carrots
3–4 stalks celery
50 g (2 oz) butter or
   dripping
100 g (4 oz) lean ham or
   bacon, chopped
3 litres (5¼ pints) water
1 teaspoon salt
½ teaspoon sugar
¼ teaspoon cayenne pepper
1 tablespoon flour
milk or water for mixing
150 ml (¼ pint) Burgundy
   or dry Madeira

Consommé madrilène

France

TO SERVE SIX

INGREDIENTS
900 g (2 lb) ripe tomatoes
1 medium-sized onion,
   chopped
1–2 stalks celery
1 medium-sized turnip,
   diced
1.7 litres (3 pints) meat
   stock
bouquet garni
6 peppercorns
225 g (½ lb) lean minced
   meat
2 egg whites, lightly beaten
2 crushed egg shells
salt (optional)
1 lump of sugar

32

This soup is rich, thick and sustaining and should be served as a main course.

Wash the oxtail, rub dry on kitchen paper, cut into 5-cm (2-in) pieces unless the butcher has already done this for you, and sprinkle lightly with salt and pepper. Peel and chop the onions and carrots and slice the celery stalks into thin rounds. Heat the butter in a large saucepan, add the ham, the oxtail and vegetables and cook over a moderate heat, stirring from time to time until all the ingredients are lightly browned. Add the water, the measured quantities of salt, sugar and pepper and cook over a low heat until the oxtail is tender, about 4 hours. Take the oxtail from the pan, strip off the meat from the bones, dice and return it to the pan. Mix the flour with enough milk to make a thin paste. Add this to the soup, stirring all the time until the stock thickens. Add the wine, bring the soup slowly to the boil and serve hot. For some tastes, the soup might seem a little fatty, and much depends on the oxtail. If this is so, I suggest skimming from time to time while the soup is cooking. The Germans serve oxtail soup either with hot toasted rolls, which is excellent, or garnished with macaroons, a rather specialized taste. To the above ingredients may be added 1–2 bayleaves, a small piece of fresh ginger and a pinch of allspice. Instead of Burgundy or Madeira, you may use brandy, port, a dry sherry or a dry Marsala.

Top: oxtail soup
bottom: consommé madrilène (hot and chilled)

This is one of the classic soups of the world. The meat does not require to be of the finest quality.

Cut the tomatoes into quarters and put with the remaining vegetables into a large pan. Add the stock, bouquet garni and peppercorns and cook until the tomatoes are very soft. In the meantime mix the meat with just enough water to make a lump. Add this to the pan. Add the egg whites and shells and whisk the soup until it comes to the boil, lower the heat to simmering and continue cooking for 30 minutes. Strain through the finest possible wire sieve or a damp cloth. Return the soup to the pan to reheat. Test for seasoning, add salt if required – there may be enough in the stock – and the sugar. Stir until the sugar has dissolved. To serve, garnish with croûtons or peeled diced tomatoes (flesh only, no seeds) and finely chopped chives. About 150 ml (¼ pint) of Madeira can be added to great advantage.

The consommé can be served hot or chilled. If chilled it will jell. It should then be broken up, served in *bouillon* cups, generously sprinkled with finely chopped fresh green herbs, such as chervil, parsley or chives.

Mulligatawney

Milagu-tannir
India

TO SERVE SIX–EIGHT

INGREDIENTS

For the stock
450 g (1 lb) chicken
6 dried chilli peppers
6 peppercorns
175 g (6 oz) onions,
    coarsely chopped
1–2 teaspoons cumin seeds
2–3 sprigs fresh coriander
    or parsley
2–3 cloves garlic, chopped
200 g (7 oz) tomatoes,
    chopped
1–2 bayleaves
water (*see recipe*)

For the seasoning
425 ml (¾ pint) coconut
    milk (*see page 185*)
pinch saffron (optional)
3-cm (1-in) piece fresh
    ginger
1 teaspoon ground turmeric
6 peppercorns
25 g (1 oz) clarified butter
225 g (8 oz) onion, sliced
225 g (8 oz) long-grain
    rice, cooked
1 lemon, thinly sliced

The word mulligatawney is a corruption of the Tamil words roughly translated as 'pepper water' (*milagu* = pepper and *tannir* = water). This soup should, therefore, be well flavoured with hot peppers or cayenne. Its origin in the dim Indian past is to be found with the yogis and gurus when it was a basic part of their diet. Later it descended from this hallowed position to be taken over by the tribes of southern India who began to add, as did the yogis, stimulating spices and peppers into their otherwise simple dishes. With the coming of the British Raj, *milagu-tannir* was introduced to the British memsahibs by their Indian cooks, became called mulligatawney in English and so it was launched on a new career. Finally, it was so worked upon by successive mems and their cooks so that no reincarnated yogi of the ancient world would have recognized it. Like the Indian *kicheri* (kedgeree), pepper water has changed its character.

Instead of chicken, about 450 g (1 lb) of stewing mutton may be used. Failing fresh coriander, use 1 tablespoon of coriander seeds. Should fresh ginger be difficult to find, ground ginger can be substituted, but not more than a level teaspoon of it, or better still dried ginger which has been soaked for about 30 minutes.

Put all the stock ingredients into a large pan with plenty of water, about 2–3 litres (4 pints). Cook until the chicken is tender enough to make a really strong stock, of about 2–3 litres (3 pints). Take the chicken from the pan, strip off the meat and cut this into small pieces. Strain the stock and return it to the pan, add the chicken meat and gently simmer. Prepare the seasoning. Make the coconut milk (*see page 185*). Soak the saffron, if using, in warm water for 15 minutes. Chop and crush the ginger, combine with the turmeric, peppercorns and saffron and pound or grind to a paste. Stir this paste into the coconut milk, add to the soup and stir well. Continue cooking for about 15 minutes, or until the soup begins to thicken slightly. Meanwhile heat the butter and fry the onions to a dark brown, almost black for some tastes. A few minutes before the soup is ready to be served, add the rice, stir well, reheat, add the fried onion and serve the soup hot. Garnish each bowl of soup with a slice of lemon.

Pot-au-feu
France

TO SERVE TEN–TWELVE

INGREDIENTS
1½ kg (3 lb) rump, shoulder
  or topside of beef
3.5 litres (6 pints) water
450 g (1 lb) beef bones
bouquet garni
100 g (4 oz) carrots
225 g (8 oz) turnips
225 g (8 oz) leeks
225 g (8 oz) parsnips
450 g (1 lb) onions
4 cloves
450 g (1 lb) cabbage
pinch of salt
12 peppercorns
1 clove garlic

There are no hard-and-fast rules for the preparation of this typical French family dish, as in the making of national dishes all cooks have their 'tricks' according to where they live. I have a dozen or more recipes for *pot-au-feu* and I do not doubt there are many dozens more. Usually a *pot-au-feu* is cooked in an earthenware pot.

Wash the meat in cold water, then put into a large stew pan or earthenware pot. Add the water, bones and bouquet garni. Bring this to a fast boil, skim until all the fat has been removed and the stock looks clear. Lower the heat and continue cooking for 1 hour. Meanwhile prepare the vegetables. Peel or scrape the carrots, turnips and parsnips and cut into chunks, or if small enough leave whole, this is a matter of preference. Slit the leeks down the middle, wash thoroughly in cold running water, cut into halves and tie into 2 small bundles with string. This is simply to help when

taking them out of the pan. Leave the onions whole but stick a clove into each one. Wash and trim the cabbage but leave it whole. Add all the vegetables to the pan, the salt, peppercorns and garlic and continue cooking slowly for 3–4 hours. To serve, take out the meat and cabbage, put aside but keep hot to be served separately. Take out the remaining vegetables and cut into small pieces. Put these into a soup tureen. Add the stock. Serve separately as a soup and garnish, if liked, with croûtons. Serve the meat thickly sliced as a main course, together with the cabbage.

Alternatively, you can drain off all the vegetables and serve them as a garnish to the meat and serve the stock simply as a clear soup. French bread generally accompanies a *pot-au-feu*, which is both a soup and a main course.

Top: pot-au-feu
bottom: cock-a-leekie

Cock-a-leekie
Scotland

TO SERVE EIGHT

INGREDIENTS
1 boiling fowl
2.6 litres (3½ pints) white
  stock or water
450 g (1 lb) leeks
100 g (4 oz) long-grain rice
salt and pepper

In the poetry of the North we are told that the leek is the badge of high-spirited honour, and where today it might be said that 'our James is the flower of the family', in days gone by in Scotland they said, 'our Jamie is the leek of the family'. Times change, and so have the many recipes for this well-known Scottish soup, which has had its royal admirers for, according to Sir Walter Scott, James VI of Scotland (James I of England) cried: 'And, my lords and lieges, let us all to dinner for the cockie-leekie is cooling.'

Cook the fowl in the stock until very tender. Take from the pan and put aside. Wash the leeks thoroughly under running water and cut into 5-cm (2-in) pieces. Put them into the broth, add the rice, salt and pepper and bring to the boil, continue cooking over a moderate heat for 30 minutes. Meanwhile cut the fowl into at least 8 small pieces, and return it to the pan. Bring again gently to the boil and serve the soup very hot.

Chicken, prawn, mushroom and quails'-egg soup
China

TO SERVE FOUR

INGREDIENTS
225 g (8 oz) boned
   chicken breast
Chinese wine
cornflour (see recipe)
175 g (6 oz) small shelled
   prawns
8 button mushrooms
2 litres (3½ pints) clear
   chicken stock
8 quails' eggs, shelled
dash of monosodium
   glutamate (optional)

It is fair to say that all Chinese soups are delicious, yet most of them take less than 30 minutes to prepare, provided you have stock in the larder. The following recipe is a classic example of a simple yet elegant soup that can be served for special occasions. Quails' eggs are neither difficult to find, nor unduly expensive. A glass jar of quail's eggs holds 8–9 hard-boiled eggs. Failing Chinese wine, use a pale dry sherry or Italian grappa.

Pound the chicken breasts and cut into thin strips and sprinkle lightly with Chinese wine and about a teaspoon of cornflour. Sprinkle the prawns in the same manner with wine and cornflour. Slice the mushrooms thinly. Bring the stock to the boil, add all the remaining ingredients, bring the stock once more to the boil and serve immediately.

Quarter-of-an-hour soup
Sopa de cuarto de hore
Spain

TO SERVE FOUR

INGREDIENTS
1.2 litres (2 pints) strained
   fish stock
100 g (4 oz) long-grain rice
salt and cayenne pepper
225 g (8 oz) cooked peeled
   shrimps
100 g (4 oz) ham, diced
2–3 hard-boiled eggs,
   coarsely chopped

Bring the stock to the boil, add the rice, salt and pepper and when the rice is half cooked add the remaining ingredients. Continue cooking until the rice is soft, between 15 and 20 minutes. Serve the soup steaming hot.

A garnish of finely chopped herbs such as dill, chervil or fennel may be sprinkled over the soup immediately before serving, and a glass of dry sherry added at the end of cooking time would certainly not come amiss. A chicken version of this soup can be made, using clear chicken stock instead of the fish stock, and 225 g (8 oz) of raw chicken breast, cut into thin strips, instead of the shrimps and put into the pan at the same time as the rice. Continue as for the shrimp version.

New England clam chowder
USA

TO SERVE FOUR

INGREDIENTS
225 g (8 oz) tinned or
  frozen clams
75 g (3 oz) fat bacon or salt
  pork, diced
100 g (4 oz) onions, diced
750 g (1¾ lb) potatoes,
  peeled and diced
a little salt
generous quantity of white
  pepper
275 ml (½ pint) milk
150 ml (¼ pint) single
  cream

There are several versions of clam chowder, the main variation being the addition of tomatoes. In New England it is insisted that tomatoes, being strong in flavour, ruin the delicate flavour of the clams. However, clam chowder, with or without the tomatoes, is one of the Americans' favourite dishes and in some parts of the country it is the Friday 'must', and certainly so in New England where they claim that their clam chowder is actually world renowned. But while Americans blithely argue the whys and wherefores of clam chowder, they cheerfully ignore the fact that it is not of American origin at all. The word chowder comes from the French *chaudière*, which means cauldron or kettle; French fishermen and peasants had been cooking in cauldrons for centuries before the discovery of America. These French *chaudières* were communal, everyone producing an ingredient, fish, milk, vegetables, usually potatoes, and herbs. Today's American chowder is not communal but there is much that is reminiscent of that French communal or large family pot.

Clams are important in the American diet and there are several varieties. Usually fairly large ones are used in chowders, either chopped or minced. I have also made clam chowder with the tiny Italian *vongole*, or baby clams, and these of course are added whole to the dish. Their flavour is delicate indeed.

Drain the clams (if using frozen clams, defrost according to instructions). Reserve the liquid. If they are very small, leave them whole, if large, coarsely chop them. Fry the bacon in a large heavy pan until all the fat runs out and the bacon is crisp and brown. Take out the bacon with a perforated spoon and put aside on paper to drain. Add the onion to the pan, stir well and cook until soft but do not let it brown. Add the potatoes. Measure the reserved clam liquid and add enough water or dry white wine to make it up to 275 ml (½ pint). Pour this into the pan over the potatoes, add salt if required – the clam liquid may well be salty enough – and pepper. Cook until the potatoes are tender. Add the milk and cream, stir gently, then add the clams and bring gently, but very gently, to the boil. Check seasoning, adding extra salt and pepper only if required.

The chowder can be served at this point but connoisseurs prefer to keep it for several hours, being of the opinion that its flavour improves with standing. When serving, ladle into deep soup bowls, sprinkle the bacon over the top and serve with water biscuits or crackers.

Prawn bisque

Bisque de crevettes
France

TO SERVE FOUR

INGREDIENTS
450 g (1 lb) prawns, cooked and peeled
50 g (2 oz) butter
75 g (3 oz) carrots, diced
75 g (3 oz) onions, finely chopped
50 g (2 oz) mushrooms, cleaned and diced
750 ml (1¼ pints) fish stock
2 tablespoons finely chopped celery leaves
1 bayleaf
salt, pepper, cayenne pepper and nutmeg
150 ml (¼ pint) single cream
150 ml (¼ pint) dry white wine
2–3 tablespoons brandy (optional)
Garnishing
a few prawns and croûtons

A *bisque* usually means a thick shellfish soup, although there are mushroom and tomato *bisques*. Originally the name was applied to a purée of poultry and game, and some authorities claim it is a word of Provençal origin. However, whatever its origin there has been much praise for the *bisque* by some of the world's best-known gourmets. Dumas *père* wrote that it is the most royal of dishes; the eccentric Grimod de la Reynière observed it was a food for princes and financiers, which indeed it is today. Brillat-Savarin preferred crayfish *bisque* for he was of the opinion that if there was justice in this world, then cooked crayfish would be the subject of divine worship.

Chop the prawns into small pieces. Melt the butter, add the carrots, onions and mushrooms, stir together, and then add the prawns. Cook gently for 3 minutes. Add the stock, celery leaves, bayleaf, salt, pepper, a little cayenne pepper and a good grating of nutmeg. Cook gently for 15–20 minutes, then rub the mixture through a sieve into another pan. Bring to a gentle boil and boil for 2–3 minutes. Scald the cream. Take the soup from the heat, add the cream and wine, also brandy if using, and stir well. Reheat to boiling point and serve at once. Or, if preferred, cool and chill the soup and serve cold.

Garnish with whole or chopped prawns and/or croûtons. If you use small prawns, leave these whole.

Belgian fish soup

Waterzooi
Belgium

TO SERVE FOUR

INGREDIENTS
100 g (4 oz) butter
225 g (8 oz) carrots, finely chopped
225 g (8 oz) onions, finely chopped
3 cloves
1 sprig parsley
1 sprig thyme
1 bayleaf
900 g (2 lb) assorted fish (*see recipe*)
575 ml (1 pint) water
275 ml (½ pint) dry white wine
salt and pepper
1 lemon

From top to bottom: New England clam chowder; prawn bisque; Belgian fish soup

This is essentially a Flemish soup. In Belgium among the assorted fish used are carp, eel, tench, roach, perch and barbel and these are mixed to make a genuine Flemish *waterzooi*. If the suggested fish are not available, use any that are, and it will still make a very good soup. The fish are cleaned and their heads and tails are cut off, but these are cooked and served with the fish.

Heat the butter, add the carrots, onions, cloves, parsley, thyme and bayleaf. Stir well, then add the heads and tails of the fish and simmer for a few minutes. Add the water, wine, salt and pepper and cook gently for 15 minutes. Meanwhile cut the fish into equal-sized pieces, add to the pan, raise the heat and cook quickly for 20 minutes. Slice the lemon, discarding the pips, and add to the pan 5 minutes before the soup is ready.

Serve the *waterzooi* with or without the heads and tails (I prefer to serve without) and with thinly sliced buttered bread.

The cheese market in Alkmaar in Holland

Cheese and egg dishes

Cheese is a condensed, highly concentrated and solid form of milk, but it may be stored for a much longer period than milk itself. It is impossible to say with exactitude how many different types of cheeses there are in the world, as so many are nameless products of tiny villages and it is not easy to categorize them. As a rule, they can be classified as soft or semi-soft, firm or semi-firm, hard or semi-hard. All cheeses are made from one essential ingredient, milk, which when curdled separates into firm but soft curd and whey. There are some cheeses which are made from the whey itself. Cheese differs in the main according to the type of milk used as well as in its preparation. Most cheeses are made from cows' milk, either whole milk or skimmed milk. Skimmed milk cheeses are lower in fat content and higher in protein, therefore are useful for special diets. Many countries also use goats' and ewes' milk, either alone or mixed, to produce cheese with a sharp and piquant flavour.

The great cheese-producing area is Europe, the main producers being the French, Italians, British, Swiss and Dutch. The Scandinavians also have a large cheese industry, so too the Germans. In the Far East, cheese as we know it is almost unknown. Various types of cottage or soft cheese do exist there, but for some reason the Orientals have not taken kindly to it.

There are certain rules which must be followed in order to achieve success.

1 Too much heat or over-cooking will cause cheese to become stringy or leathery. This can be prevented by shredding or breaking cheese into small pieces before cooking, enabling the cheese to cook more rapidly.

2 Cheese takes less time to cook if brought to room temperature before being used.

3 Adding cream to some cheeses assists in cooking, so does using a double-boiler.

4 Mature cheeses have more flavour than younger cheeses. This is of especial importance when making a soufflé or similar dish when a less mature cheese is required.

5 Many cheeses are interchangeable in cooking. For example, if a recipe calls for a Bel Paese, which is not available, then use a cheese with a similar texture. Almost all of the good melting cheeses are interchangeable, such as Gruyère, Cheddar and Lancashire. The flavour of the resultant dish will be changed but not the texture.

Modern refrigerated transport enables cheeses to be dispersed throughout the world, since most of them travel well. Storing cheese in the home is not difficult. It has always been thought that keeping cheese in a refrigerator or a freezer was fatal to the taste and texture. Today this has been disproved. All cheese will stay fresh and retain its flavour and moisture if kept in a cold larder or refrigerator (on the coolest shelf) either well wrapped in cling film or a similar wrapping. To obtain the maximum flavour and aroma, take the cheese out of the refrigerator at least one hour before serving to reach room temperature.

The cheeses which take most kindly to freezing are the very soft cheeses such as Brie or Camembert. They too must be wrapped in cling film. Well sealed, they will keep for up to eight months at least. For freezing, slightly underripe cheeses are usually suggested, but I remember a very ripe Brie I had to freeze on one occasion which, when defrosted, was still fine and very runny. Defrost for 1–2 hours before serving at room temperature.

Eggs are thought of today only in terms of nutritional value. No other single food has such a wide and varied use. They can be served at any meal and, as a breakfast or supper dish, eggs are unsurpassed since they are quickly and easily prepared.

The lore of cooking eggs is important. Eggs will separate more easily when cold than when warm. Egg whites beat up more easily at room temperature, and adding a generous pinch of baking powder to the whites just before beating will produce a firmer meringue. To boil a cracked egg, add a few drops of vinegar or lemon juice or a good pinch of salt to the pan to seal the crack. When frying eggs, sprinkle a little flour into the pan to prevent them sticking. This is particularly important when frying them in the dripping from bacon or ham previously cooked in the same pan.

Cheese fondue

Switzerland

TO SERVE FOUR

INGREDIENTS

1 clove garlic
kirsch (*see recipe*)
350 g (12 oz) Gruyère
cheese
350 g (12 oz) Emmenthal
cheese
2–4 level teaspoons
cornflour
½ bottle dry white wine
1 teaspoon lemon juice
(optional)
freshly ground black
pepper
freshly grated nutmeg
(optional)
½ loaf French bread, cubed

I have pages of recipes and instructions on how to make the one and only correct cheese fondue, a dish that I have been served again and again in Switzerland; there are many versions but it is generally agreed by the Swiss that the fondue of the city of Neuchâtel can claim to be the best.

Since in the making of fondue there is a ritual which should be obeyed, I will digress a little. You need a fondue set, available almost everywhere today in Britain. This consists of a spirit stove, a chafing dish, which is a small pan, preferably of heat-resistant ceramic, earthenware, or even enamel-covered cast iron, and a set of fondue forks, which have long handles and sharp prongs to enable you to pick up cubes of bread. Instead of kirsch, other spirits, such as vodka or a Swiss liqueur called Williamine, are also suitable. A fondue party has its sacred rules and traditions. The fondue is served from the casserole in which it is cooked. The table is usually covered with a bright washable cloth for it is surprising how much of the fondue is spilled, even by the experts. On the table are small baskets filled with cubes of bread, fondue forks and small glasses for kirsch. A Swiss habit is to drink a glass of kirsch, which is known as the *coup du milieu*, halfway through the meal, and a final glass at the end.

If you should let fall a piece of bread from your fork, you must pay a forfeit. If it is a man, this means a bottle of white wine; if a girl, she must pay her forfeit with a kiss. Dropping a piece of bread twice means the victim has to give another fondue party with the same guests – so be warned.

Fondue parties in Switzerland are good fun with plenty of friendly warm atmosphere and no one minds paying a forfeit.

As a fondue takes only a little time to make do not start cooking it until just before serving. You can start the cooking on top of the stove and transfer the casserole to the spirit stove after you have added the kirsch, or start bravely at the table on the spirit stove. Smear the casserole with garlic or, as in Lucerne, with a piece of cloth dipped in kirsch. Shred the two cheeses finely into the casserole. Add the cornflour, stir, add the wine and, if liked, 1 teaspoon of lemon juice. Bring to a quick boil, stirring all the time with a zig-zag movement until the cheese has dissolved. As soon as the fondue begins to simmer, add the pepper, still stirring. Then add the kirsch – a small glass is suggested – and if liked some grated nutmeg. Let the fondue simmer during the meal over a low heat. To eat, spike a cube of bread on to your fork, dip it into the fondue and turn it round and round in the dish – it should not be a plunging movement – for the constant turning of the bread cubes keeps the fondue thick and creamy to the last. It is important to use bread of a consistency that will not crumble; French-style bread is the most widely used.

Garnished cheese

Liptòi körözött

Hungary

TO SERVE FOUR

INGREDIENTS
225 g (8 oz) dry curd
  cheese
100 g (4 oz) butter
½ teaspoon each caraway
  seeds, paprika pepper,
  dry mustard
4 capers, chopped
a little chopped chives or
  onion
ale or beer

Liptòi is a cream cheese prepared from goat's or sheep's milk and owes its name to the Liptòi range of mountains in Czechoslovakia where it was first produced. The cheese has a slight acid flavour and always is served *körözött*, meaning garnished. Similar concoctions are made in Austria and Rumania. The German name, *Liptauer*, is often used in shops and restaurants in Hungary and Austria, and sometimes it is to be found under this name in Britain and elsewhere. The mixture can be prepared in the kitchen, which usually is more convenient, but sometimes, especially in restaurants, all the ingredients except the beer are served on your plate around the cheese so that it can be mixed personally at table.

Rub the cheese through a sieve to remove any lumps. Cream the butter and mix into the cheese, beating until the mixture is smooth. Add the remaining ingredients, remembering that the quantity of paprika must only be sufficient to colour the cheese a faint pink, and only enough ale be used to loosen it. Serve piled on a dish garnished with radishes and slices of brown bread.

Baked cheese dreams

New Zealand

TO SERVE THREE–SIX

INGREDIENTS
50 g (2 oz) butter
6 thin slices bread
100 g (4 oz) grated
  Cheddar cheese
salt and pepper to taste
1 egg, well beaten
6 small, thin rashers bacon

Travelling through the Commonwealth forty years ago, when afternoon tea was a popular meal and hostesses vied with each other not only to produce sandwiches and cakes but also a few hot delights, I discovered that this recipe was one of the most popular. Either brown or white bread may be used.

Preheat the oven to 220°C, 425°F, Gas Mark 7. Soften the butter and spread it thinly on the bread. Mix the cheese, salt and pepper with the egg. Spread this mixture over the sliced buttered bread. Roll each slice firmly and secure with cotton. Arrange the rolls on a well-greased baking sheet, cover each roll with a rasher of bacon and bake in the oven for about 5 minutes, or until the rolls are a golden brown. Remove the cotton before serving.

Welsh rabbit or rarebit

Wales

TO SERVE SIX

INGREDIENTS

6 slices buttered toast
350 g (12 oz) Cheddar
   cheese
50 g (2 oz) butter
2 tablespoons ale
1 teaspoon made mustard
pinch of cayenne pepper

This is a homely dish, dubbed 'The Welshman's Delight'; but homely or not it can boast an international reputation. Andrew Boorde (1490–1549), a writer on food and diet, relates a pretty story of Welsh rarebit or rabbit. It seems that there were a number of Welshmen in Heaven who were quarrelling among themselves until God could no longer tolerate it. He spoke to St Peter who had recently been made custodian of the Heavenly Gates and asked his advice. St Peter had an immediate solution. Clutching his golden keys he went outside the gates loudly crying 'Toasted cheese, toasted cheese'. Out ran the chattering Welshmen, whereupon the wily saint dashed back inside and slammed the gate shut, leaving them outside.

First make the toast and keep it very hot. Grate the cheese. Heat the butter in a small saucepan, add the cheese and stir over a moderate heat until it thickens. Gradually add the ale, mustard and cayenne pepper. Continue cooking until the mixture is smooth and creamy. Spread this over the toast and serve at once with a 'fine' glass of beer. Many people put the toast, after it has been spread with the cheese, under a hot grill.

Top: welsh rabbit or rarebit
bottom: baked cheese dreams

Quiche Lorraine

France

TO SERVE FOUR

INGREDIENTS
225 g (8 oz) flour
100 g (4 oz) butter
pinch of salt
1–2 tablespoons cold water
or, better still, brandy or
dry sherry
Filling
15 g (½ oz) butter
6 rashers streaky bacon,
chopped
2 eggs
275 ml (½ pint) single cream
salt and pepper
butter for garnishing

A quiche is an open-faced flan or tart of ancient origin. Originally it was prepared with a risen bread type of dough, but over the years this has been changed to a rich short or flaky pastry. The fillings in the pastry shell vary enormously, from sweet fruit to savoury fillings of all kinds, such as fish, potatoes and onions. However, it is the quiche from Lorraine that has become internationally famous. It is usually served lukewarm, although some local cooks prefer to serve it very hot, or even cold. Another, more recent, innovation is the baking of quiches in small individual tins and offering them as an hors d'oeuvre. The correct filling for a quiche Lorraine is of eggs, cream and bacon. The correct wine to serve with it is the Alsatian *vin gris*.

Sift the flour into a bowl and rub in the butter until the mixture looks like breadcrumbs. Add a pinch of salt, then just enough cold water to mix to a firm paste. Leave to chill for about 1 hour. Preheat the oven to 190°C, 375°F, Gas Mark 5. Lightly grease a 23-cm (9-in) quiche or flan tin. Roll out the pastry and line the flan tin. To make the filling, heat the butter in a small pan, add the bacon and lightly fry. Sprinkle this over the pastry. Beat the eggs until smooth, mix into the cream, add a little salt and pepper and pour this mixture into the prepared pastry shell over the bacon. Add a few slivers of butter, not too much, and bake in the oven for 30 minutes, or until the top is a rich brown.

Egg ragoût

Oeufs ragoût
Switzerland

TO SERVE FOUR

INGREDIENTS
25 g (1 oz) unsalted butter
2 tablespoons flour
1.2 litres (2 pints) meat
stock
100 g (4 oz) onions,
or 1 small onion
4 cloves
1 bayleaf
8 eggs
lemon juice

This is a pleasant little dish from Switzerland and useful when there is no meat in the house but plenty of eggs and some meat stock.

Heat the butter until it begins to change colour, add the flour and stir continuously until it is blended into the butter to make a light *roux*. Gradually pour in the stock, stirring all the time to make a thick sauce. Spike the onion with the cloves, add to the sauce with the bayleaf and cook gently for 20 minutes. Meanwhile boil the eggs until they are hard and shell them as soon as possible. Cut into halves and arrange in a shallow serving dish. Take the onion and bayleaf from the pan and discard, add a dash of lemon juice to the sauce and pour it at once over the eggs. Serve hot with triangles of toast or fried bread.

Baked eggs

Yaitsa v chashkye
USSR

TO SERVE FOUR

INGREDIENTS
Method 1
butter for greasing
grated cheese to taste
4 tablespoons finely
chopped ham
4 eggs (size 2)
salt and pepper
chopped chives to taste
Method 2
butter for greasing
4–6 eggs, lightly beaten
salt and pepper
plenty of finely chopped
chives or the green of
spring onions

Method 1
Preheat the oven to 190°C, 375°F, Gas Mark 5. Generously rub 4 ramekin dishes with butter and sprinkle the bottom of each with grated cheese and chopped ham. Drop 1 egg into each dish, sprinkle lightly with salt, pepper and chives. Bake in the oven until set, about 15 minutes. Or, if preferred, the eggs can be steamed on top of the stove.

Method 2
Preheat the oven to 190°C, 375°F, Gas Mark 5. Generously rub 4 ramekin dishes with butter. Mix the eggs with salt, pepper and chives, pour into the ramekins and bake in the oven until set, about 15 minutes.

   Although it is not a Russian custom, I add a little crushed garlic to the egg.

Savoury custard

Jing daahn
China

TO SERVE FOUR

INGREDIENTS
100 g (4 oz) cooked pork, minced
1 tablespoon pale dry sherry
1 tablespoon soya sauce
6 eggs
425 ml (¾ pint) warm stock
salt and pepper to taste
1 teaspoon sesame oil
1 teaspoon soya sauce

Savoury egg custards are used throughout the Far East. Sometimes, as in Japan, they are cooked in small individual dishes with lids which are called *chawan-mushi jawan*. Here is a typical savoury custard that can be served in the West as a starter to a meal and is exceedingly good. Instead of pork, chicken or flaked cooked lobster, crab or fish may be used. The ingredients may also be mixed but there are no hard-and-fast rules. The Chinese, Japanese and the Koreans are able to eat these custards with chopsticks, but it is more usual to eat them with teaspoons.

Mix the meat with the sherry and the soya sauce. Beat the eggs lightly and combine with the stock, stirring all the time. Add the meat, pepper and salt, the last very cautiously since the soya sauce is salty. Put the ingredients into a Pyrex dish, and place it on a stand in a pan, 5 cm (2 in) wider than itself, containing boiling water. Cover the pan and steam over a good heat for 20 minutes, or until set. Sprinkle with the sesame oil and the remaining soya sauce.

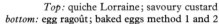

Top: quiche Lorraine; savoury custard
bottom: egg ragoût; baked eggs method 1 and 2

Scrambled eggs with anchovies

Tojas szardellaval
Hungary

TO SERVE FOUR

INGREDIENTS
6 eggs
150 ml ($\frac{1}{4}$ pint) soured cream
white pepper to taste
6 anchovy fillets, finely chopped
25 g (1 oz) butter

This recipe from Hungary is both simple and appetizing and vastly different from English scrambled eggs. Failing soured cream, a natural yogurt may be substituted.

Lightly beat the eggs in a mixing bowl, add the soured cream, blend into the eggs, then add the white pepper (no salt) and the anchovies. Heat the butter in a small, shallow pan. Pour in the egg mixture and cook slowly until the mixture begins to set, then lift up the egg mixture from the bottom with a spatula so that the mixture from the top flows gently through to the bottom and thickens. Cook until the eggs are set and creamy.

It is not a Hungarian custom to serve the scrambled eggs on toast.

Scrambled eggs

Woon dow chow daahn
China

TO SERVE SIX

INGREDIENTS
2 tablespoons oil (*see recipe*)
1 spring onion, finely chopped
100 g (4 oz) smoked ham, diced
100 g (4 oz) bacon, diced
225 g (8 oz) cooked peas
1 teaspoon salt
$\frac{1}{4}$ teaspoon pepper
6 eggs
1 tablespoon Chinese wine or pale dry sherry

In this recipe frozen or tinned peas may be substituted for fresh peas. Chinese cooks use either peanut or sesame oil for cooking.

Heat the oil in a pan, add the spring onion, ham, bacon and peas. Sprinkle with salt and pepper. Lightly beat the eggs and add to the pan, stir gently over a low heat, add the wine and cook until the eggs begin to set but are still moist. Turn into a hot serving dish: it must be hot for by the time the eggs come to the table they must be completely set. They can be served with or on toast.

Scrambled eggs

Achoori
India (Parsee)

TO SERVE SIX

INGREDIENTS
3–4 green chillies
1 clove garlic
3-cm (1-in) piece fresh ginger
450 g (1 lb) onions
6 eggs
50 g (2 oz) butter or ghee
1 teaspoon ground turmeric
pinch salt
3 tablespoons finely chopped fresh coriander or parsley

Parsee scrambled eggs are usually served on fried straw potatoes but can also be served with toast. If green chillies are not available, use about $\frac{1}{4}$ teaspoon of chilli or cayenne pepper.

Chop the chillies finely, discarding the seeds. Finely chop the garlic and ginger. Chop the onions coarsely. Beat the eggs until frothy. Heat the fat, add the onions and garlic and fry until soft and a golden brown. Add the chopped chillies, turmeric and ginger, stir well, then add the eggs and salt. As the eggs begin to set, gently stir, mixing them well into the onions. Just before the eggs are cooked, add the coriander, stirring well.

From top to bottom: scrambled eggs with anchovies; Chinese scrambled eggs; Indian scrambled eggs

Egg curry

Baida mooli

India

TO SERVE FOUR

INGREDIENTS

50 g (2 oz) ghee or other
  cooking fat
225 g (8 oz) onions, sliced
1 teaspoon ground turmeric
6 thin slices fresh ginger
pinch of salt
275 ml ($\frac{1}{2}$ pint) thick
  coconut milk (*see page*
  185)
2–3 green chillies
275 ml ($\frac{1}{2}$ pint) chicken
  stock
1 tablespoon vinegar
8 hard-boiled eggs, shelled

This egg curry of Portuguese-Goan origin is one of the nicest of the Indian egg curries. Failing fresh ginger, 1 teaspoon of ground ginger may be used, and $\frac{1}{2}$ teaspoon of chilli or cayenne pepper may be used instead of green chillies.

Heat the fat and fry half the onion until a golden brown. Add the turmeric, ginger and salt, stir well, gradually add the coconut milk and cook for about 5 minutes. Add the chillies and the rest of the onion, stir well, add the stock and vinegar and cook for about 10 minutes. Add the eggs and continue cooking for another 10 minutes. Serve with rice.

A fish mooli is made in precisely the same manner except that white fish, cut into small cubes or squares, is used instead of eggs, and fish stock used instead of chicken stock.

47

Rice dishes

As rice is the staple food of much of the world's population, it is not surprising to learn there are estimated to be some 7000 varieties, although more modest estimates put it at a mere 4000. Rice varies from field to field, much as wine does from vineyard to vineyard. These differences, although of vast importance to the rice growers and connoisseurs, seldom enter into the calculations of the Western consumer. Listening to Orientals discussing their favourite methods of cooking rice, it is easy to assume that there are as many methods as there are varieties of rice, but whichever way is used the rice is always served with each grain separate. In an Oriental house rice is usually bought in large quantities and when a new sack is opened the experienced cook will only need to cook it a couple of times before he gets its measure and can cook it perfectly. The number of different types of rice that can be obtained in British shops is growing and most of the rice imported into Britain comes from the United States, already packaged, washed and ready for use. However, it is sometimes possible, especially in Oriental shops, to buy loose rice, which is generally cheaper and sometimes stronger in flavour. Loose rice should be rinsed under cold, running water and soaked in cold water for about 30 minutes before use. Before cooking it must be drained and dried. The types of rice required for recipes in this book are as follows and all are easily obtainable.

An early nineteenth-century miniature of a travelling cook in China

Long-grain rice
The grains are four to five times as long as they are wide. The rice should come from the pan light and fluffy, and with each grain separate. This is the rice used in most savoury dishes, pilaus, fried rice, salads, soups and stews, but not risotto, however.

Round, short or medium-grain rice
These are used in the preparation of sweet rice dishes, for rice croquettes, or any rice dish that is to be moulded. Since this rice is rather starchy and the grains lightly cling together, it can also be made into risottos, although the Italians themselves would use their own short-grain rice, *arboria* or *vialone*.

Patna rice
This has always been a misnomer. It was merely long-grain rice that was shipped out of India from Patna. Such rice exports came to an end years ago. Today so-called Patna rice is simply long-grain rice made from a Patna seed type.

Carolina rice
This short, stubby-looking starchy rice is from a Carolina seed type. However, many firms still package rice under the name Carolina rice.

Appetites vary, especially between the Western and Eastern rice eater. For the former, allow about 75 g (3 oz) of uncooked rice per portion, i.e. about 450 g (1 lb) for 6 portions. Rice trebles its volume when cooked, so remember that 1 cup of uncooked rice will give you 3 cups of cooked rice. One standard cup of uncooked rice is 225 g (8 oz).

Shellfish risotto

Risotto con frutti di mare
Italy

TO SERVE FOUR–SIX

INGREDIENTS
450 g (1 lb) mussels
450 g (1 lb) clams
1 tablespoon olive oil
200 g (7 oz) large prawns
75 g (3 oz) butter
a few strips each celery,
    carrot and onion
75 ml (3 fl oz) brandy
255 ml (½ pint) dry white
    wine
salt and pepper
1 small onion, finely
    chopped
450 g (1 lb) short-grain rice
1.2 litres (2 pints) hot fish
    stock

This risotto is a favourite along the Italian Adriatic coast. It must be served hot and piled on to a hot serving dish in a pyramid shape and garnished with the remaining ingredients. This recipe uses fresh fish, but tinned or frozen fish may also be used.

Thoroughly wash the mussels and clams and put them into a large pan with the olive oil and cook, covered, over a good heat until the shellfish open. Discard any that do not open. Take them from the pan and strain, reserving the resulting liquid. Shell the mussels and clams and put aside. Shell the prawns. Heat 50 g (2 oz) of butter in a deep frying pan, add the strips of vegetable, then the brandy and stir well. Add the wine and cook until this has been reduced by half. Add the shellfish, salt, pepper and about half their liquid. Stir and cook over a moderate heat for 15–20 minutes. While this is cooking, start preparing the risotto.

In a fairly large saucepan heat the remaining butter with the finely chopped onion, then add the rice and cook this for about 5 minutes, stirring frequently. Then add the fish stock, a little at a time, still stirring frequently, adding more stock as the rice absorbs the liquid. When all the stock has been used up, continue to cook the rice for a few minutes longer until it is *al dente*, i.e. neither too hard nor too soft. As soon as the rice is ready, put it on to a hot round plate, shape it like a pyramid and garnish it with the shellfish and the sauce.

If you find shaping the rice difficult, put it into a hot pudding basin, press it down lightly and then turn out.

Pilau

Turkey

TO SERVE SIX

INGREDIENTS
150 ml (¼ pint) olive oil
450 g (1 lb) long-grain rice
salt and black pepper
575 ml (1 pint) boiling
    meat stock
unsalted butter for
    garnishing (*see recipe*)

Pilaus of all kinds are found throughout the Balkans, the eastern Mediterranean, the Middle East and as far as the Far East: as my Muslim cook once told me sententiously, 'There are as many pilaus as there are stars in the sky,' and I almost believe he did not exaggerate. This recipe comes from Turkey, typical of most plain pilaus and, once mastered, becomes a way of cooking rice that does not fail. It is a basis for many a main dish of meat, fish and vegetables – all can be added to it with impunity. Long-grain rice is absolutely essential in the preparation of a pilau.

Heat the oil in a saucepan. Add the rice and fry it for 5 minutes, stirring all the time to prevent it from sticking. Add salt and pepper, and then the stock, which will sizzle rather alarmingly as it hits the bottom of the hot pan. Stir well, cover the pan with a cloth, then with the lid and cook over the lowest possible heat for about 30 minutes, by which time all the liquid should have been absorbed into the rice. Stand the pan away from the heat but keep on the stove, still with its cloth on, for 15 minutes. By this time the rice should not only be thoroughly cooked but each grain separate and the rice fluffy. The butter can be stirred into the rice or, rather better, turn the rice out on to a large hot dish and top it with a single large piece of butter, preferably not less than 100 g (4 oz).

To make chicken pilau, garnish the rice with cooked, chopped chicken and grilled tomatoes and use a chicken stock.

Left: shellfish risotto; *right:* pilau

La paella

Spain

TO SERVE EIGHT

INGREDIENTS

1 1-kg (2¼-lb) chicken
1–2 dozen mussels
225 g (8 oz) Spanish
  smoked ham (see recipe)
450 g (1 lb) tomatoes
225 g (8 oz) chorizo
  sausage
1–2 cloves garlic, chopped
pinch of saffron
olive oil for frying
450 g (1 lb) onions,
  coarsely chopped
675 g (1½ lb) red peppers
salt and black pepper
450 g (1 lb) short-grain
  rice
225 g (8 oz) cooked green
  peas
225 g (8 oz) lobster meat
  (optional)

Spain's most famous dish according to some Spaniards, reaches its peak of perfection in Valencia, although it would be unwise to repeat this in Barcelona, for the two cities are jealous rivals on the subject of paella. However, despite Valencia's claim, the paella itself originated rather south of the city amid the vineyards and orange and lemon groves. Its origins are peasant, for it was cooked by the women working in the groves over an open wood fire in a shallow large pan called a paella. The large surface of the pan comes into direct contact with the heat and this is important when cooking a paella for the heat must be strong enough to brown and cook the meats and set the rice steaming without burning or drying. As the fire burns low the rice is gently steamed. The pan is never covered and the rice should not be stirred. For paella there were no set ingredients, the peasants simply popped into the pan whatever came to hand and at the table everyone dipped into the pan with a spoon, eating directly from it. The dish became popular and having no name was simply called after the pan in which it was cooked. Paella is still basically a simple dish and recipes for its preparation vary throughout Spain, not only from town to town but from cook to cook and it is doubtful whether the housewife or cook prepares her paella today in the same manner as her mother did yesterday. The seasons obviously also decide on what goes into a paella and, therefore, having learned how to make a basic paella, then you simply put into it more or less of what you fancy. The only essential, of course, is the rice. More often than not there will be chicken; smoked Spanish ham from the mountains; or Galicia sausages (chorizos), which are both sweet and spicy; tomatoes, which should be fresh and not from a tin; and one or two other vegetables at least, more if you want, in the average Spanish paella. I have given a simple recipe using peas, but beans, artichokes and other similar vegetables may be included. Not all paellas include mussels and other crustaceans. Saffron is optional and used rather more in southern Spain than the north.

Although generally the Spaniards use their own brand of fine short-grain rice for this dish, it can also be cooked with long-grain rice. If using short-grain, however, it is advisable to rinse it well under running water in a sieve and soak in cold water for 30 minutes before cooking. This removes all the starch and ensures that each grain of the rice will be separated. Considered the finest of Spanish smoked ham is the jamón serrano which is cured in the cold dry air of the Sierra Morena mountains. It is eaten raw. There are other good hams, such as that from Galicia; both are available in many delicatessens in Britain.

A paella pan is two-handled and about 6 cm (2½ in) deep and can be bought in a wide range of sizes from most kitchen shops throughout Britain. For this recipe the pan should be about 30 cm (12 in) in diameter. Failing such a pan, use a large but heavy frying pan. After being garnished, a paella should be served in the pan in which it is cooked. Crustaceans when used are usually left on the half shell but, if preferred, can be shelled first. Also it is usual to serve a bowl of assorted olives as an accompaniment, and a dry strong red wine to drink with it. Finally, the oil must be olive oil for, without this, say the Spaniards sternly, a paella is not a paella.

Cut the chicken into at least 8 pieces, or use chicken pieces. Wash the mussels in several waters, remove the beards and cook in a large pan with enough water to reach about 3 cm (1 in) up the side of the pan. Cover tightly and cook over a high heat for 5–6 minutes, or until they are all open. Discard any that refuse to open. Put the cooked mussels aside and strain but reserve the liquid. Cut the ham into narrow strips. Peel, seed and chop the tomatoes. Cut the sausage into thick slices. Chop the peppers, discarding seeds and core. Soak the saffron in a little water or mussel stock. Heat the oil in a paella or large frying pan. Add the garlic, cook this until it begins to brown, take out and discard. Add the onions, tomatoes, red peppers and the pieces of chicken to the oil, turn them over in the oil and sprinkle with pepper (or, if preferred, hot paprika pepper) as you do so. Cook gently for 10 minutes, stirring frequently. Take out half the peppers, put aside but keep hot. Add the rice, stir this well into the mixture to coat each grain with oil, raise the heat slightly and cook for 3 minutes, then add the saffron and its liquid. Reheat the mussel liquid, measure and if necessary bring it up to 1.2 litres (2 pints) by adding boiling water. Gradually pour this into the pan, stir well, raise the heat, bring to the boil, lower the heat, add salt (very little if using mussels) and the peas, stirring gently and cook for about 15 minutes, or until the rice has absorbed all the liquid. Do not be tempted either to cover the pan or stir the rice. Serve in the paella pan, garnished with the mussels, preferably on the half shell, and the reserved red peppers arranged on top. If available, and if making the paella for a special occasion, cooked lobster meat can be added as a garnish, or a dozen shelled and cooked prawns.

Kedgeree
Britain

TO SERVE FOUR–SIX

INGREDIENTS
175 g (6 oz) long-grain rice
450 g (1 lb) cooked fish
  (*see recipe*)
2–3 hard-boiled eggs
50 g (2 oz) butter
salt and black pepper to
  taste

Kedgeree is a development of the ancient Indian dish of *kicheri*, 'a mess of rice cooked with lentils, flavoured with a little spice, shred onion and the like: a common dish all over India and often served at Anglo-Indian breakfast tables. . . . In England we find the word is often applied to a mess of re-cooked fish, served for breakfast; but this is inaccurate. Fish is frequently eaten *with* kedgeree but is no part of it.' I quote from *The Glossary of Anglo-Indian Words*, more affectionately known as Hobson-Jobson. It does show how far today's kedgeree has changed to bear almost no relationship with the original *kicheri*.

The fish most often used today for a kedgeree is smoked haddock but this is a recent development. Mrs Beeton in her recipe of 1886 says that any fish may be used, and no curry powder; neither do the Indians use curry powder in their own *kicheri*. Mrs Beeton used cayenne pepper instead of black pepper, also 1 teaspoon of dry mustard. She says that this dish is seasonable at any time 'and it costs 5d to make'. It can be served at breakfast, at lunch, or as a light supper dish.

Wash the rice and soak it for 30 minutes in cold water, this releases the starch and the rice will cook with each grain separate. Drain well and put into a pan with just enough water to come about 3 cm (1 in) above the rice. Cook rapidly uncovered for 2–3 minutes, then cover tightly and leave over the lowest possible simmering heat for 20 minutes. By this time the rice will be dry and fluffy, each grain separate. Cool and leave until quite cold. Flake the fish, removing all skin and bones. Separate the egg yolks from the whites. Chop the whites and crumble the yolks. Put aside and keep separate. Heat the butter in a pan, add the fish, stir gently, then add the rice, salt and pepper and again stir gently, a too vigorous stirring will produce a mush. Add the chopped egg whites, stir again and cook until the mixture is hot. Pile on to a hot serving plate, sprinkle with the crumbled egg yolks and serve hot.

Mutton with rice

Biryani

Pakistan

TO SERVE SIX–EIGHT

INGREDIENTS
900 g (2 lb) lean boneless mutton

2 teaspoons salt

1 teaspoon powdered coriander

3 cloves garlic, crushed

450 g (1 lb) mild onions

5-cm (2-in) piece fresh ginger

3 blades mace

pinch saffron

275 ml (½ pint) yogurt

100 g (4 oz) butter or vegetable fat

4 cloves

12 peppercorns

6 cardamom seeds

450 g (1 lb) long-grain rice

This is a typical Pakistani dish. For festive occasions it is often garnished with shimmering gold or silver leaf, which is usually obtainable in shops selling Indian and Pakistani foods. Although the leaf has no flavour, it gives a very exotic and pleasing appearance not only to rice dishes but also to many of the Pakistani and Indian types of sweet dishes (*see page* 189). Failing saffron, a little turmeric may be used, roughly in the same proportion. Failing fresh ginger, use dried ginger, which is better than ground ginger; 1–2 cardamom pods will produce 6–8 seeds. Pakistanis would use curd or soured milk rather than yogurt but yogurt is easier to obtain.

Wipe the meat with a damp cloth and, without cutting it up, put into a pan with ½ teaspoon of salt, the coriander, garlic half the onions, ginger and mace. Add 1½ litres (2¾ pints) of water, cover and bring to the boil. Take off the lid, wrap it in a cloth and tightly clamp it on the pan again. Continue cooking until the meat is tender: the timing depends on the quality of the meat but it is advisable not to keep taking off the lid, otherwise much of the aroma

will disappear. It will probably take about 1 hour until the meat is tender. Soak the saffron in a little water. Take the meat out with a perforated spoon when tender and cut into stew-size pieces. Put aside but keep hot. Strain the stock through a sieve, return it to the pan and add the meat. Stir in the yogurt and leave to simmer. Heat the butter in a separate large pan. Slice the remaining onions, add to the butter and simmer until brown and soft. Take out half and put aside. Leave about 3 tablespoons of butter in the pan. Add 2 cloves and the peppercorns, stir for a minute, then add the meat with the stock, stirring well and cook over a slow fire. In another pan put 1 litre (1¾ pints) of water, flavour with salt, add the remaining cloves, onion and cardamom seeds and bring to the boil. Add the rice and cook this rapidly until almost tender, about 10 minutes. Drain and spread the rice over the meat. Add the saffron, and stir it into the rice so that some of the rice is coloured yellow. Again clamp the lid on tightly and leave over the lowest possible heat until the rice grains are dry and separated, 15–20 minutes.

Fried rice

Nasi goreng
Indonesia and Holland

TO SERVE SIX

INGREDIENTS

3 tablespoons peanut or
    vegetable oil
100 g (4 oz) shelled cooked
    prawns
225 g (8 oz) cold cooked
    mixed meats, shredded
2 tablespoons clear stock
6 cups cold cooked rice
    (450 g (1 lb) uncooked
    rice)
salt and pepper
40 g (1½ oz) butter
Seasoning
1 teaspoon chilli pepper
225 g (8 oz) onions, peeled
    and finely chopped
3–4 cloves garlic, chopped
1 tablespoon finely
    chopped fresh coriander
    or parsley
2 tablespoons soya sauce
1 tablespoon brown sugar
Garnishing
2 eggs
2–3 tablespoons vegetable
    or peanut oil
10 small onions or 1 large
    one, 175 g (6 oz)
50 g (2 oz) prawn crackers
    (optional)
1 small cucumber, 225 g
    (8 oz)

This dish of Javanese origin is a favourite among the Dutch, many of whom spent long periods in Indonesia and returned to Holland with a taste for the dishes of the country. Today there are many Indonesian restaurants throughout Holland and dishes such as *nasi goreng* have become nationalized. Indeed, *nasi goreng* is so popular that it has become a takeaway dish and is served in snack bars and lunch counters. It was formerly served as a late breakfast on Sundays by Dutch families when they lived in Indonesia before the Second World War. Today many Dutch families eat it at least once weekly. The hot seasoning or *sambal* can be bought ready mixed in jars. The rice used in this dish should be a long-grain variety and cooked the day before serving.

First prepare the garnish. With the eggs make 2 extra-thin omelettes, roll each up separately and cut into thin strips. Put aside but keep warm. If using small onions, cut into halves or thirds; a large onion should be thinly sliced. Heat 2–3 tablespoons of oil in a pan and fry the onions until they are soft and a golden colour. Take from the pan, put aside but keep warm. If using prawn crackers, cook them (*see page* 188). Peel and dice the cucumber. Now make the seasoning by either pounding all the ingredients in a mortar with a pestle or, much simpler, in a small grinder. Heat the 3 tablespoons of oil, add the pounded seasoning and fry, stirring constantly, for a minute or two. Add the prawns, meat and stock and again stir. Cook over a moderate heat until the meat and prawns are hot, then add the rice, salt, pepper and butter. Stir well and simmer for 10 minutes, stirring frequently. Pile the rice on to a hot plate, garnish with the remaining ingredients and serve at once. Instead of shredded omelette, fried eggs are often used as a garnish. In Holland, instead of including the hot seasoning *sambal* in the cooking, very often a jar of it is placed on the table.

Top: fried rice
bottom: Chinese fried rice

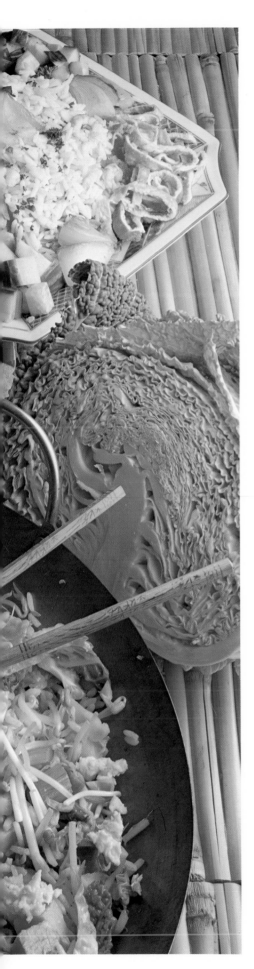

Chinese fried rice

Chow fan

China

TO SERVE SIX–EIGHT

INGREDIENTS

450 g (1 lb) long-grain rice
150 ml (¼ pint) peanut oil
225 g (8 oz) cooked pork, diced
3 stalks celery, chopped (optional)
2–4 spring onions, finely chopped
½ small crisp white cabbage, finely shredded (optional)
1 cup bean sprouts
pepper to taste
2 tablespoons soya sauce
4–6 eggs

Rice, one of the staple foods of China, and consequently precious, has had dozens of proverbs and superstitions spring up about it during the past centuries. To upset a rice bowl brings bad luck, and nothing could be worse than for someone deliberately to upset a bowl of rice on to the ground. Children are told that for every grain of rice they waste a pock mark will appear on their faces. I have some half-a-dozen recipes for this favourite Chinese savoury dish of rice. It makes a very acceptable luncheon or light supper dish.

Basically all recipes for Chinese fried rice agree on the way in which the rice should be cooked, but it is in the other ingredients that they differ. The rice should be boiled and then left after this for several hours or, better still, overnight before being fried. Fried rice can take its place as a dish alone or served with other Chinese dishes. Salt is not required as soya sauce is salty enough.

Wash the rice and soak for 30 minutes. This releases much of the starch and ensures that the grains will be well separated when cooked. Drain well. Put into a pan with enough cold water to reach 3 cm (1 in) above the top of the rice. Wrap the lid in a piece of cloth and clamp it as tightly as possible on the pan. Cook slowly until the rice is tender and all the liquid is absorbed. Do not attempt to peek at the rice until it has been cooking for about 20 minutes. It is ready when the rice at the top is flaky and cooked through and natural steam holes are formed in the dry surface of the mounds of rice. Do not stir the rice while it is cooking. Take the pan from the stove, cool the rice and leave in a covered bowl until the next day.

Heat the oil in a heavy frying pan, add the pork, vegetables, bean sprouts, pepper and soya sauce and cook for 5 minutes. Add the cold rice, stir vigorously to break up any lumps and thoroughly coat with oil. In another pan scramble the eggs, add to the rice and serve immediately, very hot.

Variations

Omit the cabbage and instead use 2–3 sprigs of chopped parsley. Use half pork and chicken meat, or omit both and use chopped prawns or whole shrimps. Instead of bean sprouts, 1–2 thinly chopped bamboo shoots may be used. Some cooks add shelled cooked peas, others dried Chinese mushrooms, which have been soaked in water and then drained. Also, instead of scrambling the eggs separately, you can make a well in the centre of the rice, add the eggs and as they begin to set stir them into the rice.

Unloading fish on to the quayside in Aberdeen, Scotland

Fish

Fish is nature's harvest of the seas, lakes and rivers and with today's refrigerated trawlers and fast transport, it is available to everyone. Fish is rich in protein; 25 g (1 oz) of fish are equal in protein to the same amount of meat, cheese or egg. It is appetizing, nourishing, light in texture, delicate in flavour and easily digested. The flavour of fish varies according to the type of water from which it is fished. Fish taken from cold seas is generally considered to have more flavour than that taken from warmer waters. Most fish lovers agree that fish caught in fresh water is superior to that taken from salt water, and all agree that fish taken from a sandy bed is finer than that coming from a muddy one.

Fish deteriorates more quickly than other flesh and must be bought when absolutely fresh. After being out of the sea for a short while, it will take on the tang of seaweed; but when it gives off a strong smell, do not buy it. If a fish is fresh, its eyes should have a bold bulging stare, never a dull one. The gills must be bright red and the body, when slightly pressed, show no imprint. It is not always easy to tell how fresh a sole or other types of flat fish may be for the eyes and gills are almost invisible.

Although in the following recipes exact details are given for the preparation of the dishes, a few generalizations might be helpful.

Boiling. Although we use the term boil, what we really mean is poach. Fish for so-called boiling should be dropped into a simmering *court-bouillon* or water and cooked gently at simmering point.

Frying. A popular method for cooking fish, especially smaller fish and fillets. They can be dipped into a light batter, into egg and fine breadcrumbs, or simply into seasoned flour and fried either in a light oil or butter.

Baking. The fish can be wrapped in foil or greaseproof paper, or simply placed in the pan covered with herbs, tomatoes, onions, or cooked in a fish brick. The oven temperature should be around 180°C, 350°F, Gas Mark 4.

Grilling. Excellent for whole fish. Make sure the grill is very hot before you start to cook the fish, otherwise it will stick. Slash the fish diagonally two or three times across its body and rub well with oil before grilling.

More often than not fish are interchangeable in recipes so, for example, failing the *bangus* (*see page* 65), use a similar white fish as suggested. This may result in a dish of slightly different flavour but this is not important, as improvisation is the art of good cooking. The term 'white fish' is a general term for fish which has indeed a white flesh, like cod, halibut, turbot, hake and even sole and plaice; but don't be confused by the American freshwater whitefish, so called because its flesh and skin are white.

Shellfish is the name given to edible crustacea of which prawns, lobsters, mussels, scallops, crayfish and clams of all types are typical examples. Shellfish deteriorates rapidly and should be fresh when bought and cooked as soon as possible. Generally all shellfish should feel heavy in proportion to their size.

Demand for such fish varies considerably. In the United States mussels receive short shrift but clams are rated highly. So are oysters, of which some of the finest are to be found in the United States as well as in Australia and, of course, in Britain and in France.

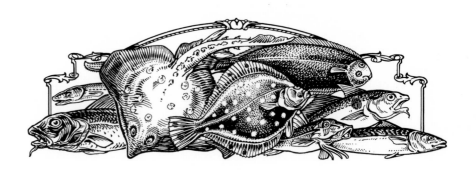

Poached salmon

Britain

TO SERVE FOUR

INGREDIENTS
900 g (2 lb) fresh salmon
wine *court-bouillon* or salt
water (*see recipe*)

Court-bouillon with vinegar
1.2 litres (2 pints) water
75 g (3 oz) carrots, diced
1 100-g (4-oz) onion stuck
   with 1 clove
bouquet garni
6–8 peppercorns
2 tablespoons wine vinegar
1 teaspoon salt

Court-bouillon with wine
100 g (4 oz) onions
150 g (5 oz) carrots
425 ml (¾ pint) dry white
   wine
2 litres (3½ pints) cold
   water
bouquet garni
salt and pepper
1 bayleaf

If a salmon were capable of blushing it would spend all its life doing just that, so much praise has been lavished on it. It is admired as a splendid game fish and a source of valuable and highly palatable food. It can be cooked and served with a simple sauce; it can be smoked, dried, tinned or frozen. The classic manner in which to cook salmon for the table is to poach it either in a *court-bouillon* or in salted water, but cooks disagree on which method is the best. The salt-water supporters say that a *court-bouillon* spoils the delicate flavour of the fish. Cooking times vary slightly from cook to cook but the following times are generally accepted.

Whole fish over 2.3 kg (5 lb): 8–10 minutes per 450 g (1 lb).

Whole fish or salmon steaks under 2.3 kg (5 lb): 10 minutes per 450 g (1 lb).

If necessary, scale the fish, clean and wash it. It can be cooked in one piece or cut into cutlets. Prepare the *court-bouillon*, making sure that there is just enough liquid to cover the fish rather well. If you are the fortunate owner of a fish kettle, place the fish in this on the grid and cover with tepid liquid (i.e. *court-bouillon* or salted water). Failing a kettle with a grid, wrap the fish in a piece of muslin with long dangling ends so that you can lift it out unimpaired when cooked. Bring the liquid to a simmering boil – when it just starts to bubble – and continue to simmer for the required time. If the salmon is to be served cold, let it cool in the liquid in which it has been cooked and then skin it before the fish is quite cold, or not, as you prefer. Serve with a cucumber salad, wedges of lemon, mayonnaise, or a *ravigote* or *rémoulade* sauce. If serving the salmon hot, take carefully from the pan and place for a moment on a dry cloth to drain. It can be skinned or not as you prefer. Place on an oval dish and serve with thinly sliced cucumber, boiled new potatoes and an *hollandaise* or *béarnaise* sauce. Make the sauce while the fish is cooking.

Salmon trout can be poached and presented in the same manner: many consider it has more flavour than salmon and is more tender. If cooking a whole salmon trout or large portions, the procedure is precisely the same as salmon but cooking time is slightly longer by 2–3 minutes. Other fish such as trout, char and the so-called white fish or gwyniad can be poached in the same way.

Court-bouillon with vinegar
There is no English translation for this liquid in which the French almost invariably cook their fish, especially fresh-water or delicately flavoured fish. I have chosen this particular recipe from the many because it is one of the simplest.

Put all the ingredients into a saucepan and bring gently to the boil. Cover the pan and cook for 20–30 minutes. Strain and cool before using.

Court-bouillon with wine
Slice the onion, and scrape and thinly slice the carrots. Put all the ingredients into a pan and bring slowly to boiling point. Reduce the heat to simmering point and cook gently for 45 minutes. The *bouillon* should be used hot; if it is cooled before using, bring it once again to boiling point before adding the fish.

Trout in soured cream

Risted ørret med kremsaus
Norway

TO SERVE FOUR

INGREDIENTS
4 trout, about 225 g (8 oz)
   each
50 g (2 oz) flour
pinch of salt
50 g (2 oz) butter
2 tablespoons oil
150 ml ($\frac{1}{4}$ pint) soured
   cream
1 tablespoon lemon juice or
   wine vinegar
1 tablespoon finely
   chopped parsley

You can use frozen trout in this dish if fresh ones are not available.

Clean the fish but leave the head and tail intact. Do not wash but wipe the inside only with kitchen paper; this prevents the fish from becoming soft inside while cooking. Roll the fish in the flour and salt and shake them to remove excess flour. Heat together in a heavy frying pan half the butter and all the oil until the mixture begins to foam. Stir well, lower the heat to moderate, add the trout and fry them two at a time, unless your pan will take all four, for about 5 minutes on each side, turning them carefully with a spatula. When the trout are fried, keep them in a warm oven.

Pour off all the fat from the pan, add the remaining butter, stir this over a low heat and, with a wooden scraper, scrape up the brown drippings in the pan, mixing them well into the butter. Add the cream and continue cooking and stirring for about 3 minutes, but do not allow the cream to come to the boil, if you do it will curdle. Stir in the lemon juice quickly and at once pour the sauce over the fish. Garnish with the parsley and serve at once with boiled potatoes.

Mackerel with a gooseberry sauce

Britain

TO SERVE FOUR

INGREDIENTS
4 small mackerel
butter and oil
The sauce
450 g (1 lb) gooseberries
150 ml (¼ pint) cooked
  spinach water or milk
sugar to taste
15 g (½ oz) butter
grated nutmeg to taste
butter and oil for frying

Mackerel and gooseberries have been cooked together for centuries. It was an old Norman practice to eat green gooseberry sauce with mackerel, and the French use the expression *groseille à maquereau* to distinguish gooseberries from currants. If the mackerel are small, have them cleaned but left whole. If really large, have them filleted or sliced. Whole mackerel will take 15–20 minutes to cook; filleted or sliced 10–15 minutes. If frying the mackerel whole, cut slits along both sides of the fish at intervals of about 4 cm (1½ in) to prevent the fish from curling up.

First prepare the sauce. Wash, top and tail the gooseberries and put into a saucepan with just enough water to prevent them from burning. Cook slowly until soft. Drain well and rub through a sieve or purée in a liquidizer. Return the purée to the pan, add the spinach water or milk, sugar, butter and nutmeg and simmer, stirring all the time until the sauce is reheated. Heat enough butter and oil mixed together to cover the bottom of a fish frying pan. Add the mackerel and fry first on one side until browned, then turn and brown the other side. When the fish are well brown all over they are ready. If unable to fry all the fish in the pan at one time, fry two at a time and when they are ready keep hot in a warm oven. Serve the mackerel with the hot sauce poured over it.

Variation
Large green grapes can be used to make a sauce for mackerel; the quantity is the same, so is the method, but the pips must be removed first.

Herring salad

Haringsla

Holland

TO SERVE SIX–EIGHT

INGREDIENTS
1 head of lettuce
3 pickled herrings, filleted
  and chopped
3 firm sour apples, chopped
3 hard-boiled eggs,
  chopped
2 medium-sized cooked
  beetroots, diced
6–8 cold boiled potatoes,
  chopped
4 dill pickles, sliced
  lengthwise
100 g (4 oz) onions, finely
  chopped
salt, pepper, oil and
  vinegar to taste
mayonnaise
Garnishing
2 hard-boiled eggs
sliced dill pickles to taste
1 tablespoon finely
  chopped parsley

Amsterdam is criss-crossed with canals and it seems to me that every bridge spanning the waterways is flanked with a herring stall where everyone flocks, from the errand boy on his bicycle to the tycoon passing in his Rolls. They come simply to swallow green (i.e. fresh) herrings, holding the prepared slithery fish by its tail and, tossing their heads back, gulping it down in one. It takes a bit of skill to do this. As one travels through the country one realizes that herrings are part of the Dutch economy and way of life. When the herring fleet sets out from the seaports at the beginning of the season in May it is a brave sight, the boats dressed with bunting and flags. The skipper who brings home the first herrings of the season is allowed to present the Dutch monarch with a cask of traditional design filled with herrings. And from this day on everyone eats fresh herrings, from breakfast through to evening, until they are out of season.

Wash and dry the lettuce, break up the leaves and spread these over a serving dish. Mix the remaining seven ingredients together, adding salt, pepper, oil and vinegar to taste. Spread this mixture over the lettuce and coat well with mayonnaise.

Separate the yolks from the whites. Rub the yolks through a coarse sieve directly over the salad. Finely chop the whites and sprinkle over the top. Cut the pickle into strips (failing dill pickle, pickled gherkins will make a good substitute), add these and finally sprinkle with parsley. Many cooks in Holland mash the potatoes instead of dicing them which makes, for my taste, a far too solid salad.

Top: skate in black butter; *bottom:* bouillabaisse

Skate in black butter

Raie au beurre noir
France

TO SERVE FOUR

INGREDIENTS
900 g (2 lb) skate, cut into strips
bouquet garni
1 teaspoon salt
¼ teaspoon white pepper
100 g (4 oz) butter
2–3 sprigs fresh parsley, washed and dried
1 tablespoon wine vinegar

This large flat fish, of which there are many varieties, is recognized by its large wing-like pectoral fins. Not all species are edible and for some people none are edible. I recall one Scottish lady in an Edinburgh fishmonger's remarking as I asked for skate, 'I'd no gie it to ma cat.' In Britain skate is sold cut into fairly large pieces and crimped. The usual method of cooking it is to cut the wing into wide strips right through the gristle that forms the 'bones'.

Put just enough water into a fish pan to cover the strips of fish, add the bouquet garni, salt and pepper and cook over a moderate heat for 10 minutes. Reduce the heat and continue cooking gently until the skate is quite tender, 15–20 minutes. Heat the butter until it is brown and fry the sprigs of parsley. Drain the fish on absorbent paper and gently pull off the skin. Put the skate on to a hot dish, pour the butter with the parsley over the top and put into a warm oven to keep hot. Add the vinegar to the frying pan in which the butter has been browned, bring to the boil and boil for 2 seconds. Pour this over the fish and serve.

The best accompaniments to this popular French dish are boiled potatoes and a green salad. Capers are sometimes sprinkled over the skate at the same time as the butter and parsley.

Bouillabaisse

France

TO SERVE FOUR

INGREDIENTS
500 g (1 lb 2 oz) filleted flat fish (*see recipe*)
250 g (9 oz) carrots
350 g (12 oz) potatoes
butter
250 g (9 oz) onions, chopped, preferably large spring onions
1–2 tablespoons each finely chopped parsley, chives and mint
salt and pepper to taste
2 litres (3½ pints) hot water or, better still, fish stock

Although recipes for a *bouillabaisse* usually appear among the soups in most cook books, it is not intended to be a soup. It is a fish dish in which a large variety of fish are cooked and served whole. There are dozens of recipes for its preparation and those who have travelled along the Mediterranean coast of France no doubt will have met with fierce arguments as to the merits of a particular town's own *bouillabaisse*. As an example, the Marseillais are convinced that anyone attempting to make a *bouillabaisse* outside their port is undertaking a fruitless task: an excellent fish stew might well result, they will concede, but a *bouillabaisse*, never.

Stews of this kind have been made through the centuries and the Greeks claim that their *kakavia* is the mother of them all. As the Greeks occupied the region around Marseilles centuries ago, it seems fair to assume that they left their recipe behind.

The following recipe does not come from the south of France but from Brittany, and bears no relationship to the Marseilles or other Provencal versions. It is simple to prepare, and can be served as it comes from the pot, or the fish can be rubbed through a coarse sieve and returned to the pot to make a soup. It is all a matter of taste.

Remove the head, and bone and cut the fish into pieces small enough to be eaten with a spoon. Scrape and slice the carrots into rounds, peel and dice the potatoes. Heat the butter, add all the vegetables, herbs and seasonings and cook gently until the onions begin to brown. Add the fish, cook gently for a minute or two, then add the liquid and cook over a moderate heat for 20 minutes. Serve hot in deep bowls with coarse soft brown bread or toasted French bread.

Braised fish

Tinolang bangus
Philippines

TO SERVE FOUR

INGREDIENTS
350 g (12 oz) potatoes
1.5 kg (3 lb) whole fish or steaks (*see recipe*)
25 g (1 oz) fat
3–4 cloves garlic, chopped
225 g (8 oz) onions, chopped
575 ml (1 pint) rice water or fish stock

The fish used in this recipe is the milk fish, or *bangus*, probably the most common fish to be found in the markets in Manila and, indeed, an all-the-year-round fish in Far Eastern waters. It has the same bone structure as the herring. Failing *bangus*, use a whole small cod or similar fish. Rice water is simply the water in which rice has been cooked and is used a great deal in Far Eastern cooking.

Peel and slice the potatoes into thin rounds. Cut the fish into thick rounds or steaks. Heat the fat in a casserole, add the garlic and let it brown before discarding; then add the onions and half cook them. Add the fish, cover with the potatoes, pour in the liquid and cook over a moderate heat for 20–30 minutes until the fish and potatoes are tender.

Sole bonne femme

France

TO SERVE TWO

INGREDIENTS
butter for greasing
50 g (2 oz) mushrooms,
  finely chopped
1 shallot, finely chopped
1 tablespoon finely
  chopped parsley
1 450-g (1-lb) sole
150 ml (¼ pint) dry white
  wine
salt and pepper

Hollandaise sauce
2 egg yolks (size 2)
1 tablespoon cold water
100 g (4 oz) unsalted butter
1 tablespoon lemon juice
salt and pepper

The term *bonne femme* more or less means
'as the good wife does it', in other words, it
should indicate a rustic or country dish;
however, there does not seem to be much
rusticity about this one which has been
described as 'the dreamiest and creamiest
of dishes ever' and a great French pisca-
torial triumph. Ask your fishmonger to
pull off the black skin, cut off the head and
tail and generally trim the sole but keep it
whole – although I have seen recipes for
sole bonne femme using fillets. To bake the
fish use either a shallow earthenware dish
or ovenproof dish.

Preheat the oven to 180°C, 350°F, Gas
Mark 4. Rub the dish generously with
butter. Sprinkle with the mushrooms,
shallot and parsley. Lay the fish on top of
this, add the wine, salt and pepper, cover
with well-buttered greaseproof paper and
bake for about 15 minutes in the oven.
Meanwhile prepare the *hollandaise* sauce.
Take the sole from the oven and transfer it
to an ovenproof serving dish. Add the
hollandaise sauce to the liquid in the baking
dish, stir well, then pour this sauce over the
fish. At this point you can return it to the
oven, with the heat raised to 220°C, 425°F,

Gas Mark 7, or put it under a grill until the
top is brown. But take care that the sauce
does not curdle, which it will if the fish is
kept too long under the grill or in the oven.

Hollandaise sauce
This is a French housewife's version of a
famous sauce.

Combine the egg yolks and water and pour
into the top of a double boiler or bain-
marie. Over a moderate heat, without
allowing the water in the bottom half to
come to the boil, whisk briskly until the
mixture begins to thicken. Remove the
pan from the heat. Cut the butter into small
pieces and add to the egg mixture. Return
the pan to the heat and stir constantly until
the sauce thickens. Warm the lemon juice,
remove the pan from the heat again, add
the juice, salt and pepper, stir and serve hot.

Pickled fish

Ingelegde

South Africa

TO SERVE SIX

INGREDIENTS

1.5 kg (3 lb) white fish
½ tablespoon salt
¼ teaspoon pepper
575 ml (1 pint) water
350 g (12 oz) onions
3 tablespoons sugar
3 tablespoons curry
  powder
2 tablespoons flour
575 ml (1 pint) malt
  vinegar

This is a popular dish in South Africa and will keep almost indefinitely in a cool place. It is particularly useful for dealing with fairly tasteless fish. Care must be taken in its presentation for, although the flavour is good, it can look unattractive. This dish is considered also a speciality of the South Sea Islands.

Preheat the oven to 220°C, 425°F, Gas Mark 7. Wash the fish, wipe it dry and cut into neat 2-cm (½-in) slices. Sprinkle lightly with salt and pepper. Arrange carefully in a large shallow ovenproof dish, add half a cup of water and bake in the oven until the fish is tender, 15–20 minutes. Meanwhile make a curry sauce. Peel the onions and slice fairly thickly. Put into a

pan together with the rest of the water, bring to the boil and cook for 2–3 minutes, but do not let the onions become soft. Mix the dry ingredients, add the vinegar, stir well, then pour this mixture into the onions (with the water) and stir well. Cook the sauce for 2–3 minutes, stirring continuously until it is smooth. Pour a layer of the sauce into a shallow glass dish, then add the fish, arranging it carefully either in layers or neatly piled up in the centre. Cover with the rest of the sauce and leave for at least 2 days in the refrigerator before serving. Serve garnished with wedges of lemon and springs of parsley. As a variation, many cooks fry the fish first before adding it to the curry sauce.

Halibut in a piquant sauce

Cozumel

Mexico

TO SERVE FOUR

INGREDIENTS

1 tablespoon coriander
  seeds
225 g (8 oz) tomatoes
1 small sweet pepper
900 g (2 lb) halibut or
  similar fish
3 tablespoons olive oil
100 g (4 oz) onions, diced
¼ teaspoon cayenne pepper
150 ml (¼ pint) lime juice
salt and pepper
butter or oil for greasing

Lemon juice may be used instead of lime juice, and cod instead of the more delicate and expensive halibut.

Preheat the oven to 190°C, 375°F, Gas Mark 5. Pound or grind the coriander seeds to a powder. Peel and quarter the tomatoes, discarding the seeds. Cut the pepper into strips, discard the seeds, core and stems, and dice the flesh. Rinse the fish under cold running water, pat dry and put aside. Heat the oil in a shallow pan, add the onions and fry over a moderate

heat until they begin to soften and become translucent. Do not let them brown. Sprinkle in the coriander seeds and cayenne pepper and stir well until blended. Add the sweet pepper. Again stir and cook for 5 minutes. Add the tomatoes, stir, then add the lime juice, stir, add salt and pepper and stir once more. Take the pan from the heat, rub a shallow ovenproof casserole with butter, arrange the fish in this and cover with the sauce. Put into the oven and bake for 20–25 minutes, or until the fish flakes when tested gently with a fork.

Top: pickled fish; *bottom:* halibut in a piquant sauce

Fish in coconut milk

Fiji

TO SERVE THREE

INGREDIENTS

450 g (1 lb) white fish
lime juice to cover (see
    recipe)
275 ml (½ pint) thin
    coconut milk (see page
    185)
salt and pepper to taste
1 chilli pepper, chopped
1 tablespoon chopped
    onion

For most of us the cooking of the South Sea Islands can only be armchair cooking, for many of the ingredients are hard to come by, even in these days of transport in freezer containers. However, there are one or two recipes we can add to our culinary repertoire, such as the following which I have cooked in many parts of the world. In this dish the fish is pickled or soused in lime juice (if impossible to obtain, lemon juice makes a good substitute), which tenderizes the fish tissues by the 'cooking' action of the citric acid and the fish is flavoured with the coconut milk. When the fish is served it has the appearance of having been superbly poached and not a scrap of its fishy flavour has gone. In the Bahamas there is a similar recipe called Desert island fish. The fish can be cut either into fillets or cubes, and almost all white fish can be prepared in this manner.

Put the fish into a shallow bowl and cover with strained lime juice. Leave overnight in the refrigerator. Next day make the coconut milk (see page 185), add a little salt and pepper, the chopped chilli pepper and onion. Put this mixture into a small pan and bring gently to the boil. Cool and then chill. Two hours before serving the fish, drain off all the juice and pour the chilled coconut sauce over it. Serve cold with a potato or green salad.

Tempura

Japan

Preparing tempura at Ikeda, a Japanese restaurant in Mayfair, London

There are some important internationally known recipes that are as well to be aware of, even though it is not always possible to make them in your own home. Tempura is one such recipe and indeed even Japanese housewives, although they know how to make a tempura, which simply means fried food, prefer to eat it in a restaurant.

Some people declare that it is a dish of Portuguese origin that has become naturalized in Japan as well as nationalized. There is some argument in Japanese culinary circles as to where it first appeared: some say it was in Nagasaki, others in Edo (Tokyo). But whichever town can truly claim its beginnings (and I suspect none can), it was in Edo that it was brought to its present perfection, and a well-made tempura is perfection indeed.

Tempura is a mixture of foods, mainly fish and vegetables, dipped in a batter and fried. Some cooks use sesame oil for frying, others prefer a mixture of olive oil and sesame. In the making of the batter, some cooks declare that salt must be added to make it crisp; others hold exactly the opposite view: but, curiously, both seem to turn out a fine tempura. This batter is not what we in the West would call a batter. It is deliberately lumpy, gossamer thin, light and lacy. To the Japanese tempura implies, 'wearing a crust of batter, as a woman wears silk gauze, stimulating the desire of the beholder by the glimpses of the beauty beneath.' So, obviously, it is no easy task to make tempura batter.

The usual fish chosen for a tempura is shellfish, exquisitely fresh, straight from the sea and not precooked. Tempura can also be made with cuttlefish and crisp fresh vegetables, cut into small pieces for easy eating with chopsticks. As the pieces come piping hot from the pan to your plate you take them up one by one with chopsticks and dip each piece into the sauce.

Le grand aïoli

France

TO SERVE FOUR

INGREDIENTS

900 g (2 lb) poached or
    boiled fish (*see recipe*)
4–8 cloves garlic
salt and pepper
2 egg yolks
275 ml (½ pint) olive oil
1 tablespoon lemon juice

Le grand aïoli, which is a meal of fish and vegetables served with *aïoli* sauce, is the classic Friday dish of the Mediterranean and of Provence in particular. The Provençal poet, Frédéric Mistral, wrote that for him *aïoli* '. . . concentrates in its essence the warmth, the energy and joy of the Provençal sun.' Others talk of its digestive excellence, that as a winter dish it is a great comforter; in the summer many Provençals indulge in *le grand aïoli*, or even *le petit aïoli*, instead of the regular luncheon. The quantity of garlic, they say, helps to send them to sleep when taking the essential siesta in the summer heat.

The ingredients for a meal which makes *le grand aïoli* are traditionally poached fish, such as cod, or in its season salt cod. It is also excellent with hard-boiled eggs, perfect with lobster and with vegetables, in particular globe artichokes, which are served hot or cold. The vegetables vary with the seasons but a most frequent combination is with boiled jacket potatoes, carrots and string beans. However, at Christmas *aïoli* sauce is often served with a dish of snails. *Le grand aïoli* is a meal in itself and you follow it only with a green salad, maybe a small piece of goat cheese, or a salad made of fennel and celery cut into *julienne* strips and flavoured with fennel seeds, which supposedly freshen the breath.

The *aïoli* simply as a sauce turns up all over Provence. In Aix-en-Provence it is served with somewhat underdone roast lamb, which is very good, or with grilled lamb chops. Often it is mixed into one or other of the many local fish soups. It is served with fish on Ash Wednesday, after carnivals, and at many village festivals.

Indeed, there are fêtes in which *aïoli* is the main attraction and the fish and vegetables served with it are simply an excuse to indulge in an *aïoli* session.

What then is this sauce, sometimes called the butter of Provence? It is an unctuous mayonnaise flavoured with crushed garlic to satisfy the Provençal palate. *Aïoli* is made with the local sweet, first-pressed Provençal olive oil and with the dead-white local garlic, which grows in the sandy soil and is sold in all Provençal markets in September. Vinegar is never used in its preparation. The quantity of garlic used varies: tradition decrees 2 cloves per person, but today some Provençals find this rather too much, so it is often made with 1 clove per person.

Peel and crush the garlic with a pestle in a large mortar, adding salt and pepper to taste. Add the egg yolks, one at a time, whisking them with a wire whisk all the time. Leave for 10 minutes. Add the oil, drop by drop as for mayonnaise, until the eggs and oil have thickened. Once this has happened, the oil can be added in a steady stream. Finally add the lemon juice. *Aïoli* can also be made in a liquidizer. Some Provençals also add crushed sea-urchin eggs when they are obtainable; this gives the *aïoli* a fish flavour, plus some colour. Serve in a bowl, with the fish and vegetables on a large dish.

Apart from the fish and vegetables, a chunk of French bread is served. And the wine? Preferably a local *rosé*.

Lobster mayonnaise
France

TO SERVE TWO–FOUR

INGREDIENTS
1–2 cooked lobsters
mayonnaise
lettuce leaves

Alexander Dumas's sauce

4 tablespoons olive oil
1 tablespoon French
mustard, preferably
Dijon
2 tablespoons mixed finely
chopped parsley, tarragon
and chives
1 generous tablespoon
finely chopped shallot or
onion
12 drops soya sauce
freshly ground white
pepper
1–2 tablespoons Pernod or
Pastis

Today lobsters are most frequently sold already boiled, although it is possible sometimes to buy them alive. However, generally speaking unless living within yards of the lobster baskets, ready-boiled lobsters are the better buy as many of the so-called live creatures we see in the larger cities away from the sea are rather more dead than alive.

Wipe the lobster with a damp cloth. Twist off all the claws and legs. Crack the claws with a nutcracker at the broadest part of each. Put aside, still with their flesh inside. Put the lobster on to a large chopping board with the shell uppermost and the tail well spread out. With a strong pointed knife pierce the head just behind the eyes and drive the knife downwards along the middle of the lobster and split it into halves. Turn it flat on the board and pull out the intestinal cord, a dark line that runs the length of the tail. Then take out the dark stomach sac, which lies near the head, as well as the sponge-like gills.

The traditional method of serving the lobster is to leave it in its shell, the head upright on a dish, with the cracked shell around it, and garnished with lettuce and a mayonnaise sauce served separately. In Scandinavia they serve very thinly sliced brown buttered bread, or white buttered toast, with lobster. Some people prefer to take all the meat out of the lobster, slice the tail meat into rounds and dice the rest. This does stretch the quantity a little and, whereas one lobster does only for two when halved and retained in the shell, it can be made just enough for three when cut and taken out of the shell. If you are doing this, place the lobster meat along the length of a plate and on either side arrange thinly sliced cucumber and hard-boiled egg. Pour the dressing over the lobster immediately before serving. Instead of mayonnaise, lobster can be served with a salad dressing, or a sauce tartare, or the following sauce, which Alexander Dumas *père* recommends in his *Grand Dictionnaire de Cuisine*.

Alexander Dumas's sauce

Put the oil into a small sauce bowl, add the mustard and mix this thoroughly, then add the herbs and onion, again stir well, add the soya sauce, pepper and finally the Pernod. It is very good.

Lobster Newburg
USA

TO SERVE FOUR

INGREDIENTS
meat from 1 large lobster
50 g (2 oz) butter
1 teaspoon salt
1 teaspoon cayenne pepper
2 tablespoons dry sherry
1 tablespoon brandy
75 ml (3 fl oz) milk
275 ml (½ pint) double
cream
2 egg yolks
2 tablespoons milk

Top: lobster with Alexander Dumas's sauce; *bottom:* lobster Newburg

Lobster Newburg, it is said, was created in New York at the turn of the century by a well-known man-about-town, Ben Wenburg, who spent much of his time eating at Delmonico's, then one of New York's most famous restaurants. The story goes that Wenburg would gather together a group of cronies and prepare for them at table his own special creamy sauce for lobster. In time it became well known and a house speciality, called by the chef Lobster à la Wenburg. However, one day Delmonico and Wenburg quarrelled and to spite Wenburg the dish was renamed Lobster Newburg, a reversal of the first three letters. The dish was considered in those days a splendid one for a man-about-town to order in his bachelor apartment, cooked and served in a chafing dish, together with a bottle of well-iced champagne: 'the perfect prelude to a quiet seduction' it was claimed.

Naturally, as with all famous recipes, there are variations but among my books I have one written by Filippini, formerly of Delmonico's, in 1906. His should be the most authentic, for he was *the* chef of this famous establishment at the end of the last century. Mr Filippini would have us plunge 2 live lobsters into boiling water with 1 tablespoon of salt and boil for 20 minutes.

Then remove the meat from the claws and tail. But as today lobsters are generally bought already cooked, we must perforce omit this piece of advice, good though it is. Tinned lobster can also be used.

Take the meat from the lobster and cut it into 2-cm (½-in) pieces. Heat the butter in a heavy frying pan, add the salt and cayenne pepper and cook gently for 5 minutes, letting the meat lightly brown, but turning it again and again to avoid overcooking. Add the sherry and brandy and cook for 3 minutes. Combine the first quantity of milk with the cream, add to the pan, let it come to a slow boil and boil slowly for 6 minutes. Beat the egg yolks together with the remaining milk, take the pan from the heat, and add the egg and milk, stirring gently all the time with a wooden spoon. Return the pan to the heat, cook the sauce gently for 2 minutes without letting it boil, pour into a chafing dish, or a deep dish (Filippini suggests a soup tureen) and serve at once.

Devilled crab
USA

TO SERVE THREE—FOUR

INGREDIENTS
450 g (1 lb) crabmeat
4 tablespoons lime or
  lemon juice
2 teaspoons finely chopped
  onion
1 teaspoon black pepper
2 dashes Tabasco sauce
pinch of salt
25 g (1 oz) butter
2 tablespoons each finely
  chopped onion and sweet
  pepper
100 g (4 oz) tomatoes,
  peeled and chopped
1 small clove garlic,
  crushed
1 tablespoon finely
  chopped parsley
1 pinch each dry mustard,
  mace and basil
2 tablespoons dry pale
  sherry
2 tablespoons fine
  breadcrumbs
crab shells
1 tablespoon grated cheese
butter for slivers

There are over a thousand different varieties of crab scattered throughout the world, many of which are edible. The edible crab we know is *Cancer pagurus*, a descendant of the courageous crab who lost his life saving the goddess Juno from Hercules. As a reward, she gave him a place among the celestial constellations, or the Zodiac. Use cooked, frozen or tinned crabmeat (but not dressed) for this recipe. Tinned tuna fish can also be devilled in the same way. If possible either use crab shells or, failing these, cleaned scallop shells, or even ramekin dishes for the final baking in the oven. If basil is not available, forget about it; some cooks prefer Worcestershire sauce to Tabasco – it is all a matter of taste.

Marinate the crabmeat in a bowl in the lime juice with the finely chopped onion, black pepper, Tabasco and salt to taste. Leave this in the refrigerator for 2–3 hours. Preheat the oven to 180°C, 350°F, Gas Mark 4. Shortly before serving, heat the butter in a pan, add the onion and sweet pepper, tomato, garlic and parsley and cook gently until the onion and pepper are soft. Add the mustard, mace and basil, stir well, add the sherry and half the breadcrumbs. Stir gently and cook over a low heat for a minute or two. Add the crabmeat with its marinade and cook gently until the mixture is hot. Fill the mixture into the shells or ramekins, sprinkle lightly with the remaining breadcrumbs mixed with the cheese, dot with slivers of butter and bake in the oven for 8–10 minutes or until the top is brown.

Black crabs
Jamaica

These are land crabs which go down to the sea for the breeding season. This migration is an annual event, and as the crabs at this time are at their best they fall victim in considerable numbers to the local gourmets. The crabs cross the island like an invading army. Driving along the Jamaica roads during such an invasion is an extraordinary experience. Although the car wheels crush hundreds of the creatures, more and more plough on like a relentless black cloud.

Black crabs are reckoned a great delicacy and each planter's family has 'the best recipe on the island'. For every dozen black crab backs (shells) filled you will need about 18 crabs.

When you are ready to start cooking, drop them into a cauldron of boiling water, which usually is established in the garden (this is an exciting moment as the crabs are very agile, and, as soon as their cages are opened, they swarm all over the garden chased by screaming servants who con-

sider it all part of the fun).

Scrape all the meat from the cooked crabs, take out the eggs and put these aside, remove the gall and discard it. Keep the black liquid. Flake the crabmeat into a basin, add plenty of black pepper, a little cayenne pepper as well as some white pepper, salt, grated nutmeg, a little Worcestershire sauce and the black liquid. Mix lightly together and fill as many crab shells as you require. Put one or two crab eggs into each shell, sprinkle with very fine breadcrumbs, dot with butter and bake in a quick oven for 15 minutes.

As black crabs are not available outside the Caribbean, I suggest you either use small undressed crabs and mix the flesh as above, or regard it as a good way of dealing with tinned crab. Put into shells and deal with as above. However, you will have to omit the crab eggs and, instead of the black liquid to moisten the crabmeat, use a pale dry sherry, Pernod or Pastis.

Steamed clams with ham and sausages

Ameijõas na cataplana
Portugal

TO SERVE FOUR

INGREDIENTS
900 g (2 lb) small clams
100 g (4 oz) smoked ham
100 g (4 oz) *chorizo*
  sausage
25 g (1 oz) butter
1 tablespoon olive oil
350 g (12 oz) onions,
  thinly sliced
1 tablespoon *piri-piri*
  (*see recipe*)
1 teaspoon paprika pepper
1–2 cloves garlic
4 tablespoons finely
  chopped parsley

Left: devilled crab;
right: steamed clams with ham
and sausages

If fresh clams are not available, mussels may be used or, perhaps better still, either frozen or tinned clams. *Piri-piri* is a seasoning made from small hot peppers steeped in olive oil for at least one month before using. If not available, use enough Tabasco sauce in 1 tablespoon of olive oil to make the oil pepper-hot. The type of ham used in this recipe in Portugal is called *presunto* and is similar to Italian smoked ham. A *cataplana* is a favourite cooking vessel in Portugal and is rather like a deep, round metal frying pan with no handles and with a tight-fitting lid, which is clamped on with metal fasteners. Any deep frying pan or shallow pan with a tightly fitting lid can be used instead.

If using fresh clams wash them thoroughly, removing any beards or barnacles. Discard any that are open and will not close when tapped as this means the clams are dead. Coarsely chop the smoked ham and *chorizo*. Heat the butter and oil in a pan over a moderate heat, add the onions and cook these with the *piri-piri* and paprika until they are soft but not browned. Add the clams, ham, *chorizo*, garlic and parsley. Tightly cover the pan and cook over a moderate heat for 20 minutes. Serve immediately as a first course, uncovering the pan at table, so that, as one writer put it, the steam comes rushing out like Vesuvius.

If the pan is not suitable for serving at table, serve on hot deep plates. Some recipes suggest adding about 100 ml (4 fl oz) of a dry white wine to the pan at the same time as the clams.

Prawn pie with mashed potato crust

Prawn pie with mashed potato crust

Torta de camarão
Brazil

TO SERVE FOUR–SIX

INGREDIENTS
450 g (1 lb) mashed
  potatoes
2 tablespoons flour
3 egg yolks
4 tablespoons grated
  Parmesan cheese
1 teaspoon salt
good grating of nutmeg
4 tablespoons oil
225 g (8 oz) shelled prawns
4 artichoke hearts, sliced or
  coarsely chopped
10 olives, stoned
2 hard-boiled eggs, sliced
1 teaspoon capers

Brazil is reckoned to be a paradise for lovers of shrimp and prawn and there are, it is claimed, hundreds of Brazilian recipes for cooking them.

Preheat the oven to 200°C, 400°F, Gas Mark 6. Mix the mashed potatoes with the flour, 2 egg yolks, grated cheese, salt and nutmeg. Line a large but shallow pie dish with about two-thirds of the potato mixture. Heat the oil in a frying pan and lightly fry the prawns. Arrange the prawns on top of the potato, then cover with the artichoke hearts, olives, slices of eggs and capers. Cover with the remaining potato, smoothing it down with a knife. Brush with the remaining egg yolk and bake in the oven for 20–25 minutes. Serve hot.

Prawn stew

Gulai guisado
South Pacific

TO SERVE FOUR–SIX

INGREDIENTS
450 g (1 lb) shelled prawns
1–2 tomatoes
1 large onion
225 g (8 oz) white cabbage
225 g (8 oz) green beans
1 clove garlic
575 ml (1 pint) water
salt to taste

This dish can be served as a starter to a meal, rather like a soup, or as a light mid-day meal. Frozen prawns can be used when fresh ones are not available.

If the prawns are large, cut them into two. Peel the tomatoes and cut into thick chunky pieces. Thinly slice the onion and shred the cabbage. Trim the beans. Pound the garlic. Bring the water to a rolling boil, add the tomatoes, onion, beans and garlic and boil for 2–3 minutes. Add the cabbage, prawns and salt and continue cooking for about another 15 minutes. Serve hot with boiled rice.

Prawn curry

Jhinga ki kari
India

TO SERVE SIX–EIGHT

INGREDIENTS
275 ml (½ pint) thick
  coconut milk (*see page*
  185)
275 ml (½ pint) thin
  coconut milk (*see page*
  185)
1 small piece tamarind or
  3 tablespoons lime or
  lemon juice
3 tablespoons water
½ teaspoon cumin seeds
2 teaspoons coriander
  seeds
8 dried chillies
3-cm (1-in) piece fresh
  ginger
1 teaspoon ground
  turmeric
8 peppercorns
2 sprigs fresh coriander or
  parsley, chopped
1 teaspoon dried mustard
75 g (3 oz) ghee (*see recipe*)
pinch of salt
24 large prawns, cooked

This Indian curry, one of many hundreds, comes from the west coast, known as 'Bombay-side', where the prawns are good and plentiful. Tamarind is usually available in Oriental stores; its flavour is sour so that lime or lemon juice makes a good substitute. Instead of ghee you can use vegetable fat.

Make the coconut milk. If using tamarind, it should be soaked in 3 tablespoons of cold water, which dissolves it into a sour liquid, and squeezed well before using. Toast the cumin and coriander seeds in a dry pan until they are brown, this brings out the flavour. Make a curry paste by pounding or grinding the chillies, ginger, turmeric, cumin and coriander seeds, peppercorns, fresh coriander and mustard with the tamarind, or lime juice, to a smooth paste. It should be thin and add a little water if necessary. Heat the fat, add the paste and fry for about 5 minutes, stirring all the time, add the salt and bring slowly to the boil. Add the prawns, stir and cook gently for 5 minutes. Add the thick coconut milk, stirring as you add. If a more liquid curry is preferred add a little water. Simmer for about 5 minutes. It is important that once the prawns have been added to the pan, the mixture is only simmered, otherwise the prawns will toughen. Serve with rice, pappadums and chutney. Bottled chutney can be used with this dish but I suggest using a home-made cucumber chutney (*see page* 94).

Top left: prawn stew
top right: scallops au gratin
bottom: prawn curry

74

Scallops au gratin
Coquilles St Jacques
France

TO SERVE SIX

INGREDIENTS
9 scallops
bouquet garni
75 g (3 oz) butter
100 g (4 oz) mushrooms
1 tablespoon chopped
  parsley
1 tablespoon chopped
  onion or shallot
25 g (1 oz) flour
150 ml ($\frac{1}{4}$ pint) dry white
  wine
1 egg, well beaten
salt and pepper to taste
fine breadcrumbs

The story of how the scallops came by their saintly name is a charming one. When the body of St James of Santiago de Compostela was being carried by sea from Joppa (now called Jaffa) to Galicia in northwest Spain, miraculously, without sails or oars, we are told, it passed gently by the village of Bonzas on the coast of Portugal. It so happened that on this day an important but non-Christian marriage was taking place and the young bridegroom, a noble knight, and his gallants were having a light-hearted gallop along the sands. Suddenly the bridegroom's horse bolted out of control and dashed headlong out to sea and straight at the little boat. On board were some of the disciples of the saint who were able to save him, telling the grateful knight it was not they who did so but the miraculous intervention of God. They were so convincing that the knight, his bride and all the followers embraced the Christian faith and were baptized on the spot. But, why the scallops? When the knight and his horse emerged from the waves both were covered with scallop shells, clinging to them like armour. This was seen as an omen and from that day on the Galicians took the scallop shell as the sign of St James and scallop shells have been worn ever since by pilgrims travelling to Santiago de Compostela.

When alive, scallops have their shells tightly closed but it is usual to buy them already opened and the shells cleaned.

Preheat the oven to 220°C, 425°F, Gas Mark 7. Take the scallops from their shells and lightly wash in cold water. Dry carefully. Prepare a pan of boiling, salted water, just enough to cover the scallops, add the scallops and bouquet garni and cook for 3 minutes. Take the scallops from the pan and either thickly slice or quarter them. Discard the bouquet garni but keep the liquid. Heat 40 g ($1\frac{1}{2}$ oz) of the butter, add the mushrooms, parsley and onion. When cooked keep hot. Melt 25 g (1 oz) of butter in a small pan, add the flour and stir well to a white *roux* (it is important that it should not brown). Add the wine and enough of the scallop liquid, about 275 ml ($\frac{1}{2}$ pint), to make a thick sauce. Cook gently for 5 minutes, take the pan from the heat, and beat well, beating in at the same time the egg. Add salt and pepper. Add the scallops and mushroom mixture and put this into the shells. Sprinkle the scallops lightly with breadcrumbs, top with the remaining butter cut into slivers and bake in the oven until the top is brown, about 10 minutes. The edges of the shells can be piped with a border of creamed potatoes, added before or after the browning.

Sucking pig being roasted in the Philippines

Meat

The principal meats we eat are beef, pork, lamb, veal and, of course, all their accompanying offal. Meat for cooking is usually classified as dark red meat, e.g., beef and lamb, and white meat, which embraces most other meats.

It is not easy for the layman to judge for himself whether his piece of meat is going to be tough or tender. To be able to do this you must know something of the muscle structure of the animal. When meat is tough, the muscles will be seen to be thick and there is more connective tissue present. This means the meat comes from a mature, active beast. In young, immature animals whose muscles have not been well exercised, the meat is more tender. The most tender cuts of meat are those from the ribs and loin. However, they are no more nutritious than a tougher cut coming from the neck and hind legs.

When buying meat it is important to note its colour. Beef should be bright red, well marbled or streaked with fat. Lamb varies in colour from a light to a dark pink, since the meat darkens as the animal grows older. The fat of the lamb is slightly pink, while that of mutton is dead white. Also lamb is a finer grained meat than mutton. Pork is the fattest meat and should be relatively firm, well marbled and, in Britain at any rate, covered with a firm white fat. Veal is a controversial meat for, to be true veal, it should come only from an animal up to 12 weeks old. The meat is fine grained with no marbling.

It is impossible to be precise regarding cuts of meat, since not only does butchering differ from country to country but also from region to region, or even from town to town. Even in Britain there are eight recognized schools of butchering. In France and Italy meat cuts are totally different from those of Britain, and indeed of each other, while the United States and Canada tend to butcher as did their ancestors before them, e.g., in New York and Pennsylvania they butcher as they did and still do in Holland, and in Quebec as they do in France. In countries where the meat is not always of the finest quality, cuts tend to veer towards small pieces, and in the Far East, in India for example, there are no butchering styles at all, just a simple hacking at meats. In countries where chopsticks are used, meat is methodically cut into very small pieces for easy eating.

Cooking meat should not present problems. Tough meat is best dealt with by long, slow cooking in liquid to bring out its flavour and ensure tenderness. Such meats can be made more interesting with the addition of spices, such as paprika pepper as they do in Hungary, or with the addition of plenty of vegetables, as in the Middle East and the Balkans. Tough meats can be marinated, which is a very popular Austrian and German method of tenderizing meat. In Britain lamb and mutton is cooked rather longer, for example, than in France and Italy. In Italy and Greece kid rates as high if not higher than lamb in many of their dishes, and these two meats are interchangeable in recipes. Offal includes liver, kidney, brains and sweetbreads. In France, Italy, also the Balkans, we find some excellent recipes for cooking offal together with aromatic herbs.

Boiled beef

Tafelspitz

Austria

TO SERVE FOUR

INGREDIENTS

100 g (4 oz) carrots

1–2 celery stalks

225 g (8 oz) onions

450 g (1 lb) tomatoes

225 g (8 oz) parsnips

750 g (1¾ lb) leg of beef

salt to taste

1½ litres (2¾ pints) water

chopped chives to taste

A very important dish in Austria consisting of fine-grained quality prime beef cut from the leg. It was a favourite dish of the long-reigning Emperor Franz Josef and, because of his royal patronage, this dish, which started life among the discerning peasantry, was elevated to noble households.

Prepare the vegetables; scrape the carrots and cut into pieces, wash the celery and cut into short lengths, cut the onions into quarters, the tomatoes into halves, and the parsnips into thick rounds. Put into a large pan, add the meat, salt and water.

Bring gently to the boil, lower the heat and let the water simmer so gently it scarcely moves for 3–4 hours, or until the meat is very tender. To serve, take the meat from the pan, cut into medium-thick slices and sprinkle with chopped chives. Serve with horseradish sauce and hot vegetables such as carrots, potatoes or turnips; or with a cold chive sauce, apple sauce, red-cabbage salad, or coleslaw; or with fried, roast or sautéed potatoes, or with roast onions. The stock can be rubbed with the vegetables through a sieve and used separately as a 'soup', garnished with croûtons.

Boiled beef and vegetables

Hutspot
Holland

TO SERVE SIX

INGREDIENTS
675 g (1½ lb) beef brisket
575 ml (1 pint) water
1 tablespoon vinegar
675 g (1½ lb) carrots
675 g (1½ lb) potatoes
225 g (8 oz) onions
salt and pepper

This is probably the Dutch national dish and is traditionally served on 3 October to commemorate the raising of the siege of Leiden in 1574. (The University of Leiden was founded as a reward for the citizens' courageous defence against the Spanish.) A dish of stewed beef and vegetables, history relates, was the first food the starving populace was given after the long months of siege.

Wipe the meat with a damp cloth and put into a large pan with cold water to cover. Add the vinegar and bring slowly to the boil. Lower the heat and simmer. Scrape or peel the carrots, chop finely and add them to the meat after it has been cooking for about 2 hours. Peel the potatoes; if large, cut into halves or quarters. Peel and coarsely chop the onions. Add the potatoes and onions to the pan and continue cooking for 20–30 minutes until the vegetables are tender. Add salt and pepper to taste shortly before serving.

Spiced beef

Sauerbraten
Germany

TO SERVE SIX–EIGHT

INGREDIENTS
100 g (4 oz) salt pork or bacon
1.5 kg (3 lb) topside or silverside of beef
1 litre (1¾ pints) wine vinegar or half vinegar and red wine
pinch of salt
2 teaspoons sugar
8 juniper berries, crushed
3 cloves
1 bayleaf
75 g (3 oz) cooking fat
100 g (4 oz) onions, thinly sliced
2–3 stalks celery
1–2 leeks
chopped parsley to taste
1 tablespoon tomato purée
3 thickish slices black or ginger bread

Spiced beef is one of the great German dishes. The perfect *Sauerbraten* takes several days of preparation. *Sauerbraten* is served thickly sliced, accompanied by noodles, potato dumplings, or a small type of noodle the Germans and Austrians call *Spätzle*, but Italian *gnocchi* can be used instead. Quite often stewed, dried and soaked apple rings, apricots, prunes, raisins and chopped almonds also accompany a *Sauerbraten*.

Cut the pork into fine strips. Wipe the beef with a damp cloth and lard it with the pork. Put into a bowl. Pour the vinegar into a saucepan, add the salt, sugar, juniper berries, cloves and bayleaf and bring to the boil. Pour it at once over the meat. Cover and leave in a cool place for 3–4 days, turning it over once during this time. Drain thoroughly. Heat the fat in a large saucepan, add the meat and brown it all over. Strain the marinade and pour it over the meat and cook over a moderate heat. Meanwhile prepare the vegetables, washing, peeling and slicing where required, and add with the parsley and tomato purée to the pan. Continue cooking until the meat is very tender, 2–3 hours, the cooking time depending on the quality of the meat. Take the meat from the pan, place on a hot serving dish, and put aside but keep hot. Add the bread to the pan and stir well until the bread is very soft, then rub everything through a sieve or mouli-légumes to make a thick, spicy, somewhat sweet-sour sauce, which is served separately.

Top: boiled beef and vegetables; *bottom:* spiced beef

Pot roast

Virgin Islands

TO SERVE EIGHT

INGREDIENTS
1.5 kg (3 lb) topside of beef
1 teaspoon salt
1 teaspoon pepper
2–3 cloves garlic, finely
  chopped
a little fresh thyme or
  1 teaspoon dried
1 blade mace, chopped
freshly grated nutmeg to
  taste
2–3 sprigs parsley, finely
  chopped
350 g (12 oz) onions, thinly
  sliced
350 g (12 oz) tomatoes,
  peeled and coarsely
  chopped
3 tablespoons vinegar
25 g (1 oz) butter
½ cup boiling water
parsley for garnishing
  (optional)

My own memories of the lovely Virgin Isles are of long ago, when they were gentle and happily cool, for I was there during the so-called winter. I remember in particular one heavenly evening eating in the smallest possible patio of an equally small restaurant under aged trees, and eating well, for the owner was a dedicated elderly Dane who had lived a lifetime in the islands.

Wash the meat, dry it well and cut into fairly large stew-size pieces. Mix the salt, pepper, garlic, thyme, mace and nutmeg and rub this well into the meat. Put the meat into a shallow bowl, add the parsley, onions, tomatoes and vinegar; stir well, then leave for 2–3 hours. Take out the meat, pat dry and reserve the marinade. Melt the butter in a large casserole, add the meat and brown it well over a good heat. Lower the heat, add the boiling water and the reserved marinade. Cover and cook over a low heat for about 1½ hours, longer if necessary, until the meat is very tender. Serve with rice or puréed potatoes.

Beef Stroganov

Byefstroganov
Russia

TO SERVE FOUR

INGREDIENTS
750 g (1¾ lb) fillet of beef
salt and pepper
flour for coating
50–75 g (2–3 oz) butter
175 g (6 oz) onions, finely
  chopped
275 ml (½ pint) soured
  cream
150 ml (¼ pint) clear meat
  stock

Beef Stroganov is now a dish of international repute but the recipe is supposed to have been created by a Russian general named Stroganov. He came from a powerful family of adventurers-turned-industrialists who pioneered mining in Siberia and the Urals and who were given great privileges and monopolies by Ivan the Great.

Slice the beef thinly, pound gently and cut into 5-cm (2-in) strips. Sprinkle the strips with salt and pepper and roll lightly in flour. Heat the butter, add the meat and brown. Take from the pan but keep hot. In the same pan fry the onions to a light brown. Return the meat to the pan, add the soured cream and the stock. Cook covered over a low heat for 15–20 minutes. If desired, 10–12 chopped mushrooms may be added with the onion. Although not traditional, extra soured cream may be added before serving as decoration.

Top: beef Stroganov; *bottom:* beef goulash

Beef goulash

Gulyás
Hungary

TO SERVE FOUR–SIX

INGREDIENTS
900 g (2 lb) boneless lean
  beef
50 g (2 oz) lard or other fat
350 g (12 oz) onions,
  preferably red, sliced
pinch of salt
1 tablespoon mild paprika
  pepper
2 tablespoons tomato purée
1 teaspoon caraway seeds
warmed stock or water
  (*see recipe*)
900 g (2 lb) large potatoes
15 g (½ oz) butter
½ teaspoon strong paprika
  pepper or to taste

The *puszta*, the wide plain that lies at the foot of the Carpathian mountains in eastern Hungary, is the birthplace of many Hungarian dishes. The word *gulyás* in Hungarian means a cowherd and the original stews and soups now called *gulyás* were the dishes cooked by the cowherds in cauldrons, called *bogràcs*, at night when they gathered round their fires. Goulash became popular in Austria simply because the cowherds had to come to Austria, usually Vienna, to do their military service and nostalgically they brought their *gulyás* with them. In early days paprika pepper was unknown but a goulash without it today would be unthinkable. Austria, which has adopted the goulash, favours using veal instead of beef. The finest goulash I think I have been served was away high in the Carpathian mountains in Ruthenia, in a remote village almost on the Czechoslovakian frontier in those pre-Second World War days. It was winter and the snow 'lay round about' and I literally followed in the steps of my husband. We found the local inn: it was really a house where a village housewife cooked for her family, the village priest when he was there, and he was the day we arrived, and the local customs' officers who also used it to take a nap between hours of frozen duty. We all ate, naturally at the same table, and a goulash of great aroma and flavour was ladled out to us from an enormous cauldron hooked over a wood fire. This is but one of the several varieties of goulash dishes, popular not only in Hungary but internationally.

Wash the meat, do not dry it but cut into cubes, as equal as possible. Thoroughly warm a thick pan (copper or iron preferably), add the fat and, when melted, add the onions. Fry these until they begin to change colour and are soft but do not let them brown. Add the meat, shake the pan and cook, stirring all the time until the meat changes colour and the onions are soft, about 15 minutes. Add salt, the mild paprika pepper, tomato purée, caraway seeds and just enough warm liquid to

cover. Cook gently, covered, until the meat is tender, for 2–2½ hours. While the meat is cooking, cook the potatoes separately in their skins until tender. Cool, peel and quarter. When the meat is quite tender, add the potatoes to the pan, mix well and continue cooking gently for another 10 minutes. Just before serving, melt the butter in a small pan, add the strong paprika pepper, stir well and add to the pan immediately before serving to give the goulash its traditional bright red colour.

Beef cooked in foil

Gingani yaki

Japan

TO SERVE SIX

INGREDIENTS
6–8 dried Chinese mushrooms (*or* if not available, small button mushrooms)
salt and pepper
butter or other fat, softened
900 g (2 lb) tender beef, cut into 4-cm (1½-in) strips
6 25-cm (10-in) squares of aluminium foil
450 g (1 lb) sweet peppers, seeded and diced
1–2 stalks celery, cut into small pieces
Sauce
1 tablespoon each lemon and orange juice
2 tablespoons soya sauce
2 teaspoons horseradish, grated
1 tablespoon sweet pepper, diced (taken from above)
stock from the mushrooms

Beef is a favourite meat in Japan, and of Kobe beef it is claimed that the cattle are fed on beer, massaged to distribute their flesh evenly, and generally cosseted. By the time these spoiled creatures are ready for the slaughterhouse they are contented and have been fattened.

Preheat the oven to 220°C, 425°F, Gas Mark 7. Soak the mushrooms in water for 30 minutes and drain. Rub salt, pepper and butter into the meat. Divide all the ingredients into 6 portions but put aside 1 tablespoon of the diced pepper for the sauce. Place a layer of meat in the centre of each piece of foil, then add the mushrooms, sweet peppers and celery in that order. Sprinkle lightly with salt. Wrap securely and cook in the oven for 20–25 minutes. Serve the beef and vegetables in the foil, one packet per person.

Meanwhile make the sauce, which is served separately. Mix together the lemon and orange juice with the soya sauce, the horseradish, 1 tablespoon of the reserved diced sweet peppers and enough strained stock to make this into a thin sauce. If sweet pepper is not available, use grated or chopped radishes in the same quantity.

Other tender meats can be cooked in the same manner. For those who like their meat less rare, prolong the cooking time.

Spanish stew

Cocido

Spain

TO SERVE SIX

INGREDIENTS
450 g (1 lb) stewing beef
150 g (5 oz) Spanish
  smoked ham
125 g (5 oz) salted belly of
  pork
2 pieces beef marrow
  (optional)
200 g (7 oz) *chorizos*
275 g (10 oz) chick peas
pinch of salt
3 leeks
225 g (8 oz) carrots
1 225-g (8-oz) turnip
900 g (2 lb) cabbage
garlic to taste (*see recipe*)
750 g (1¾ lb) potatoes
75 g (3 oz) pasta (*see recipe*)

This dish, probably the oldest in Spain and perhaps the national dish of the country, can be described as either a stew or even a soup. It is a first cousin to the French *pot-au-feu* and the Italian *bollito*. It has other names such as *puchero, pote, cazuela* and *olla porido*, for example. The name derives, as do so many ancient dishes, from the type of pot in which it was originally cooked, a round-bellied earthenware pot which was left over a low fire with embers placed on the lid and the stew allowed to cook for hours while the peasants went about their work. Such earthenware pots are still to be bought in local Spanish markets and can be used over a gas flame with an asbestos mat. However, a *cocido* can be cooked in a modern crock pot. This stew is obviously elastic in the choice of ingredients used, but there are some rules to adhere to. Chick peas, dried beans or lentils must be included, as many fresh vegetables as are available, and *chorizo*, which is absolutely essential as it is this that gives the dish its special flavour, also its red-brown colour. If salted belly of pork is not available use bacon. The Spaniards use *tocino*, salted bacon fat.

Cocido is not a dish for hot weather and should be served as two main dishes: the stock with the pasta as a soup, the meats separately on one plate, the vegetables on another. It is a dish that cannot spoil with overcooking, and is expandable and excellent for large appetites. The French in the past have scorned *cocido*, saying it consisted of 'two old cigars stewed together', but as it is remarkably like their own *pot-au-feu*, such scorn may be wondered at. However, the Spanish do not appear to have taken much notice of this French witticism at the expense of their *cocido*.

Soak the chick peas overnight. Put the beef, ham, pork, also marrow if using, and the sausages into a large pot, cover with water and cook over a good heat. When the liquid comes to the boil, drain the chick peas and add to the pan with a little salt. Lower the heat and continue cooking slowly for 2–3 hours. Meanwhile prepare the vegetables; thoroughly wash the leeks and slice roughly, using as much of the green part as possible. Scrape and coarsely chop the carrots and turnip. Add to the pan. Wash and trim the cabbage and cut

into large pieces. Add to the pan. Add the garlic 'to taste': in Spain a head of garlic would not be thought too much, added to the pan whole, not cut up at all. Continue cooking slowly for another hour. Peel and cut the potatoes into halves or quarters, according to their size. About an hour before serving the *cocido*, take out most of the liquid in the pan leaving only enough to cook the potatoes. Add the potatoes to the pan and continue cooking until they are tender. Bring the liquid you have taken from the pan to the boil in another pan, add the pasta and cook this until tender, 15–20 minutes, according to the shape you are using. Pasta takes longer to cook in stock than in water as the boiling point differs.

To serve, take out and discard the garlic. Take out the meats and sausages and cut into serving pieces. Put on to a hot dish and keep hot. Take out the chick peas and remaining vegetables, drain them well and arrange neatly on the plate and keep hot. Pour a little of the remaining hot broth over the meats. Serve the soup in the usual manner and follow it with the meats and vegetables. Follow with a green salad.

Lobscouse

Labskovs
Denmark

TO SERVE FOUR–SIX

INGREDIENTS
900 g (2 lb) stewing steak, not too lean
1.5 kg (2½ lb) potatoes
stock
1 bayleaf
salt and pepper
butter

Beef stew with peaches and pears

Carbonada criolla
Argentina

TO SERVE SIX

INGREDIENTS
50 g (2 oz) butter
1 large onion, chopped
1 large tomato, peeled and chopped
900 g (2 lb) beef, finely chopped
1 teaspoon salt
¼ teaspoon pepper
150 ml (¼ pint) meat stock or water
4–6 pears
4–6 peaches
4 medium-sized potatoes
25 g (1 oz) seedless raisins

Left: Spanish stew; *top right:* lobscouse; *bottom right:* beef stew with peaches and pears

This was a seaman's dish of meat stewed with vegetables, plus a hard ship's biscuit. The name is of obscure origin but it occurs in several northern countries, in Sweden as *lapskojs*, with mashed potatoes, salted beef, ham and onions all mixed together; the Danish version is as below; the Germans have two *Labskaus* recipes, one claimed as a speciality of the Rhineland, the other from Oldenburg. England calls it lobscouse, a mixture of beef, onions and potatoes all fried together which was served in Cumbria on Twelfth Night; in Liverpool, where it is still eaten, the name has been shortened to 'scouse', a name also familiarly applied to the people of that city and their dialect.

Cut the beef into small stew-size pieces. Peel the potatoes and cut into pieces of a similar size. Put with the meat into an iron pot (or other type of heavy pan), cover with stock and add the bayleaf. Bring gently to the boil, lower the heat still further and continue cooking until the meat is tender, about 2 hours, by which time the potatoes also will be mushy. Stir well, add salt and pepper and serve in a hot deep dish. Top each portion when on the plates with a generous knob of butter.

The Argentinians love to eat well and many are the dishes that combine meat and fruits as in this typical Argentinian recipe. Other fruit such as apples may also be used instead of peaches.

Melt the butter in a large pan, add the onion and cook fairly quickly until it begins to brown, then add the tomato. Stir well, add the meat, stir again and let it brown extremely slowly. Add salt, pepper and stock, cover and simmer for 1 hour. Meanwhile peel and core the pears and cut into halves. Peel and stone the peaches and cut into halves or quarters, depending on their size. Peel and quarter the potatoes. Add these ingredients to the pan, cover and continue cooking until everything is tender. Finally add the raisins. The *carbonada* should not be too juicy; if it seems to be so, uncover and let it cook until the surplus liquid evaporates. Serve with boiled rice or a pilau (*see page* 51).

Chile con carne

Mexico and USA

TO SERVE FOUR–FIVE

INGREDIENTS
350 g (12 oz) sweet peppers
675 g (1½ lb) beef or pork
450 g (1 lb) onions
2–4 cloves garlic
100 g (4 oz) beef suet or
    other fat
salt and pepper
4 dried chillies
275 ml (½ pint) hot water
    or stock

Is this an American or Mexican dish? Even the American cookery experts seem to disagree. Some say that it is a North American development, as typical of American cooking as apple pie; others describe how when frost and sleet sweeps across the plains from Texas into Mexico the Mexican *peón* wraps himself in his blanket and gets down to a bowl of steaming *chile con carne* held between his knees. This recipe comes from Mexican sources but there are as many ways to make *chile con carne* as there are makers. It should be a kind of slightly mushy stew.

Soak the peppers in boiling water for 20 minutes to soften them before using. Cut the meat into small cubes or dice. Thinly slice the onions. Drain the peppers, cut into thin strips and discard the pith, cores and seeds. Chop the garlic. Heat the fat, add the onion, garlic, peppers, salt and pepper and fry together until the onions are soft but do not let them brown. Take from the pan with a perforated spoon and put into a saucepan. Add the chopped meat to the pan and cook this over a good heat until it browns, stirring almost constantly to prevent scorching. When the meat is seared, turn it with the remainder of the fat into the saucepan. Add the chillies and the liquid, cover the pan and cook until the meat is tender – the timing depends entirely on the quality of the beef, but it can take as little as 30 minutes or up to 2 hours. Check from time to time to see whether extra hot liquid is required.

You can serve *chile con carne* either with rice, with crackers or water biscuits, or with sour pickles. Instead of dried chilli peppers, you can use chilli powder: here cooks disagree wildly, some saying 3 teaspoons of this fiery pepper, others 4–8 tablespoons, which is violent. Some cooks also like to add a little dried oregano or cumin; quantities of both are a matter of taste. There is a large school of thought that adds about 450 g (1 lb) green or slightly unripe tomatoes to the above quantity, which gives the dish a strange piquancy. If the tomatoes are small, simply chop them into tiny pieces, if large, they must be blanched and peeled as well. Many recipes call for dried beans, soaked overnight (or else use tinned ones), cooked and served separately.

Top: chile con carne; *bottom:* Königsberg meatballs

Königsberg meatballs

Königsberger Klopse
Germany

TO SERVE FOUR

INGREDIENTS
450 g (1 lb) stewing beef
1 large onion
4 tablespoons chopped suet
15 g (½ oz) butter
2–3 slices white bread
1 large cooked potato
2 tablespoons capers,
    chopped
8 anchovy fillets, chopped
1 egg, beaten
1 bayleaf and 1 clove
juice of ½ a lemon
1 tablespoon flour

Pass the meat with the suet twice through the mincer. Finely chop the onion. Heat the butter in a frying pan and fry the onion until soft but not brown. Remove the crusts from the bread. Mash the potato. Soak the bread in water until soft, then squeeze dry. Mix the meat, bread, potato and onion to a smooth paste. Add half the capers and half the anchovies. Mix well and bind with the egg. Break off small pieces about the size of a golf ball and shape into balls. Bring a fair quantity of water to the boil in a large wide shallow pan; do not use too much water or the *Klopse* will float. Add the bayleaf, clove, lemon juice, the remaining capers and anchovies. Carefully arrange the *Klopse* at the bottom of the pan. Bring the water very slowly once more to the boil, lower the heat and cook gently for 30 minutes. Take the meatballs

from the pan with a perforated spoon, strain the stock and return to the pan. Bring to the boil. Mix the flour with enough water to make a thin paste, add this to the stock when it is boiling, and stir well until the stock thickens. Return the meatballs to the pan and cook for 5 minutes. Serve the meatballs in a deep dish with their sauce, accompanied by rice or boiled or puréed potatoes.

Steaks with huancaina sauce

Lomo huancaina
Peru

TO SERVE SIX

INGREDIENTS

100 g (4 oz) curd cheese
3 hard-boiled egg yolks, crumbled
½ teaspoon chilli or cayenne pepper
½–1 teaspoon salt
3–4 tablespoons olive oil
150 ml (¼ pint) double cream
½ teaspoon lemon juice
150 g (5 oz) onions, finely chopped
6 beef steaks
12 green or black olives, stoned
3 hard-boiled eggs, quartered

It is the unusual thick, creamy yellow sauce with a strong flavour that distinguishes this dish. I have also served this sauce with lamb chops and with pork. Instead of using three hard-boiled eggs, cut the leftover egg whites into thick slices. I find that the sauce can take 1 teaspoon of chilli pepper, but tastes differ. Wine vinegar can be used instead of lemon juice.

Beat the cheese until smooth, add the egg yolks, beat these well into the cheese, then add the chilli pepper and salt and continue beating until the mixture is smooth again.

Add the oil, drop by drop, steadily beating all the time with a wooden spoon until well blended. Add the cream, the lemon juice and onions, mixing well. Put this mixture into a small saucepan and cook gently until it is hot. Do not let it boil. Meanwhile grill or fry the steaks. Place on a serving dish, cover with the sauce and serve at once, garnished with the olives and quartered hard-boiled eggs or sliced egg whites.

The sauce has a strong onion flavour for these are hardly cooked.

Top: steaks with huancaina sauce
bottom: tournedos

Tournedos

France

TO SERVE FOUR–SIX

INGREDIENTS

4–6 slices white bread
4–6 tournedos steaks
fat or oil for frying
salt and pepper
lemon juice

Tournedos are small steaks cut from the fillet. They should weigh between 75 and 100 g (3–4 oz). Usually the butcher will shape them into small rounds, wrapping round each one a thin layer of fat. There are many garnishes for tournedos, such as mushrooms and asparagus. One typical French garnish is *sauce béarnaise*, and another is chopped tarragon and tomato sauce. Rossini, the great Italian composer, of whom it was said that he was more fond of inventing new dishes than composing music, created his own version of tournedos which has become famous. His tournedos were grilled and the bread was fried quickly until brown on both sides, on top of which he laid thin slices of sautéed *foie gras*, and for full measure he added truffles. He mixed port wine into the fat in which the bread and *foie gras* had been

fried and poured this over the lot. He is also credited with inventing the name tournedos. He asked his cook to prepare some minute steaks in the dining room; the cook protested that such a procedure was too banal, at which Rossini, ever ready for a pun, exclaimed: 'Eh bien, tournez-moi le dos'.

Cut the bread into rounds a little larger than the tournedos. Grill the tournedos on both sides until brown, or if preferred, sauté them quickly in hot fat until well browned on the outside but pinkish inside, about 4 minutes on either side. Put aside but keep hot. Fry the bread in hot fat or oil until brown on both sides. Sprinkle lightly with salt, pepper and lemon juice. Place a tournedos on each round of bread and serve with a garnish.

Lamb on skewers

Sis kebabi
Turkey

TO SERVE FOUR

INGREDIENTS
675 g (1½ lb) boned rump
  of lamb
olive or vegetable oil for
  marinade (*see recipe*)
100 g (4 oz) onions
salt and peppercorns

Sis kebabi, pronounced *shish kebabi*, is clearly the national dish of Turkey. It is easily prepared in the home, in the country and even on the battlefields, for the Turkish army at one time was always on the march. With the present-day return to popularity of the spit or *rôtisserie*, preparing kebabs of all kinds should present no problem.

Lightly pound the meat and cut into squares. Leave these for an hour or so in a marinade with enough oil to cover, adding the onions, salt and peppercorns. Drain the meat and impale on skewers and grill over a fierce heat – charcoal if possible. Turn the skewers frequently to ensure even browning. Serve hot on the skewers, or with the meat slipped off them – this is a matter of preference – usually without a garnish, although quite often coarsely chopped raw onion is served with kebabs.

Grilling can be varied by putting a bay-leaf, a small tomato or onion, or a chilli pepper between each piece of meat.

Braised leg of lamb

Gigot d'agneau
France

TO SERVE FOUR–SIX

INGREDIENTS
1½ kg (3 lb) boned and
  rolled leg of lamb
salt and pepper
50 g (2 oz) butter, fresh
  pork fat or oil
575 ml (1 pint) water
150 ml (¼ pint) brandy
½ calf's foot sawn into
  small pieces (optional)
bouquet garni
450 g (1 lb) carrots

Braising is an excellent way to cook meat, whatever its quality, as it can be simmered without much attention until it is tender. For French taste, by the time the meat is ready, it should be so tender that it almost melts and the gravy has become a fine glaze. Leg of lamb with the bone can be cooked in the same manner.

Wipe the meat and rub generously with salt and pepper. Heat the butter in a braising pan or large saucepan, add the meat and brown it all over. Add the water, brandy, calf's foot and bouquet garni. Bring to the boil, reduce the heat, cover the pan and simmer. Scrape or peel the carrots and cut into rounds, add these to the pan and continue cooking until the meat is very tender, 3¼–4 hours. Baste frequently and if necessary add more stock or water. When the meat is ready, put it on to a hot serving dish, surround it with the carrots and pour over the top the gravy in which it was cooked.

Serve with boiled potatoes. Instead of only carrots, half onions and half carrots may be used. Braised lamb is often served with white haricot beans. These are cooked separately, drained and served with the lamb and carrots.

Lamb and cabbage casserole

Får i kål

Norway

TO SERVE SIX–EIGHT

INGREDIENTS

1 large firm cabbage, 900 g (2 lb)

2 kg (4½ lb) mutton or lamb on the bone, middle neck or breast

salt and flour

2 tablespoons black peppercorns (*see recipe*)

I was served this dish during a stay in Villajoyosa in Spain where there is a large Norwegian community. My Norwegian hostess explained it is the national dish of her country and 'please do not be afraid of the quantity of peppercorns called for'; she actually said 'a small cupful of them'. Both lamb and cabbage play an important role in Norwegian cooking and this vigorous stew is typical of the local cooking. Cabbages, which in Norway are crisp and beautifully flavoured, can grow to a height of more than 30 cm (12 in). A similar dish rejoices in the delicious name of *pusa pass* and adds carrots and potatoes as well. The following recipe is, I was assured, *the* classical version. According to Norwegians, this dish is better made a day in advance of serving, by which time the cabbage will have taken on a darkish hue.

Trim the cabbage, wash it well and cut into half. Slice into thin strips. Trim the meat and chop into small chunks. Fill the bottom of a large pan with a layer of cabbage, add a layer of meat, sprinkle with salt, flour and peppercorns; repeat these layers until all the cabbage and meat are finished, with a layer of cabbage on top. Add enough water to come one-third up the pan. Cover and cook gently for 4 hours, or until the meat is almost in shreds 'nearly falling to pieces'. Stir from time to time. Serve with boiled potatoes, ice-cold aquavit *and* beer.

Top: lamb and cabbage casserole
bottom: braised leg of lamb

Lamb in an egg and lemon sauce

Agneshko v yaitse i limonov sos
Bulgaria

TO SERVE FOUR

INGREDIENTS
1 medium-sized onion,
  150 g (5 oz)
1 medium-sized carrot,
  100 g (4 oz)
small bunch parsley
1–2 cloves garlic, peeled
1 stalk celery
1 bayleaf
½ teaspoon dill seeds
  (optional)
salt and pepper to taste
900 g (2 lb) lamb or
  mutton, boned
50 g (2 oz) butter
50 g (2 oz) flour
275 ml (½ pint) natural
  yogurt
2 eggs
juice of ½ a lemon
¼ teaspoon paprika pepper

Peel and cut the onion in half and scrape or peel the carrot. Into a large pot put about 1.5 litres (2¾ pints) of water, half the onion, the carrot, a little of the parsley, garlic, celery, dill seeds, salt and pepper. Bring to the boil. Meanwhile wipe the meat with a damp cloth, cut into stew-sized pieces, add to the pot and cook over a moderate heat until the meat is tender, 1–1½ hours. Finely chop the remainder of the parsley. Take the meat from the pot with a perforated spoon, and put aside but keep warm. Strain the stock and return it to the pot. Cook over a moderate heat. Finely chop the remaining onion. Heat half the butter, add the onion and fry until it is soft but not brown. Add the flour, cook and stir well with a wooden spoon until there are no lumps. Add this to the stock, stirring all the time, then stir in the yogurt. Bring to a gentle boil, return the meat to the pot and cook over a low heat until reheated. Meanwhile beat the eggs, add the lemon juice and paprika pepper. Take the pot from the stove, add the lemon-egg mixture and stir well but gently until it is blended into the sauce. Add the rest of the butter and continue stirring until this has melted. Sprinkle with the parsley and serve at once. Serve with boiled rice or boiled potatoes.

Irish stew

Eire

TO SERVE SIX

INGREDIENTS
1½ kg (3 lb) breast or neck
  of mutton
575 ml (1 pint) meat stock
1 teaspoon salt
900 g (2 lb) potatoes
450 g (1 lb) onions
white pepper

Irish stew belongs to that large tribe of dishes that have been sadly mutilated but the traditional version is made with mutton, lamb being considered too good. The 'secret' of an Irish stew is that it is cooked in very little liquid, only just enough to give the meat a start. Then the meat and vegetables cook in their own juices. When the meat is done, it is embedded in a thick mush of potatoes and onions and all the liquid is absorbed.

Trim the meat, cut into neat pieces and discard any surplus fat and gristle. Put the meat into a saucepan, add the stock, and 1 teaspoon of salt, and bring gently to the boil. Skim off any scum that may arise on the top of the pan and cook steadily but gently for 30 minutes. Meanwhile wash, peel and slice the potatoes thickly. Peel and thinly slice the onions. Add the potatoes and onions to the pan, with a little more salt if required and freshly milled white pepper to taste. Cook over a low heat for 1½–2 hours without stirring but shake the pan from time to time. At the end of the cooking time the meat should be very tender, almost falling off the bone, and the potatoes and onions soft. Serve the meat on a hot serving dish surrounded by the vegetables.

Fresh coarsely chopped parsley may be sprinkled over the stew immediately before serving, and triangles of toasted bread added as a garnish.

If preferred, the meat, potatoes and onions can be put into the pan in layers, each layer sprinkled with salt and pepper. It is all a matter of taste and preference. In this case the stew usually is served from the casserole in which it has been cooked. Irish stew also can be cooked in a moderate oven, 180°C, 350°F, Gas Mark 4, and will take about the same cooking time. The traditional accompaniments to serve with an Irish stew are boiled carrots and pickled red cabbage.

eft to right: Irish stew; lamb in an egg and lemon sauce; lamb stew with prunes

Lamb stew with prunes

Tagine

Morocco

TO SERVE SIX

INGREDIENTS

1.5 kg (3 lb) boned lamb
50 g (2 oz) butter
2 tablespoons olive oil
1 teaspoon each ground cinnamon and ginger
½ teaspoon each powdered saffron and turmeric
425 ml (¾ pint) water
4 tablespoons finely chopped parsley
4 tablespoons finely chopped coriander (optional)
350 g (12 oz) onions, thinly sliced
450 g (1 lb) dried prunes
4 tablespoons honey
salt and pepper to taste
2 tablespoons sesame seeds

A *tagine* (pronounced *tageen*) is a stew that is vastly different from those we are accustomed to. It is a mixture of meat, vegetables, fruit and spices and can be made with lamb or chicken. It is a way of cooking especially attributable to Morocco where the *tagine* is cooked in a large earthenware dish with a conical cover that looks like a dunce's cap, or perhaps a Mexican's hat. When the meat and vegetables are on the dish, it is covered with this high lid and the contents cook slowly and with plenty of steam, losing none of their aroma. These *tagine* are sold in the markets of Morocco in all sizes, even tiny ones with enamel decorations for tourist souvenirs. The *tagine*, or stew, can be served in the earthenware pot and uncovered at the table when the whole delicious aroma wafts out. Failing an earthenware *tagine*, use a flame-proof casserole that can be used for serving at table.

Wipe the meat with a damp cloth and cut into stew-size pieces. Heat the butter and oil together in the pan over a low heat, add the spices and mix well. Add the meat to the pan, stir it well into the fat and spices, and cook gently for about 20 minutes, until the meat is lightly coloured. Add the water, parsley and coriander, bring the liquid

slowly to the boil, cover the pan and simmer for about 1 hour. Add the onions, re-cover the pan and continue cooking for a further 30 minutes. Meanwhile stone the prunes. When the meat has been cooking for 1½ hours, add the prunes, honey, salt and pepper, partially cover the pan and cook gently until the prunes have swollen and the liquid is slightly reduced. While the prunes are cooking, toast the sesame seeds in a dry pan until they are brown and give off an aroma, a matter of a minute or so. Either serve the stew in the casserole in which it is cooked, or transfer to a deep, hot dish and sprinkle lightly with the sesame seeds.

The recipe given here is basic. Quinces can be cooked with lamb in the same manner, giving the dish a Persian flavour. Another favourite fruit cooked in the above manner is the apricot, either fresh or dried. Whether the dried fruits should be presoaked or not depends on the type of fruits used. If it is oversoaked, the fruit will not hold its shape and this, according to local tastes, spoils the dish.

Couscous

North Africa

TO SERVE EIGHT

INGREDIENTS

450 g (1 lb) stewing lamb
450 g (1 lb) chicken pieces
225 g (8 oz) onions,
  quartered
100 g (4 oz) chick peas,
  soaked overnight
225 g (8 oz) turnips,
  quartered
225 g (8 oz) carrots, sliced
2 tablespoons olive oil
salt and pepper to taste
¼ teaspoon ground ginger
  and saffron (optional)
450 g (1 lb) *couscous*
75 g (3 oz) raisins
4 tablespoons finely
  chopped parsley
50 g (2 oz) butter
cayenne or chilli pepper to
  taste
paprika pepper

Red pepper sauce

15 g (½ oz) dried chilli
  peppers
½ teaspoon salt
1 teaspoon ground cumin
  seeds
about ½ coffeespoon
  caraway seeds
1 teaspoon medium-strong
  paprika pepper
2–3 tablespoons olive oil
2 tablespoons lemon juice

Couscous is a dish eaten all over North Africa, from the Red Sea to the Atlantic; in Sicily, where the Arabs occupied the island for a long time; and now in France, especially in the south, the recipe having been brought back by French settlers from Tunisia, Algeria and Morocco. Until fairly recently it was always prepared as it was centuries ago, and still is in many homes in the region, in the primitive way, with wheaten flour on which cold water was sprinkled, then mixed lightly and swiftly by the hands of the cook, usually a woman. The idea was to increase the size of the particles of wheat, also to prevent the grains from clotting. It was then put into a basket of palm leaves and placed over an earthenware pot, the *couscousier*, containing boiling water, meat and vegetables. In the *Book of Judges* we read that Gideon used a pot and basket in his simple cooking. Many Provençal restaurants put aside one day a week for the serving of *couscous* and the locals flock to eat it with that same nostalgia many British express for a real Indian curry. There is not one *couscous* recipe, but many, and as far as the ingredients go, almost anything may be included in it: for example, in Tunisia they specialize in a fish *couscous*; in Morocco they add a lot of fruit. In many Arab homes in Morocco, *couscous* is still served in a communal dish and eaten, as is an Indian curry and rice, with the fingers, with everyone sitting on the carpeted floor. This can be a harrowing experience for most non-Arabs who leave behind them a sordid heap of *couscous*. Those experienced in the local manner of eating with the fingers feel that by not doing so something of the essence of the dish is lost. Nowadays a *couscous* is prepared in a *couscousier*, which comes in two halves, a fat-bellied pot topped with a steamer, traditionally made of glazed earthenware or copper but today more often of aluminium. Such pots, imported mainly from Morocco, are available in Britain. The stew is cooked in the bottom section, the *couscous* in the steamer. Failing a *couscousier*, a steamer with small holes lined with muslin that fits easily on the top of a large pan does equally well. The following recipe is Algerian. *Couscous*, also often written as *kuskus harissa*, the *harissa* sauce and chick peas are available in many shops specializing in Oriental and Middle Eastern foods in London's Soho and elsewhere.

Put the meat and chicken, with the onions, chick peas, turnips and carrots into the bottom half of the pot, cover with water, add oil, salt, pepper, ginger and saffron (if used), then bring to a gentle boil, lower the heat and simmer for about 1 hour. Meanwhile prepare the *couscous*. Put it into a deepish plate and moisten it lightly with water. Work it with the fingers until the grains separate. After the stew has been cooking for an hour, put the *couscous* into the top half of the pot, i.e. the steamer, and clamp this on top of the pot. Stir the grains through with a wooden fork or the fingers to give them air and allow for swelling. Steam uncovered for 30 minutes. Take the steamer from the pot, turn the *couscous* into a large bowl and stir well with a wooden spoon to break up any lumps and separate each grain. Add a little salt, if liked. Add the raisins and parsley to the meat and vegetables (some cooks also add broad beans, tomatoes and chopped courgettes as well). Return the *couscous* to the steamer, put on top of the pot and continue to cook slowly for a further 30 minutes. To serve, pile the *couscous* on to a large round dish, preferably of lightly glazed earthenware, or a large wooden dish. Add the butter and, as this melts, work it into the *couscous*. Arrange the meat and vegetables on top of the *couscous* and pour the sauce around it – and use whatever eating utensils you want, from fingers to forks. It is usual to make a really hot sauce by taking a little of the gravy from the stew and combining it with hot chilli or cayenne pepper plus a little paprika pepper and spices. Ingredients for this are strictly to taste, but the idea of the sauce is to make it fiery. You can also use a ready-made sauce, *harissa*, which also is fiery enough for most non-Arabs.

Red pepper sauce (*Harissa*)

Remove the seeds from the peppers as these are very hot. Put with the salt and the remaining spices into a liquidizer and blend at high speed to a coarse powder. With the motor still running, add the olive oil at a steady stream then, in the same manner, the lemon juice. If when the mixture is thoroughly blended it seems too thick, add a little more olive oil and lemon juice to thin it down. Pour into a small bowl. This quantity makes less than 150 ml (¼ pint) and should be used with caution as it is very hot.

Mutton curry

Gohst ki kari
India

TO SERVE FOUR–SIX

INGREDIENTS
900 g (2 lb) mutton or
   lamb
½ fresh coconut, grated, or
   100 g (4 oz) desiccated
2 teaspoons finely chopped
   fresh ginger
100 g (4 oz) onions,
   chopped
1 clove garlic, crushed
¼ teaspoon chilli pepper
1 tablespoon finely
   chopped coriander or
   parsley
1 teaspoon ground turmeric
2 tablespoons curd or
   yogurt
2 tablespoons vegetable fat
1 teaspoon ground ginger
1 tablespoon sesame seeds
1 tablespoon coriander
   seeds
salt to taste
50 g (2 oz) cashew nuts,
   finely chopped

Cucumber chutney

225 g (8 oz) cucumber
175 g (6 oz) onions
salt and pepper
mild vinegar or lemon
   juice to taste

Mint chutney

4–5 good sized sprigs of
   fresh mint
2 small green chillies,
   seeded and chopped
1 teaspoon fresh ginger,
   finely chopped
½ small onion, finely
   chopped
1 clove garlic, crushed
juice of 2 limes or 1 lemon

Cut the meat into smallish serving pieces. Make a curry paste by combining the coconut, fresh ginger, onions, garlic, chilli pepper, coriander and turmeric with the curd or yogurt. Either pound in a mortar with a pestle, or grind in a grinder (I keep a small electric grinder just for spices). Heat the vegetable fat, add the meat and sprinkle with the ground ginger. Cook until the meat is browned, turning it from time to time. Add the curry paste and continue cooking for 10 minutes, stirring continuously. Crush the sesame and coriander seeds and 'dry fry' them, that is, fry in a pan without fat, stirring all the time. Add these to the meat, stir, then add water or stock to cover, plus a little more. Add salt and simmer until the meat is very tender, about 1½ hours. Add the cashew nuts just before serving. The Indians make their curries in a pan called a *dekchie*, similar in shape to the Chinese *wok*.

Serve with rice and chutneys, also if liked with pappadums. Failing cashew nuts, other nuts such as brazil, peanuts, or hazelnuts can be used.

Chutneys

The following three chutneys are typical of real Indian cooking. Sweet bottled chutneys are not usual, although if you like them there is no reason for not using them. Between ½–1 tablespoon of chutney usually is served with each plate of curry. And usually more than one chutney.

Cucumber chutney (*Kira ki chatni*)
Peel and finely chop the cucumber and onions. Mix together, add salt and pepper and just enough vinegar to sharpen the flavour and moisten the chutney.

Mint chutney (*Pudina ki chatni*)
This chutney is a favourite throughout India and one of the easiest to make in Britain where mint abounds.

Strip the mint leaves from the stems and chop finely. Mix with the remaining ingredients and pound or blend to a paste. If green chillies are not available, use red ones, or cayenne or chilli powder.

Onion chutney (*Diaz ki chatni*)
Finely chop as many mild onions as required, add a few finely chopped mint leaves and enough lemon juice to moisten. Leave for 1 hour before serving.

Left: mutton curry; *right:*
baked curried meat casserole

Baked curried meat casserole

Bobotee
South Africa

TO SERVE SIX

INGREDIENTS

900 g (2 lb) raw or cooked
  meat (*see recipe*)
1 thick slice bread, with
  crusts removed
425 ml (¾ pint) milk
1 egg (size 2), well beaten
2 tablespoons curry
  powder
1 tablespoon sugar
salt and pepper to taste
1 tablespoon lemon juice or
  mild vinegar
25 g (1 oz) butter
225 g (8 oz) onions,
  chopped finely
extra butter for greasing
4–6 orange leaves (*see
  recipe*)
2 eggs
12 almonds, blanched and
  slivered

This recipe is also attributed to Zimbabwe but it is generally considered to be a Cape recipe of Dutch origin. There are other spellings, including *bobotie* and *babotje*. Also there are several recipes for it although the variations are not great. The minced meat can be raw or cooked, either beef, mutton or lamb. Some recipes call for raisins or a sweet chutney, about 2 tablespoons for the above quantities, and some cooks add diced apples. Very important are the orange leaves which give the dish a flavour much favoured by the South Africans. As these are not easily found in Britain, bayleaves can take their place but use not more than 4.

Preheat the oven to 180°C, 350°F, Gas Mark 4. Mince the meat. Soak the bread in a scant 150 ml (¼ pint) of milk and when soft, mash firmly with a fork until the mixture is free from lumps. Mix with the meat, stir in the beaten egg and add the curry powder, sugar, salt, pepper and lemon juice. Mix well and put aside. Heat the butter (other fat may be used instead), add the onions and fry until soft but not brown. Add this to the meat mixture. Rub a 25-cm (10-in) baking dish with butter and place 3 orange leaves on the bottom,

spread the meat mixture in the dish and distribute the remaining orange leaves throughout the mixture. Cover with buttered greaseproof paper or foil and bake in the oven for 30–35 minutes if using raw meat, 20–25 minutes with cooked meat. Meanwhile beat the 2 remaining eggs into the rest of the milk. When it is ready, take the casserole from the oven and remove the paper. Break up the meat using 2 forks and let it cool slightly. Pour the egg and milk mixture over the top of the meat, stir gently to allow the milk mixture to flow through the meat, lower the heat to 140°C, 290°F, Gas Mark 2, stick the almonds in the top of the meat, return the dish to the oven to bake, uncovered, until the custard is set, about 30 minutes. Serve with stewed tomatoes and boiled potatoes or rice.

Pork fillets with prunes

Noisettes de porc aux pruneaux

France

TO SERVE SIX

INGREDIENTS

225 g (8 oz) large dried prunes

150 ml (¼ pint) port or Madeira

salt and pepper

flour for dredging

50 g (2 oz) butter

6 thin slices pork fillet, about 450 g (1 lb)

2 tablespoons brandy

150 ml (¼ pint) double cream

This is a recipe from France peculiar to the region around Lyons. In the original recipe slices cut from the hind loin (*points de filet*) are called for but this is a rather expensive cut. In any case, for this recipe the meat must be exceptionally tender. The celebrated gastronome and essayist, Grimod de la Reynière, famous for his wit and aphorisms, was himself the grandson of a pork butcher. He liked to recount how his family made a fortune out of the sale of pork and were renowned for their extravagant dinners attended by '*tout Paris*'. Over one of these, or may be all, presided a live pig, round and fat, comfortably ensconced in an armchair with a linen napkin around his neck.

Soak the prunes for a short while in tepid water until they begin to swell. Drain and put into a pan with an equal amount of water and port or Madeira or just enough to cover, and cook gently until tender. Sprinkle the fillets with salt and pepper and lightly dredge with flour. Heat the butter in a frying pan and fry each fillet on either side for 10 minutes until brown. When all the fillets are browned, arrange on a hot dish, place the prunes in the centre, drained from their liquid. Put in the oven to keep warm. Add the brandy to the frying pan (it can be whisky if preferred), ignite and leave until the flames die down. Stir in the cream and simmer for 1–2 minutes. Pour this over the fillets and serve at once.

Triangles of fried bread and puréed potatoes may be served with this dish.

Pork and vegetable stew

Djuvec

Yugoslavia

TO SERVE FOUR–SIX

INGREDIENTS

450 g (1 lb) lean pork

225 g (8 oz) French or small runner beans

450 g (1 lb) tomatoes

450 g (1 lb) aubergines

350 g (12 oz) onions

450 g (1 lb) potatoes

225 g (8 oz) sweet peppers

3–4 tablespoons olive oil

salt, pepper and paprika pepper to taste

This is a typical peasant dish, found throughout the Balkans, in which any local vegetables are used. It is also distinguished by the somewhat liberal use of paprika pepper.

Preheat the oven to 150°C, 300°F, Gas Mark 3. Wipe the pork with a damp cloth and cut into stew-sized pieces. Wash, trim and break the beans into halves. Peel and slice the remaining vegetables and coat them well with olive oil; this is rather important but, if olive oil is rather too expensive for this, use a good-quality vegetable oil. Grease a large oven casserole with oil. Put a layer of onions at the bottom, add the remaining vegetables and the meat in alternate layers, reserving some of the tomatoes to make the top layer. Sprinkle each layer with salt, pepper and paprika pepper. Cover and put the casserole into the oven and cook for several hours until tender. The stew can be left to cook all day or night if a solid-fuel stove is used. The longer the *djuvec* cooks the more aromatic it becomes. Serve with boiled rice. A *djuvec* can also be cooked on top of the stove over the lowest possible heat.

Pork in a sour sauce

Adobo

Philippines

TO SERVE SIX

INGREDIENTS

900 g (2 lb) lean, boned pork

1 head garlic, pounded

150 ml (¼ pint) cider vinegar

1 teaspoon black pepper

1 tablespoon soya sauce

425 ml (¾ pint) water

25 g (1 oz) cooking fat

Food in the Philippines is interesting, good and quite often rich; and the Filipinos love pork dishes. A strong favourite is a whole succulent spit-roasted pig: the result is pork of a remarkable flavour, with a crisp crackling that is served separately from the pig. The Filipinos are immensely fond of entertaining and I remember one evening in Manila when it seemed everyone was celebrating someone's birthday, christening, or wedding and I found myself being escorted to no fewer than six parties, the hostesses all serving roast pig. This recipe produces a dish of subtle flavouring in which the garlic, despite the quantity, does not predominate.

Cut the pork into strips 5 cm (2 in) long and about 4 cm (1½ in) wide. Peel and separate the garlic cloves and pound them until bruised but still whole. Put the pork into a pan, add the garlic, vinegar, pepper, soya sauce (failing this, use 2 teaspoons of salt or Worcestershire sauce) and the water. Cover the pan and cook very slowly until the meat is tender and most but not all the liquid has evaporated. Drain off the gravy, put aside and keep hot. Separate the pork from the garlic and put both aside. Heat the fat in a flameproof casserole, add the garlic and fry this for 2 minutes. Add the pork and fry it for 5 minutes, then add the gravy, not more than 2 ladles of it. Stir well and serve hot with rice.

Sweet and sour pork

Tim suen goo lo yuk
Hong Kong

TO SERVE SIX

INGREDIENTS
900 g (2 lb) lean, boned
 pork
675 g (1½ lb) green or red
 peppers
1 teaspoon each brown
 sugar, salt, soya sauce
1 egg, lightly beaten
cornflower for coating
oil for deep frying
100 g (4 oz) small onions,
 quartered
3-cm (1-in) piece fresh
 ginger, thinly sliced
1–2 cloves garlic, peeled
 and crushed

Sauce
1 tablespoon cornflour
4 tablespoons mild vinegar
50 g (2 oz) brown sugar
2 tablespoons Chinese
 wine or dry pale sherry
4 tablespoons soya sauce

When the Chinese talk of meat, they mean pork or chicken, and they consider a meal without meat is fit only for the poor or vegetarians. However, Confucius, the great Chinese philosopher, once advised that man should eat more vegetables than meat, so the Chinese compromised, one-third meat to two-thirds vegetables. Sweet-sour dishes are widely known to all lovers of Chinese cooking.

Cut the pork into equal-sized 3-cm (1-in) length pieces or small cubes. Cut the peppers into half, remove the cores and seeds and cut the flesh into pieces as near in size as possible to the meat pieces. Combine the pork cubes with the sugar, salt and soya and leave until the soya has been completely absorbed. Add the egg and mix this thoroughly into the pork. Roll each piece of meat in the cornflour, put aside and leave until the cornflour coating is quite wet. It is important that the meat is not dry when fried. Heat the oil until very hot, add the pieces of pork and fry until they are a light brown. Take the meat from the pan, drain, return to the pan and

quickly fry again for about 5 minutes. The meat must be a good brown and crisp round the edges; take from the pan, drain well, then put on to a hot ovenproof plate, cover with absorbent kitchen paper and put into a hot oven while the sauce is made. Put the pan with the oil aside.

Make the sauce. Mix the cornflour with 2–3 tablespoons of water to make a thin paste, pour this into a large saucepan or *wok*, add the remaining sauce ingredients and cook, stirring all the time until you have a thick, slightly translucent sauce. Put aside but keep hot. Pour off most of the oil from the pan, add the onion, ginger, garlic and peppers and fry over a high heat for 2–3 minutes. Then add these to the hot sauce, followed by the pieces of pork. Cook for a moment or so, stir lightly and serve at once. This is not a dish meant to be smothered in a sauce.

Fish can be cooked in the same manner, so can cubed, tender pieces of boned chicken or turkey, and pork spareribs which are chopped into 3-cm (1-in) pieces and eaten with the fingers. Pineapple cubes may be substituted for the peppers.

Veal escalope

Schnitzel
Austria

TO SERVE FOUR

INGREDIENTS

4 veal fillets
salt to taste
flour for coating
fat for frying
1 tablespoon stock or water
25 g (1 oz) butter
lemon for garnishing

Top to bottom: Schnitzel;
Wiener Schnitzel; Holsteiner
Schnitzel

For most people *Schnitzel* conjures up Austria and Vienna in particular, yet it rightly belongs to Spain. This is how it all happened. According to the Vienna State Archives, there is an account by Count Attems, Adjutant to the Emperor Franz Josef, of a report from Field Marshal Radetsky on the development of the Italian campaign in which he seems to have written on food as much as war, and in particular of a *scaloppine alla milanese*. The Emperor, intrigued, asked for a demonstration. This was given to the Imperial chefs who learned their lesson so well the Field Marshal was said to have remarked he wished his military orders were carried out with the same accuracy. The Emperor, too, heartily appreciated the dish and it soon made a triumphal entry into the fashionable Viennese restaurants, with variations as always in such cases, and was finally claimed as *echt wienerisch*, with no Italian disputing the claim. However, this may well have been because the Italians knew that its origin actually was Spanish, coming to Italy with the Spanish troops of Emperor Charles V.

However, whatever its origin, a *Schnitzel* is delicate and should be prepared with veal fillets each weighing no more than 100–150 g (4–5 oz) and pounded thinly. Usually the butcher will do this for you. The meat is cut from the fillet, best end of neck or topside. Sometimes the meat is pounded until it is so thin that it loses its flavour. I have seen *Schnitzel*, especially so-called *Wiener Schnitzel*, pounded until they are the size of a dinner plate and smothered thickly with breadcrumbs until the only thing you taste is the crumb coating.

The following recipe is for a plain *Schnitzel*, without any coating at all, thus retaining all its delicate flavour. If the butcher has not pounded your meat for you, place it between sheets of waxed or greaseproof paper and beat well but not too harshly until thin and flat. Sprinkle both sides lightly with salt and one side lightly with flour. Heat just enough fat to coat the bottom of a heavy frying pan and add 2 of the fillets, no more, and fry the unfloured side quickly and as evenly as possible until brown. Turn and fry the other side in the same way. Place on a hot plate, keep warm and repeat this performance with the remaining fillets, adding if required a little more fat. Pour off any surplus fat but keep any remaining bits of juice in the pan. Add the liquid and butter and stir well until the butter has melted and the gravy hot. Pour this over the *Schnitzel* and serve at once, garnished with wedges of lemon.

Holsteiner Schnitzel. *Schnitzel* cooked as above topped with a fried egg, garnished with anchovy fillets and capers, and served with lemon.

Pariser Schnitzel. Before being fried as above, the escalopes are dipped in well-beaten egg.

Emperor Schnitzel. The escalopes are slightly smaller, fried as for plain *Schnitzel* but, after they have been taken from the pan, a few tablespoons of cream are added to the gravy and cooked until the sauce is thick and yellowish, then 2 tablespoons of lemon juice and some grated lemon rind is added and the sauce poured over the *Schnitzel* before serving.

Wiener Schnitzel. For this the escalopes are lightly coated on both sides with flour and beaten egg and fine breadcrumbs. The coating should not be too thick, so shake the escalopes lightly before adding the egg. Leave for 10 minutes to allow the coating to set before frying. Serve with wedges of lemon, sautéed potatoes and a green salad.

Chopped veal

Geschnetzeltes Kalbfleisch
Switzerland

TO SERVE FOUR

INGREDIENTS
1 medium-sized onion
100 g (4 oz) butter
450 g (1 lb) veal fillets
salt and pepper
squeeze of lemon juice

This favourite Swiss dish depends entirely on the way of chopping the meat, for it must either be chopped by hand with a knife, or cut with kitchen scissors, and never minced. The size of the pieces should be about ½ cm (⅛ in) thick. The meat must have absolutely no fat on it.

Finely chop the onion. Heat the butter in a heavy frying pan, add the onion and fry until soft but not brown. Add the meat and cook for 2–3 minutes over a high heat, the meat being cut in such small pieces that it will cook in this time. Sprinkle with salt and pepper and just a squeeze of lemon juice. Serve with *Rösti (see page* 142) or a plain risotto.

Variations
In Zürich, which claims this dish as its own, they add about 100 g (4 oz) of finely chopped fresh mushrooms to the pan as soon as the onions begin to change colour, and let these cook together with the onions until they are tender, and then the meat is added. In St Gallen they prepare the veal in the usual manner, not adding mushrooms but pouring a little cream over the veal and onions immediately before serving, and omitting the lemon juice. All three methods are good but whichever method is used, *Rösti* potatoes should be the accompanying vegetable.

Quebec veal and pork pie

Tourtière or *pâté de Noël*

Canada

TO SERVE SIX

INGREDIENTS

450 g (1 lb) minced veal
450 g (1 lb) minced pork
350 g (12 oz) onions,
  finely chopped
¼ teaspoon allspice, crushed
1 teaspoon salt
¼ teaspoon black pepper
450 g (1 lb) flaky pastry
dry fine breadcrumbs
25 g (1 oz) butter or
  margarine

Quebec veal and pork pies are of French origin, brought to Canada by settlers from France in the seventeenth century. The pies are traditionally served during the festive season between Christmas and the New Year, more particularly at the French Canadian family reunion called *le réveillon* held after Midnight Mass on Christmas Eve. It is usual to make several pies, which are served either hot or cold. They are not unlike a large minced-meat pasty. Although the traditional combination of veal and pork is reckoned to give the best flavour, some modern cooks use only chicken meat or mix it with pork.

Combine the meats in a large bowl, add the onions, allspice, salt and pepper and knead well. Turn into a saucepan and cook gently without adding either water or fat, the meat produces its own liquid. Stir from time to time and cook for about 20 minutes. Take from the heat and cool. Preheat the oven to 230°C, 450°F, Gas Mark 8. Cut off ⅓ of the pastry and put this aside. Roll out the remainder large enough to line a pie dish, 23 cm (9 in) round and about 5 cm (2 in) deep. Sprinkle with the breadcrumbs, and shake off any surplus – they are added only to ensure the pastry does not become soggy at the bottom. Add the meat, dice the butter and sprinkle it over the top. Roll out the remainder of the pastry and cover the meat. Firmly seal the edges and make a few slits on the top of the pie to release the steam while cooking. Bake in the hot oven for 10 minutes, then lower the heat to 180°C, 350°F, Gas Mark 4 and continue cooking for 1 hour and 20 minutes. Take from the oven, turn out and serve the pie hot or cold.

Ox tongue with almond sauce

Cola de buey con salsa de almendras

Argentine

TO SERVE EIGHT

INGREDIENTS

1 fresh ox tongue, about
  1.8 kg (4 lb)
1 onion 225 g (8 oz),
  studded with 4 cloves
3 sprigs parsley
4 black peppercorns
2 bayleaves
capers to garnish

Almond sauce

50 g (2 oz) blanched
  almonds
1 tablespoon olive oil
1 clove garlic, crushed
425 ml (¾ pint) beef stock
2 teaspoons finely chopped
  parsley

Rinse the tongue in cold water, put into a large pan and cover with cold water. Add the onion, parsley, peppercorns and bayleaves. Bring quickly to the boil, skim off any fat from the surface, cover and cook slowly for 3 hours. Again skim, cover the pan and continue cooking for 2½ hours, or until the tongue is absolutely tender (or you can cook the tongue in a pressure cooker according to its instructions). When tender, take the tongue from the stove, let it cool slightly in its liquid, then take from the pan, peel off the skin and remove the little bones and gristle from the root. Keep the meat warm.

Just before the tongue is ready, make the almond sauce. Cut the almonds into slivers and 'toast' in a dry pan until they are brown. Heat the oil in a small pan, add the garlic and stir well, cooking it briefly. Add the stock, almonds and parsley. Bring to a gentle boil, lower the heat and cook gently for 10 minutes.

Slice the tongue, arrange on a hot serving dish, cover with its sauce and garnish with whole capers. Serve at once. You may of course cheat and use tinned or ready-cooked tongue; in this case reheat and serve it with the almond sauce.

Grilled calves' liver

Zürcher Leberspieseli
Switzerland

TO SERVE SIX

INGREDIENTS
900 g (2 lb) calves' liver
pepper
sage leaves
4–6 rashers bacon
50 g (2 oz) butter
2–3 tablespoons hot meat
  stock

There are some delightful old guild houses in Zürich which have been converted into restaurants, large, friendly and offering good food. This dish is typical of those served, almost always together with that great Swiss favourite, *Rösti* (*see page* 142).

Remove any extraneous skin or tubes from the liver, drop into iced water and leave for 5 minutes. Drain, pat dry and cut into strips about 4 cm (1½ in) long and 1½ cm (½ in) thick. Sprinkle the strips with pepper and put 1 sage leaf on to each. Cut the bacon into as many strips as there are of liver and wrap each piece of liver in bacon. Thread on to skewers, 5–6 on each skewer,

depending on how you have cut the liver. Melt the butter in a large frying pan, arrange the skewers in this, cover the pan and cook over a medium heat for about 10 minutes. Turn the skewers once. When the liver is cooked, pour the hot stock over it and continue cooking for a couple of minutes longer.

Serve on a heated dish with the *Rösti* separately, or if preferred serve the liver, still on its skewers, over the *Rösti*.

Bernese alderman's platter

Berner Ratsherrenplatte
Switzerland

TO SERVE FOUR–SIX

INGREDIENTS
750 g (1¾ lb) potatoes
50 g (2 oz) dripping
salt to taste
100 g (4 oz) smoked, rather
  fat bacon, sliced
225 g (8 oz) onions, sliced
4 slices each calves' liver,
  beefsteak fillets and veal
  fillets (*see recipe*)
4 small frying sausages
  (*see recipe*)

One of the most famous dishes in Switzerland is the so-called *Berner Platte* in which pigs' trotters, ears and tongue are cooked with sauerkraut, bacon, ham, smoked sausages etc. It is, as the Swiss declare, a noble dish but probably for the non-Swiss cook it is better to bide time and tackle a *Berner Platte* when in Berne on a chilly day. Alderman's Platter on the other hand is reminiscent of the English mixed grill and was offered to exhausted aldermen after a long session in the town hall. However, it can be offered to the family at lunch or dinner. The liver, beef and veal should be very small indeed, each piece weighing no more than 50–75 g (2–3 oz). The sausages should be a particular variety made in Berne, but other good quality frying sausages can be substituted. The intention originally was to give the aldermen a little something to go with their beer . . . with a *real* lunch to follow.

Peel the potatoes and slice thinly. Heat half the dripping in a large pan, add the potatoes, sprinkle with salt and fry until

they are brown, turning them to brown all over. Towards the end of cooking, when they are tender and soft, do not turn any more but simply smooth down and let them continue to cook gently. In the meantime heat the remainder of the dripping in a second large pan until very hot, add the bacon and sliced onions and fry until both are brown and crisp, take from the pan, put aside but keep hot. Add the liver, the steak and veal fillets and sausages to the pan and fry until brown. Take out the liver first as this cooks more quickly than the meat or sausages and keep hot. Place the potatoes on a very hot dish, top with the onions and bacon and surround with the liver, steaks and sausages.

Meat loaf

Klops
Israel

TO SERVE FOUR

INGREDIENTS
150 ml (¼ pint) meat stock
100 g (4 oz) 2-day-old
  bread, with crusts
  removed
450 g (1 lb) minced raw
  meat (*see recipe*)
175 g (6 oz) onions, finely
  chopped
3 eggs
salt and pepper

This dish can be prepared with beef or lamb, indeed with most types of meat except pork. It can be served either with puréed potatoes, with buttered spinach, or with other vegetables in season. The loaf does not require a sauce but for those who like to have one, a tomato sauce marries well with it.

Bring the stock to boiling point. Break the bread into small pieces, add to the stock and continue to cook rapidly, stirring all the time, until the bread has completely absorbed the liquid. Preheat the oven to 160°C, 325°F, Gas Mark 3. Put the bread and the remaining ingredients into a bowl

and mix well with a wooden spoon, or knead with the hands, until the mixture is smooth. The eggs are not beaten before being added to the dish. Rub a 23-cm (9-in) baking dish generously with oil, add the meat mixture and smooth it down with a fork. Bake in the oven for about 45 minutes, or until the meat is thoroughly cooked and the top a deep, crisp, brown. Slice to serve.

Top to bottom: grilled calves' liver with Rösti potatoes; Bernese alderman's platter; meat loaf

Partridges feeding in a French field in winter

Poultry
and game

All edible domestic birds come under this heading, including duck, turkey and goose. Poultry is often more expensive than other meats on account of the large proportion of waste, such as the carcass and inedible parts. However, much of this can be used in making a stock or soup. Poultry, classified as white meat, is more easily digested on the whole than most other meat because its fibres are shorter and the flesh is not marbled with fat. The most digestible part of the bird is the meat of the breast and wing. Chickens prepared in countless ways are popular throughout the world: they are cheap, plentiful, versatile and have a relatively small carcass. In Chinese cooking, chicken and pork meat are interchangeable.

The duck is regarded by many as an extravagant bird and the gibe against it, 'too much for one and not enough for two', seems well established and often all too true. However, it is a popular bird and many are the great French chefs who have concentrated on it to produce dishes of international fame that belong to the realm of *haute cuisine*, and not to that of the home cook. Today's goose prepared for the markets is usually enough to serve a family, as well as guests. Some regard it as a greasy bird, but European cooks have long appreciated it as a delicacy and understood well how to prepare it to utilize every bit of the soft creamy fat, yet still have a dish of savoury meat. Goose fat, like chicken fat, makes an excellent shortening for pastry. Goose pie was once the Christmas treat of the British and, as, in the nineteenth century, it was every poor man's ambition to have a Christmas goose, goose clubs were started. In Central Europe today goose takes precedence over the turkey as a Christmas bird.

The strutting turkey is a jungle bird which has been domesticated for centuries. It is claimed to have first been brought to Europe by the Spaniards in about 1530 during their Mexican incursion and the first turkey eaten in France was at the wedding feast of Charles IX in 1571.

Guinea fowl, the flavour of which is a cross between that of a chicken and a pheasant, is a rather dry bird and thus requires careful basting and barding. Almost all recipes for pheasant can be applied to guinea fowl and a great many chicken recipes as well.

Tame or farm-bred pigeons make pleasant eating and one finds them far more in French or Italian poultry shops than in British ones. The wild pigeon, classified as vermin, naturally is less tender than the tame bird, which is not surprising, as he has to earn his living in the fields which is hard work. The flesh of a tame pigeon is delicate and best cooked in a casserole or in a covered pan in the oven. Young birds can be grilled, but never too fiercely, slit down the back, or cut into two pieces. Older birds are decidedly better braised.

Rabbits bred for the table should be plump, with plenty of white fat around the rather large, bright red liver. The liver is rather sweet and, if to be used for making a liver pâté, soaking it in milk overnight takes away this sweetness. The strong flavour of a rabbit, which some people find distasteful, can be obviated by soaking the rabbit for at least 12 hours in cold water. This not only removes the odour but also improves the flavour of the flesh and whitens it.

Game includes those birds and wild animals hunted for sport and which are, or should be, protected by game laws. It is a luxury in most countries and in Britain is treated with an astonishing reverence, not only in the field but also in the kitchen. The British are rather conservative in their choice of game, denying themselves some excellent game that is easily available and much enjoyed in other countries. There is no sacred rite attached to cooking game in France, Italy, Spain or Portugal; there, the game is marinated and cut into small pieces and cooked in a variety of ways, usually with plenty of wine and aromatic herbs.

With the increased technology of deep freezing, game is available all the year round and at reasonable prices. On the whole game meat is without fat, it is high in protein and therefore should be an important item in our diet.

Roast chicken with egg and parsley stuffing

Kurczeta nadziewane
Poland

TO SERVE FOUR

INGREDIENTS

2 750-g (1¾-lb) chickens
pinch of salt
juice of ½ a lemon
150 g (5 oz) butter
2 eggs, separated
1 tablespoon finely
    chopped parsley or dill
100 g (4 oz) soft
    breadcrumbs
salt and pepper
extra butter for roasting
    and greasing

Preheat the oven to 200°C, 400°F, Gas Mark 6. Rub the chickens inside lightly with salt and then with lemon juice. Put aside. Make the stuffing: soften the butter in a mixing bowl, beat in the yolks, the parsley and the breadcrumbs. Season to taste. Whisk the egg whites until very stiff and fold into the stuffing. Divide the stuffing into two, and fill the cavities of both the chickens. Sew up the openings or close with small skewers. Rub the chickens with butter and place in a roasting tin. Roast until brown, 45–60 minutes, basting frequently. To serve, cut the chickens into halves with poultry shears, serving half a chicken per person. Baked beetroot, boiled potatoes and a green salad should accompany the chickens. Instead of a pan, the chickens can also be roasted in a chicken brick.

Top: roast chicken with egg and parsley stuffing
bottom: chicken spatchcock

Chicken spatchcock

Britain

TO SERVE FOUR

INGREDIENTS

4 450-g (1-lb) poussins
salt and pepper
1 tablespoon each finely
    chopped parsley, onion
    and mixed fresh herbs
100 g (4 oz) butter,
    softened

A poussin is a young chicken between 4 and 6 weeks old with very tender flesh. It is plump and enough for one person.

Slit the chickens right through the backbone but not through the breast. Cut away the backbone and lay each chicken flat on a board, cut-side down, and lightly beat until it is flat. Rub it well with salt, pepper, the herbs and onion (if fresh herbs are not available, use dried). Use whichever herbs you like. Thread each chicken on to a skewer through the legs to keep it flat while cooking. Rub the chickens with half the butter. Heat the grill and grill the poussins (skin-side uppermost) with a moderate heat until they are a good brown. Turn them over, rub with the remainder of the butter and continue grilling until they are brown, 7–8 minutes' grilling.

To serve, take from the stove, pull off the skewers and place on a hot serving plate. Garnish with watercress and serve with either straw potatoes, game chips, or with crisply fried bacon and horseradish sauce.

Chicken kebab

Pakistan

TO SERVE TWO

INGREDIENTS
450 g (1 lb) onions, peeled
   and chopped
4 cloves garlic, crushed
3 cardamom seeds, crushed
salt and chilli powder to
   taste
1 450–900 g (1–2 lb)
   chicken
75 g (3 oz) butter, salted

The open-air cooking of kebabs can be
traced back to the mountain people of the
Caucasus in Russia, who impaled their
meat on swords and roasted it over an open
fire. This is a simple recipe and, although
all such chicken kebabs are far better when
roasted over charcoal, this kebab is still
good even when cooked on a *rôtisserie* in
an oven. When grilling, remember that the
thickness of the meat and its weight as well
as its distance from the heat are all factors
to be considered. The heat must never be
too high.

Mix the onions, garlic and cardamom seeds
with the salt and chilli powder and pound

to a paste, adding a little water. Rub this
mixture well into the chicken and leave for
30–40 minutes. If any of the paste slips off,
and it usually does, rub it back into the
chicken. Melt the butter and, when ready
to grill, rub some of this over the chicken.
Impale on the skewer and grill either over
charcoal or in the *rôtisserie*. From time to
time brush the chicken with the remaining
butter and grill steadily but not too
quickly until the chicken is tender.

To serve, cut the chicken into half and
serve one half per person with a raw onion
salad, garnished with chopped fresh chilli
peppers.

Tanduri chicken

Pakistan and India

TO SERVE TWO

INGREDIENTS

1 900-g (2-lb) chicken
Marinade
100 g (4 oz) onions, finely
  chopped
3-cm (1-in) piece fresh
  ginger
6 cloves garlic, or to taste
1 teaspoon mixed
  powdered spices
4 tablespoons lemon juice
pinch of salt
½ teaspoon chilli pepper
150 ml (¼ pint) curd or
  yogurt
fresh coriander

Today tanduri chicken is internationally known and requires little explanation. It is chicken marinated overnight, then grilled in a hot clay oven, a *tandur* (the same shape as the barrels used by the forty thieves in *Sinbad the Sailor*), heated by a charcoal fire smouldering at the bottom. The chicken is speared on to a long skewer, put into the oven and rather quickly grilled. It comes out looking rather red and naked. In India and Pakistan it is eaten with the fingers and served with a flat hot bread called *nan roti* and a pungent raw onion salad. When I was in India a whole tanduri chicken was a portion for one, but nowadays they are usually cut into half. When serving tanduri chicken, remember it must be very hot indeed.

Skin the chicken, then cut long slits into the flesh, but without reaching the bone.

Grind or pound the onion to a paste, together with the ginger, garlic, spices, salt, lemon juice and chilli pepper and mix with the curd or yogurt. Rub this mixture into the chicken. Leave, preferably overnight but at least for several hours. To cook, failing a true *tandur* oven, either grill the chicken in a *rôtisserie*, brushing it with oil from time to time, or roast in a very hot oven, 270°C, 475°F, Gas Mark 9. It should not take more than 30–40 minutes to roast or grill: it will be realized, therefore, that only a really tender bird is suitable for this sort of treatment. Sprinkle with fresh chopped coriander immediately before serving.

The onion salad is simply thickly sliced strong onions garnished generously with cayenne pepper.

Grilled chicken with peanut sauce

Sateh

Malaysia and Indonesia

TO SERVE FOUR–SIX

INGREDIENTS

2 cloves garlic
¾ teaspoon coriander seeds
a few cumin seeds
1 tablespoon shelled
  peanuts
1 teaspoon sugar
450 g (1 lb) chicken meat
peanut oil
Peanut sauce
2–3 dried chillies
100 g (4 oz) ground
  peanuts
50 g (2 oz) finely chopped
  onion, fried
garlic, crushed to taste
stock to taste

Lean lamb may be used instead of chicken in this recipe.

The sauce should be made first. Chop the chillies, discard the seeds (the Malaysians would use twice or thrice as many as I have suggested) and put into a small pan with the peanuts and fried onion, a fair amount of garlic and enough stock to make a thick sauce or paste. Instead of ground peanuts, the same quantity of peanut butter can be used.

Pound the garlic, coriander, cumin seeds and peanuts to a paste (or use a liquidizer or grinder), together with just a little water. Add the sugar. Cut the chicken meat into small cubes about 3 cm (1 in) square and rub each piece well into the paste. Thread each piece on to small skewers (in Malaysia they use thin strips of bamboo) and rub each piece with oil. Grill, preferably over charcoal, turning frequently to avoid burning. When brown the *sateh* are ready. Serve on the sticks, with the sauce in a separate bowl into which the *sateh* are dipped.

Chicken Marengo
France or Italy

TO SERVE FOUR

INGREDIENTS
1 1.5-kg (3-lb) roasting
  chicken
150 ml (¼ pint) olive oil
salt and pepper
275 ml (½ pint) dry white
  wine
150 ml (¼ pint) white stock
350 g (12 oz) tomatoes,
  peeled and chopped
1 clove garlic, crushed
100 g (4 oz) onions, finely
  chopped
8–12 button mushrooms,
  about 225 g (8 oz)
4 slices white bread
oil for deep frying
4 eggs
crayfish, cooked or tinned
  (optional)

There are dozens of stories concerning the origin of this dish and it seems that only on one point do all recipes and authorities agree – that it must be cooked with olive oil. Chicken Marengo is one of those dishes that started life rather oddly, but not humbly, and became such a success story that it has found a place in gourmet history. The dish was invented by Dumand the Younger, a Swiss by birth, who was Napoleon's chef when the Emperor defeated the Austrians at the Battle of Marengo in Piedmont. After this effort not unnaturally the Emperor felt hungry and, as he had not eaten all day, ordered Dumand to prepare something special for him. Poor Dumand was in a fix for *en route* he had lost all his provisions. However, being a resourceful man, Dumand foraged in the Italian countryside around Marengo, just southeast of Alessandria, and came back, we are told, with 3 eggs, 4 tomatoes, 6 crayfish, a small hen, garlic and olive oil, plus a small saucepan. The chef used his brains and his bread ration, which he seems to have had with him, jointed the chicken, fried it in oil, fried the eggs in the same fat together with the garlic and tomatoes. He then poured some water, laced with Napoleon's brandy, over the top and cooked the crayfish on top of them in the steam. Napoleon, we are assured, enjoyed it immensely and ordered a repeat performance. Dumand once omitted the crayfish but Napoleon would have none of it: the dish, he swore, had brought him luck and must always be served as it was on that first occasion.

Cut the chicken into pieces suitable fo lightly frying. Heat the oil, add the chicke pieces and fry them all over until a golde brown. Add the salt, pepper and win and continue cooking until the wine i reduced by half. Add the stock, tomatoes garlic and onions and continue cookin until the chicken is tender. Wash the mush rooms (peel them if you like but it is nc necessary) and cook for 10–15 minutes i salted water until tender. Meanwhile tak the chicken from the pan and arrange on hot, flat serving plate. Keep hot in a warn oven. Continue to cook the liquid in th pan until it is reduced by half. Drain th mushrooms and arrange these on top of th chicken pieces. Strain and rub the sauc through a sieve directly over the mush rooms and chicken. Keep warm. Fry th bread in hot oil or fat until brown anc crisp. Heat enough oil in a small pan fo deep frying and fry the eggs, one at a time each retaining its shape by being droppec into the centre of a whirlpool made b stirring the oil round and round with small spoon, or if this is difficult kee bunching up the white around the yolk until the yolks are almost covered and th eggs look fat and round as if in a frill shell. Garnish the chicken with the frie bread and fried eggs. At this point th good Dumand would have added hi cooked crayfish tails, which is not ofte done these days. Some recipes add slicec truffles, which I am sure Dumand did no do since the Battle of Marengo took plac in June, when even in Piedmont there ar no truffles to be found.

Alsace-style coq au vin
Coq sauté au riesling
France

TO SERVE FOUR

INGREDIENTS
1 1.5-kg (3-lb) chicken
75 g (3 oz) butter
salt and pepper
150 g (5 oz) onions, diced
1–2 cloves garlic, chopped
2 tablespoons brandy
150 g (5 oz) mushrooms,
  cleaned and chopped
2 bayleaves
2 cloves
275 ml (½ pint) Riesling or
  dry white wine
150 ml (¼ pint) double
  cream

There is not one but a dozen or more recipes for a French *coq au vin* in which any chicken may be used. The dish has earned its accolade from the quality of the wine used in making it. In many recipes the blood of the chicken is insisted upon, in others decidedly not. The main difference between the various recipes is in the type of wine used. For example, *coq au vin Chanturgue* is made with Chanturgue wine and is generally considered to be the ancestor of them all. *Nuitonne* means that a Côte de Nuits has been used and the dish has been ignited with a Burgundy marc. In the Arbois region an Arbois Rosé is used. The recipe here calls for Riesling and consequently becomes *Alsacienne*. There is indeed plenty of mystique attached to the well-known *coq au vin*: but as a dish it should not be approached with fear, it only demands and must get the right ingredients. It is no more difficult to prepare than a chicken stew.

Cut the chicken into four serving pieces Heat the butter, add the chicken pieces sprinkle lightly with salt and pepper anc cook over a moderate heat until golden al over. Add the onion and garlic, stir well cook for a minute or so, add the brandy anc ignite. When the flame dies down, add th mushrooms, bayleaves, cloves and wine Stir and cook gently for 30–45 minutes, o until tender. Take the pieces of chicker from the pan and put into a hot dish anc keep warm. Continue cooking until th pan juices are reduced to about a cup. Adc the cream, stirring all the time, and pou this sauce over the chicken.

Serve very hot with noodles, with boilec rice or puréed potatoes. In Alsace they als like to add a thin sliver or so of truffle to th pan towards the end of the cooking time

*Top: chicken Marengc
bottom: Alsace-style coq au vir*

Paprika chicken

Csirke paprikàs
Hungary

INGREDIENTS
75 g (3 oz) butter or
  chicken fat
450 g (1 lb) onions, peeled
  and thinly sliced
1 sweet red pepper, 225 g
  (8 oz), cored and cut into
  strips
1 tablespoon paprika
  pepper
2 tablespoons mild vinegar
salt and pepper to taste
2 1.3–1.6 kg (2½–3½ lb)
  broiling chickens
stock or water to cover
750 g (1¾ lb) small potatoes
3 tablespoons soured cream

The key to a successful paprika chicken lies mainly in the paprika, which must be mild and of the finest quality, and used generously. Naturally, it is important to have tender chickens, preferably broilers each weighing about 675 g (1½ lb). The dish can be prepared with a large bird suitably jointed, also with chicken pieces. If a fresh sweet pepper is not available, use one from a tin or jar but thoroughly drain it, even rinsing it in cold water to make sure it has no suggestion of brine left on it.

Heat the butter in a large saucepan, add the onions and lightly fry until they just begin to change colour. Add the sweet pepper, stir it into the onions and simmer for a few minutes; add the paprika and vinegar, salt and pepper and cook for 15 minutes. Add the chickens, enough liquid to cover them, cover the pan and cook over a moderate heat until tender, about 30 minutes. In another pan cook the potatoes until soft. Cool and peel. Just before serving, add the potatoes to the chickens, then the soured cream, and stir gently. Continue cooking over a low heat for 5 minutes. Take the chickens from the pan, cut each one in half and place on a hot serving dish. Add some of the sauce, pour the rest into a sauceboat and serve separately; garnish the chickens with the onions, sweet peppers and potatoes.

Fried chicken of Mohammed Shah

Murghi Pulao

Pakistan

TO SERVE SIX

INGREDIENTS

25 g (1 oz) fresh ginger
200 g (7 oz) curd or
  yogurt
salt and pepper
1.5-kg (3-lb) chicken
150 g (5 oz) ghee or butter
350 g (12 oz) long-grain
  rice
cloves
10 cardamom pods, crushed
2.5-cm (1-in) piece cinnamon
½ teaspoon cumin

Sauce

175 g (6 oz) curd or yogurt
100 g (4 oz) almonds,
  blanched and pounded
150 ml (¼ pint) milk
juice of 1 large lime or
  lemon

Unhappily history does not reveal the identity of Mohammed Shah, but I imagine that he was a good local cook whose speciality was this recipe. I have had to make one or two concessions in the ingredients. The Pakistanis would use ghee (*see page* 186) not butter for cooking the chicken, and those seeking authenticity can find ghee in Oriental shops.

Pound the ginger until it is a juicy mass. Mix with the curd, salt and pepper. Skin the chicken and prick it all over with a fork, then rub in some of the spiced curd. Steep the chicken in the rest of the curd for 15–30 minutes. Heat the ghee or butter in a large saucepan until very hot. Add the chicken and slowly fry for 10 minutes. Combine the sauce ingredients, add a few tablespoons of water, mix well and pour this sauce over the chicken. Simmer for 15 minutes. Take the pan from the stove.

Meanwhile prepare the rice. Cook in a little boiling salted water for 5 minutes. Drain and spread it over the chicken. Add the cardamom seeds extracted from the pods, cloves, cinnamon and cumin and, if required, a little more salt. No further liquid is required. Cover the pan tightly and simmer over a low heat for 30 minutes. Leave covered on the side of the stove for 30 minutes, or leave in a warm oven at 160°C, 325°F, Gas Mark 3. By this time the chicken will be extremely tender and the rice dry with each grain separate. Remove the cinnamon before serving.

Chicken Demidoff

Poulet Demidoff
France

TO SERVE FOUR

INGREDIENTS
1 1.5-kg (3-lb) chicken
100 g (4 oz) butter
150 ml ($\frac{1}{4}$ pint) dry
  Madeira or dry sherry
salt and pepper
225 g (8 oz) carrots, diced
175 g (6 oz) turnips, diced
225 g (8 oz) celery, thinly
  sliced in rounds
2 black truffles, finely sliced
  (*see recipe*)

This method of cooking chicken was created in France during the Second Empire for the Russian Prince, Anatole Demidoff, who preferred to frequent restaurants rather than attend the intellectual 'salon' of his wife, Princess Mathilde Bonaparte. As a regular customer of the Maison Dorée he was honoured with a new recipe for cooking a young bird, done in a casserole with a *macédoine* of vegetables and flavoured with black truffles. The recipe has remained as one of the great recipes of the world, distinguished by its truffles and its extreme simplicity. I do not suggest that mushrooms can take the place of the haunting flavour of truffles but, realizing how expensive the latter are, I suggest that a possible substitute would be Italian or Polish dried *funghi*, which have a stronger flavour than fresh mushrooms and do at least belong, if somewhat distantly, to the truffle family.

A good dry Madeira is preferable to a sherry. (The French have long been aware of the value of Madeira in cooking.)

Preheat the oven to 180°C, 350°F, Gas Mark 4. Cut the chicken into eight pieces. Melt the butter in a flameproof casserole and sauté the chicken pieces. When they are well browned, add the Madeira, salt and pepper. Let the wine evaporate, then add the vegetables, and cover and cook them for 10 minutes. Add the truffles. Cover the pan tightly and put into the oven and cook for 35 minutes, or until the chicken is tender. Serve the chicken and vegetables in the casserole in which they were cooked.

If preferred, the chicken can be cooked on top of the stove for the whole of its cooking time, over a moderate to simmering heat. Diced sweet or mild onions, or a dozen button onions, are sometimes added at the same time as the other vegetables. Serve with rice or boiled, buttered potatoes.

Left: chicken Demidoff
right: chicken Kiev

114

Chicken Kiev

Kotlyety Po-Kiyevski
Russia

TO SERVE FOUR

INGREDIENTS

4 boned chicken breasts
25 g (1 oz) melted butter
50 g (2 oz) butter, frozen
    hard
salt and cayenne pepper
2 eggs, well beaten
1 cup soft white
    breadcrumbs

Curiously it is not by any means certain that this is a Russian dish. I tried without success to discover the source of this recipe, which is also used extensively in the countries bordering on Russia. It would appear to have been a recipe of French origin, despite its name of Kiev; perhaps it was the invention of a French chef who worked in one of the Russian noble houses. This is not an easy dish to master and it is as well to try it out on the family first, although it is only a matter of correctly rolling the chicken breast round to look like a large carrot.

Each chicken breast should be divided into two, unless this has already been done by the poulterer (frozen chicken breasts are excellent for this dish). Skin them carefully and gently pound each one until the flesh is pliable but not broken. Brush the breasts with melted butter and in the centre of each put a knob of frozen butter. Sprinkle the breasts with salt and pepper, and wrap each one round its knob of butter, turning it into a hollow cutlet roughly the size and shape of a large carrot. Seal firmly to keep the knob of butter intact by overlapping the sides. Leave in the refrigerator for 2 hours. Spread the breadcrumbs out on a plate or tray. Dip each cutlet first into the beaten egg, and then into the breadcrumbs. Repeat this process, then return the cutlets to the refrigerator and leave for 30–45 minutes to let the egg-and-breadcrumb coating set.

Prepare a pan of deep, smoking hot oil and fry the cutlets for 5 minutes or until golden brown in colour. Make slits in each cutlet before serving to allow the steam to escape and, most important of all, warn the family or guests to attack the cutlets with care for there is always the danger of the butter squelching out with some force if the unwary simply pricks with a knife or fork. Serve the cutlets very hot, preferably with game chips or potato crisps and peas, garnished with sprigs of fresh parsley or watercress and wedges of lemon.

Fried chicken with walnuts

He tao chi ting
China

TO SERVE FOUR

INGREDIENTS
450 g (1 lb) boned chicken
  breast
cornflour for coating
1 egg white
2 thin slices fresh ginger
1 leek, about 75 g (3 oz)
150 ml ($\frac{1}{4}$ pint) oil for
  frying
100 g (4 oz) walnuts,
  shelled weight
1 tablespoon sugar
1 tablespoon Chinese wine,
  dry sherry or vodka
2 tablespoons soya sauce
1 teaspoon cornflour
  mixed with 1 tablespoon
  warm water

Cashew nuts or almonds, even peanuts, can be used instead of walnuts. Failing soya sauce, use Worcestershire sauce, an excellent substitute.

Pound the chicken breasts lightly and then cut into thin strips of equal size. Roll in cornflour, shake off the surplus and drop into the egg white, mix well and leave until required. Cut the ginger into thin slices. Wash and clean the leek and cut into thin rings, using the green portion as well as the white. Heat the oil, add the walnuts and fry, stirring constantly. As soon as they are brown, take from the pan with a perforated spoon and put aside. Add the ginger and leek to the oil in the pan, stir lightly, then add the chicken pieces and cook for about 8 minutes. Add the sugar, wine, soya sauce and the cornflour paste, stir well, return the walnuts to the pan, mix thoroughly and serve very hot.

Chicken à la King

USA

TO SERVE FOUR

INGREDIENTS
100 g (4 oz) button
  mushrooms
175 g (6 oz) sweet pepper
50 g (2 oz) butter
450 g (1 lb) cooked chicken
  . meat
salt and white pepper
150 ml ($\frac{1}{4}$ pint) dry
  Madeira or dry sherry
275 ml ($\frac{1}{2}$ pint) double
  cream
2 egg yolks, well beaten
cayenne pepper to taste

This simple dish has become so popular that often it is literally murdered. It is said that the late Duke of Windsor so enjoyed Chicken à la King that he devised his own recipe, which seems rather a contradiction. Use only the white meat of the chicken, cut into small chunks.

Wash and thinly slice the mushrooms. Cut the pepper into thin strips, then into dice, discarding core and seeds. Heat the butter in a medium-sized pan, add the mushrooms and pepper, stir, cover the pan and cook for 5 minutes. Add the chicken meat, stir again gently and reheat. Add salt and pepper, the Madeira and all but 2 tablespoons of the cream. Cook gently for 5 minutes. Mix the egg yolks with the reserved cream and stir into the chicken mixture immediately before serving. Add the cayenne pepper.

There are several ways in which to serve chicken à la King: hot at the table served from a chafing dish and poured over hot buttered toast; or in large hot *vol-au-vent* cases; or served with plainly boiled fluffy rice. The addition of truffle slivers as a garnish added at the last moment is often recommended.

Top to bottom: fried chicken with walnuts; chicken à la King; Viennese fried chicken; Country Captain

Viennese fried chicken

Wiener Backhendi
Austria

TO SERVE TWO—FOUR

INGREDIENTS
1 1.5-kg (3-lb) chicken
salt and pepper to taste
flour for coating
1–2 eggs, well beaten
fine breadcrumbs for
    coating
lard or pork fat for deep
    frying

The Austrians say this dish is as Viennese as the Viennese themselves. It is essential that the chicken is tender.

Cut the chicken neatly into four pieces (in Vienna the poulterer does this for his customers and leaves the head on one piece, maybe to prove that it really is a chicken). Pull off the skin to make the coating cling more firmly to the carcass. Rub the chicken lightly with salt and pepper, coat with flour, shaking off any surplus, dip into beaten egg and roll in breadcrumbs. Heat plenty of lard: there must be at least 3 cm (1 in) depth of hot fat in the pan. When the fat is very hot, carefully lower the chicken pieces into it and fry until a golden brown colour. Lower the heat to let the chicken continue cooking until tender, 10–15 minutes if the chicken is really young. Drain well on absorbent paper. Serve hot accompanied by a green salad, lemon wedges, fried parsley, sliced raw tomatoes and small whole gherkins. In Vienna the liver and stomach usually are coated in flour, egg and breadcrumbs and fried in the same fat, just before the chicken pieces are ready.

Country Captain

India and USA

This is a recipe truly without any set ingredients. It is simply chicken cut into small serving pieces, fried with chopped onion in butter and flavoured with curry spices, such as a *garam masala* (*see page* 186). The pieces of chicken are cooked in the butter until 'tender' and the cooking time depends on the tenderness of the chicken. Serve with boiled rice.

This is still an everyday way of cooking chicken in India, although the original recipe is often credited to the southern United States, Georgia in particular. There is a little mystery attached to the name Country Captain, but it would seem that since so many captains in the days of the British Raj travelled up-country, as the country parts of India were then called, and were always served chicken curry in this fashion (they still were in my days in India after the Second World War), the dish became known as Country Captain.

Usually travellers arrived at the government rest houses totally unexpectedly and the caretaker-cum-cook would dash to the yard to collect a chicken, generally chasing the protesting, scrawny creature and wringing its neck unceremoniously. The chicken was plucked and in the pot in a trice, as tough as old Harry.

Circassian chicken

Cerkes tavugu
Turkey

TO SERVE FOUR–SIX

INGREDIENTS
1 900-g (2-lb) chicken,
  boiled
450 g (1 lb) walnuts,
  shelled weight, blanched
2 thick slices crustless
  bread, soaked in milk or
  chicken broth
salt and pepper
575 ml (1 pint) cold
  chicken stock
1 tablespoon walnut or
  olive oil
mild paprika pepper

This dish is served throughout the Middle and Far East. The Turks allege that it was brought to their country by Circassian women who were taken into the harems. The Iranians regard it as a national dish, and in Hyderabad, India, it is called by its old Persian name, *fesenjan*, and served hot with a pomegranate sauce made the colour of black coffee by the application of a red-hot poker.

Strip off all the meat from the chicken carcass and cut into thin strips. Put the walnuts twice through the finest blade of a mincer. Squeeze the bread dry, mix with the walnuts, add salt and pepper and put this mixture through the mincer or, if preferred, in the liquidizer. Gradually add enough of the chicken stock to make a thick sauce. Arrange the strips of chicken in one layer on a serving dish. Pour half the sauce over the top and make sure the meat is well covered. Cover and put aside until required. Just before serving, add the remainder of the sauce, making sure the whole of the chicken meat is well blanketed. Mix the oil with enough paprika pepper to turn it a vivid red and trickle this over the top of the walnut sauce to make a pattern. Serve cold but not chilled. For a richer sauce, dispense with the bread and use extra walnuts, say half as much again plus a little cream. Serve the chicken as an early course to a meal, preferably as an *hors d'oeuvre* with no further accompaniments. It is not usual to serve any accompanying vegetable with this dish.

Casseroled chicken

Pollo Pibil
Yucatán, Mexico

TO SERVE FOUR

INGREDIENTS
1 1.8-kg (4-lb) chicken
350 g (12 oz) onions,
  sliced
450 g (1 lb) ripe tomatoes,
  thinly sliced
3 tablespoons cooking oil

Achiote paste
1 heaped tablespoon
  achiote seeds (*see recipe*)
¼ teaspoon each cumin seed
  and dried oregano
12 peppercorns
1 tablespoon coarse salt
¼ teaspoon hot paprika
  pepper
4 cloves garlic, peeled and
  crushed
1 tablespoon cold water

In the days of primitive man a favourite method of roasting meat was to wrap it in a leaf, such as a banana leaf, bury it in a deep pit in the ground, cover it with hot stones and leave it until the meat was tender, succulent and full of flavour. It is a method that still prevails in many villages all over the world and this dish of chicken is a favourite in the villages of Yucatán. However, I do not propose that Western housewives start digging holes in their gardens, for the Mexicans have developed a delicious urban version, which is remarkably simple.

The onions in the recipe should be white, but other onions may be used instead. It is important that the tomatoes, which are left unpeeled, are ripe – and the juicier the better. Start preparations either the night before serving the chicken or at least several hours in advance.

Make the achiote paste (*see recipe*). Cut the chicken into 8 pieces. Nick the pieces

all over with the point of a sharp knife and rub with ¾ tablespoon of paste. Put aside, covered, in a cool place to let the flavour of the paste penetrate. Preheat the oven to 180°C, 350°F, Gas Mark 4. Have ready a shallow casserole that will take all the chicken pieces in one layer. Heat the oil in a heavy frying pan. Add the onions and cook over a moderate heat until they are translucent but not browned. Add the tomatoes and a further ¾ tablespoon of paste. Cook for a further 5 minutes. Line the bottom of the baking dish with a layer of the onion-tomato mixture. Cover with foil or a lid and bake in the oven for 30 minutes. Uncover, baste the pieces of chicken with the liquid in the casserole (if there is not enough liquid, add 1–2 tablespoons of warm water). Leave uncovered and continue to cook for a further 40 minutes or until the chicken is tender but still firm. Avoid overcooking. Serve from the casserole, together with a bowl of rice.

In Mexico, where bananas flourish, the

Casseroled turkey

Dinde en daube
France

TO SERVE EIGHT—TEN

INGREDIENTS
450 g (1 lb) each onions
  and carrots, sliced
mixed herbs such as
  chervil, parsley and
  tarragon
1–2 bayleaves
salt and pepper
freshly grated nutmeg
1 4.5-kg (10-lb) turkey
6–8 slices fat bacon
225 g (8 oz) prunes,
  soaked and stoned
stock or water (*see recipe*)

When the early European settlers went to the New World they reported finding turkeys in the New England woodlands weighing from 13.5 kg (30 lb) and standing some 90 cm (3 ft) tall. These would seem very surprising and no doubt unlikely to people used only to small, reasonably sized farmhouse birds. But today in Italy birds of a similar size and weight are bred. A leg of these turkeys looks for all the world like a leg of lamb, and can be roasted in the same manner; well laced with garlic it makes a fine substitute for leg of lamb.

A *daube* is a French culinary term that describes a method of cooking meat, usually beef. However, other meats can be cooked in the same manner, including poultry and game. For this recipe a large casserole with a tightly fitting lid is absolutely necessary. Turkeys usually are roasted but this simple and easy recipe provides a change. Instead of stock, water or red wine is often used.

Arrange a bed of mixed onions and carrots at the bottom of a large casserole. Add half the herbs, the bayleaves, salt, pepper and a good grating of nutmeg. Lard the turkey with the bacon, place on top of this bed and cover with the remaining vegetables and herbs. Add the prunes and just enough stock to moisten – the turkey is not meant to be boiled. Sprinkle lightly with salt, pepper and nutmeg, cover the pan and gently cook on top of the stove for 3–3½ hours. Serve the turkey on a large hot dish surrounded by the vegetables and prunes, together with other fresh vegetables in season.

Casseroled turkey

local cooks line the casserole with a banana leaf. This is neatly cut into sizes to fit the dish, passed swiftly over a flame until it softens and changes colour to a rather light green. The chicken is also covered with banana leaf. This does not add so much to the flavour as to give a nicely exotic look to the dish.

Achiote paste
Grind the spices, peppercorns and salt to a fine powder. Add the paprika pepper and the garlic and mix with water to make a thickish paste.

Achiote or annatto is a main crop in South America and parts of the West Indies. The fruit, salmon red in colour, is dried in the sun and powdered. It is used in confectionery for colouring and also in Leicester and Red Cheshire cheeses. The fruit only gives colour, no flavour. It is not yet generally available in Britain, so use about half the quantity of mild paprika pepper and slightly less water.

Roast duck

USA

TO SERVE TWO

INGREDIENTS
2 large oranges
150 ml (¼ pint) rum
1 900-g (2-lb) duck
salt and pepper
1 tablespoon honey
2 sliced oranges for garnish

A duck is rather an extravagant bird and the gibe 'too much for one and not enough for two' has stuck. Even so it has a long culinary history, being offered as a sacrifice to Neptune by the Romans; Cato is said to have served his family a diet of duck whenever he felt they were not in their usual robust health. The Greeks roasted duck with wine from Chios, and the Romans, who ate only the breast and brains, garnished them with truffles. In China the bird has long been connected with Chinese superstitions. To the ancient Chinese, ducks represented fidelity. Mandarin ducks with their lovely colouring develop a strong attachment to their mates and often pine away and die when

separated. However, this little bit of sentiment has never prevented the Chinese from cooking duck in every possible manner and they were busily raising duck long before the Romans thought of sacrificing them to Neptune. The following recipe, although from the USA, is, I strongly suspect, of Italian origin for the Italians are extremely fond of cooking with rum.

Peel 1 orange and marinate it for 1 hour in the rum. Wipe the duck with a slightly damp cloth. Preheat the oven to 180°C, 350°F, Gas Mark 4. Put the marinated orange into the duck's cavity and sew up the opening. Sprinkle lightly with salt and pepper. Prick the duck lightly all over with

Duck with olives

Anitra alle olive
Italy

TO SERVE FOUR

INGREDIENTS
1 2.5-kg (5-lb) duck
salt and pepper
2–3 leaves fresh sage, or
  ½ teaspoon dried
1 bayleaf
2 tablespoons olive oil
1 each small onion and
  carrot, diced
1 tablespoon chopped
  parsley
150 ml (¼ pint) red wine
225 g (8 oz) green or black
  olives

If preferred large olives may be pitted before adding to the casserole. Small olives can be left with their stones.

Rub the duck inside and out with salt and pepper. Put the sage and bayleaf into its cavity. Heat the oil in a deep casserole and quickly brown the duck all over. Take it from the casserole and prick the skin over the breast and thighs. In the same oil brown the onion, carrot and parsley. Return the duck to the casserole, add the wine, bring to the boil and cover tightly. Lower the heat to simmering point and cook for 1½ hours, or until the duck is tender. Take the bird from the casserole, put aside but keep hot. Strain the sauce through a fine wire sieve, return it to the pan, add the olives and simmer for 3–4 minutes. Cut the duck into serving pieces and cover it with the sauce and olives.

Roast wild duck

Pecena divlja plovka
Yugoslavia

TO SERVE THREE–FOUR

INGREDIENTS
1 1.8-kg (4-lb) wild duck,
  dressed
1 tablespoon oil
juice of 1 lemon
225 g (8 oz) fat streaky
  bacon
175 g (6 oz) butter
275 ml (½ pint) water

The swamps and forests of the Vojvodina northwest of Belgrade and the game reserves of the area are famous among shooting men. The region is rich in wild life and every district has its own recipes for cooking the bag.

Put the duck on ice for 25–48 hours as is customary in Yugoslavia. When ready to roast, rub with oil and lemon juice. Cover completely and securely with the bacon rashers and leave in a cool place for 2 hours. Preheat the oven to 220°C, 425°F, Gas Mark 7. Heat the butter and water together in a shallow roasting pan and put the duck, breast down, on the rack. Tastes vary considerably in the manner of roasting wild duck. It is suggested here that the duck is roasted between 1 and 1½ hours, basting frequently. That may well be too much for some tastes as traditionally wild fowl are served slightly underdone with the breast flesh pinkish. If it seems sufficiently roasted in, say, even 45 minutes, then take it from the oven. It is a matter of personal taste. Ten minutes before the end of the cooking time, turn the duck over onto its back to brown.

Serve cut into serving pieces, with a green salad or watercress. Adding an onion and a carrot to the roasting pan improves the flavour of the gravy.

the tines of a fork, then place the bird breast-side up on the rack of a roasting pan and roast, uncovered, for 25 minutes per 450 g (1 lb) of meat. During this time prick the duck several times with a fork to release its fat. Squeeze the juice from the remaining orange and mix with the honey and marinade. With this mixture baste the duck from time to time. If there is too much fat, pour it off before the first basting – some duck can be excessively fat. When the duck is tender, take from the oven and place on a hot dish. Keep hot. Skim off as much fat as possible from the pan juices, pour these over the duck and serve garnished with sliced oranges. Serve with peas, red cabbage, spinach and potatoes.

Pheasant Normandy style

Faisane normande
France

TO SERVE TWO—FOUR

INGREDIENTS
1 900-g (2-lb) hen
  pheasant
salt and pepper
3–4 strips streaky bacon
  or larding
675 g (1½ lb) cooking
  apples
100 g (4 oz) butter
275 ml (½ pint) single
  cream
1–2 tablespoons Calvados

The pheasant is an obliging bird and lends itself to many flavours, but it is also rather a dry-breasted creature. Therefore, it is wise to lard it or cover it well with bacon or strips of larding pork, pounded flat. Although one of the finest game birds to eat the pheasant must, however, be given fair treatment. Some people like them so high that they positively repel; in the past they were hung, either from the head or tail feathers, until they dropped to the ground. However, even if the bird is too fresh it is still probably as tasty as the average chicken. A pheasant will take 3–4 days to develop its flavour in hot weather, up to 10 days in cold weather. However, the French do not hang their birds as long as do the British, so for this dish keep the pheasant underdeveloped rather than over. One hen pheasant is ample for two people but can, if necessary, be stretched to serve four.

Preheat the oven to 180°C, 350°F, Gas Mark 4. Sprinkle the pheasant inside and out lightly with salt and pepper and cover the breast with bacon or larding. Peel, core and thickly slice the apples. Heat the butter in a saucepan, add the pheasant and brown it all over. Take from the pan, put aside but keep hot. Add the apples to the pan, cook gently until they become golden. Place a layer of apples in an oval ovenware casserole, add the pheasant and arrange the rest of the apples around it. Pour the cream over the top. Cover and cook in the oven for about 40 minutes, or until the bird is quite tender. Just before serving, pour the Calvados over it.

Serve the pheasant with the apples and a bowl of breadcrumbs fried in butter separately and, if available, watercress.

Roast grouse
The Highlands of Scotland

TO SERVE FOUR

INGREDIENTS

50 g (2 oz) butter
2 tablespoons lemon juice
salt and pepper to taste
2 young grouse (*see recipe*)
4 tablespoons red
  whortleberries or
  cranberries
4–8 slices streaky fat bacon
25 g (1 oz) butter
cayenne pepper to taste
4 pieces toast

Of the leading game birds it is hard to decide whether grouse or partridge comes out as number one: but most people will agree that, good though the flavour of a young partridge is, grouse takes precedence over it. Scotland has red grouse, not to be found elsewhere except in parts of northern England, and its Latin name, *Lagopus*, has been honoured with the subtitle *scoticus*. Its flavour is exquisite; it weighs about 600 g (1 lb 5 oz) and is probably the most highly regarded and expensive game bird in the world. Grouse should hang for 3–10 days, according to its age, the weather, and personal taste, and it should be carefully plucked to avoid breaking its delicate skin. It must be drawn, not washed, but discreetly wiped inside and out. The livers should be taken out and dealt with separately.

Preheat the oven to 180°C, 350°F, Gas Mark 4. Soften the first quantity of butter with the lemon juice to make a paste and add salt and pepper. Put half of the paste into each bird cavity only, not the crop, and, if possible, add a few of the whortleberries or cranberries to help bring out its flavour

and keep it moist. Wrap each bird well in bacon, separately, then in greaseproof paper or aluminium foil and, to follow an old Highland fashion, add a sprig of heather. Put them, breast down, on to a trivet in a roasting pan and put into the oven and roast for 15–20 minutes. Remove the wrappings, dredge the birds with flour and continue to roast until the birds are brown; complete roasting time varies between 25 and 35 minutes, according to the size of the grouse. They must be taken from the oven in the nick of time, i.e. when brown, neither overdone nor underdone. Caution must be exercised.

While the grouse are roasting, cook the livers in the second quantity of butter for 10 minutes. Mash with salt and cayenne pepper and spread this mixture over the pieces of toast. Take the fat from the roasting pan. Place a piece of toast under each bird during the last few minutes of the roasting. Serve the grouse on toast accompanied by game chips, a clear gravy, fried soft breadcrumbs or fried oatmeal, slices of lemon, cranberry or rowanberry jelly and fresh watercress.

Guinea fowl with mushrooms

Faraona con i funghi
Italy

TO SERVE FOUR

INGREDIENTS
1 900-g (2-lb) guinea fowl
100 g (4 oz) butter
100 g (4 oz) onions, finely
  chopped
salt and pepper
350 g (12 oz) mushrooms
juice of 1 lemon

In sixteenth-century Britain guinea fowl were called turkeys and many literary references to the turkey usually meant the guinea fowl. In fact, not until the reign of Queen Anne was the turkey the bird we know today. Guinea fowl, once wild, are now domesticated and have been reared for several hundreds of years. They like a warm climate, perhaps that is the reason they are found so frequently in Italy. Cultivated mushrooms are called for in this recipe, but field mushrooms or wild ones may be substituted if preferred.

Preheat the oven to 180°C, 350°F, Gas Mark 4. Wipe the bird inside and out with a damp cloth. Heat half the butter in a casserole, add the guinea fowl and brown it all over. Add the rest of the butter, the onion, salt and pepper and cover with foil. Bake in the oven for 30 minutes. Wash and slice the mushrooms and put into a pan, add salt, pepper and the lemon juice. Simmer for 20 minutes and then add to the guinea fowl. Again cover the guinea fowl and continue cooking for a further 30 minutes. Remove the foil from the bird and continue to bake uncovered for 10 minutes. Take the guinea fowl from the casserole and cut into 8 pieces. Arrange these on a hot serving dish and cover with the mushrooms and the gravy in which the guinea fowl has been cooked.

Serve with small, boiled and buttered potatoes and/or peas cooked in butter.

Guinea fowl pie with grapes

Britain

TO SERVE TWO

INGREDIENTS
100 g (4 oz) streaky bacon
1 900-g (2-lb) guinea fowl,
  halved
salt and pepper to taste
450 g (1 lb) seedless grapes
2–3 whole cloves
2 small sprigs rosemary
paprika pepper
1 teaspoon sugar
225 g (8 oz) rich short
  pastry
1 egg yolk, well beaten

Fry the bacon in a heavy deep frying pan until the fat has run out, but do not let it become crisp. Take from the pan, put aside but keep warm. Add the guinea fowl to the pan and fry until it is well browned all over. If the bacon has not yielded enough fat for this operation, add some more fat, preferably bacon or butter. Add salt and pepper. Preheat the oven to 180°C, 350°F, Gas Mark 4. Arrange the guinea fowl in a deep pie dish (preferably an old-fashioned stoneware dish) skin-side up and surround with the grapes. Add the cloves, push the rosemary under the guinea fowl, sprinkle with a little paprika pepper and the sugar and spread the reserved bacon over the top. Roll out the pastry to fit the top of the dish and cover this over the bacon. Brush with beaten egg yolk and bake in the oven for about 30 minutes until the pastry is a golden brown.

Top: guinea fowl with mushrooms
bottom: guinea fowl pie with grapes

Partridges with sauerkraut

Rebhühner mit Sauerkraut
Germany

TO SERVE FOUR

INGREDIENTS
4 partridges
salt and pepper
8 slices fat bacon
100 g (4 oz) butter or
   margarine
100 g (4 oz) onions,
   chopped
275 ml (½ pint) meat stock
4 juniper berries, crushed
900 g (2 lb) sauerkraut

Pigeons can be prepared in the same manner. Instead of sauerkraut, shredded white cabbage may be used, as they do in Holland in a similar dish. Rinsing the sauerkraut reduces its briny flavour.

Clean the partridges and rub inside and out with salt and pepper. Wrap well in bacon. Melt the butter in a large saucepan, fry the birds until brown all over, add the onions, stock and juniper berries and simmer the birds until they are tender, basting from time to time in their own gravy. Meanwhile squeeze the sauerkraut dry, rinse in cold water, then cook separately in a little water for about 45 minutes. When ready to serve, cut each bird lengthwise into halves and serve on a hot dish surrounded by the sauerkraut and garnished with the bacon. The gravy can be thickened with a *beurre manié* (*see page* 184), and served separately or poured over the sauerkraut.

Pigeons in a chocolate sauce

Pichones estofados
Spain

TO SERVE FOUR

INGREDIENTS

4 pigeons or squabs
salt and freshly ground
  black pepper
flour for coating
4–5 tablespoons olive oil
12 small onions, peeled
  (*see recipe*)
2–3 cloves garlic, chopped
150 ml (¼ pint) dry white
  or red wine
275 ml (½ pint) white
  stock
50 g (2 oz) grated bitter
  chocolate
1 lemon, cut into wedges

Cooking game and rabbit with chocolate is a common Spanish practice, and produces a rich, dark and extremely good sauce. It may seem a little odd but the flavour of chocolate is not penetrating. Other small game birds can be cooked in this manner. Either chicken or veal stock may be used in this recipe. The best type of onions are the small, almost flat kind but, failing these, substitute either spring onions, which are often used in Spanish dishes, or shallots.

Wipe the pigeons with a damp cloth, and dry with kitchen paper. Sprinkle inside and out with a generous amount of salt, and then with black pepper. Roll them in flour and then shake well to remove any excess. Heat the oil in a heavy pan, add the birds and cook them until brown all over, turning them from time to time to ensure even browning. Take from the pan but keep warm. Add the onions, cook these over a high heat, turning them around again and

again to let them brown lightly and soften. Take out with a perforated spoon and keep warm together with the pigeons. Add the garlic and 1 scant tablespoon of flour to the pan. Stir well into the fat remaining in the bottom of the pan. Add the wine and stock and, stirring constantly, cook over a good heat until the sauce thickens slightly. Return the pigeons to the pan, stir them gently but thoroughly into the sauce and cover the pan tightly. Cook over a very low heat for 25–30 minutes. Add the onions, salt and pepper to taste, cover the pan again and continue simmering for a further 20 minutes. Add the chocolate, cook over a moderate heat for 2 minutes, stirring all the time but not allowing the sauce to come to the boil. Take the pigeons from the pan with a perforated spoon, arrange on a hot plate and pour the sauce over them, letting the onions fall round the sides as a garnish. Serve with wedges of lemon, with rice, potatoes or a green salad.

Rabbit with Prunes, Flemish Style

Vlaams konijn met pruimen

Belgium (Flanders)

TO SERVE FOUR

INGREDIENTS

900-g (2-lb) rabbit, jointed
Marinade made from 3 tablespoons olive oil, 275 ml (½ pint) each white wine and water, 4 each bayleaves and cloves, 2 shallots thinly sliced, a little thyme and 6 black peppercorns, crushed
Flour for coating
3 tablespoons oil for frying
225 g (8 oz) prunes, stoned
275 ml (½ pint) red wine
Salt, pepper and nutmeg

This is a popular festive dish in Flanders. When I was a child living in the country, rabbit was everyday fare. They were caught in the fields and regarded as the farmer's enemy, being rated second only to rats as a pest. As a result rabbits were later nearly exterminated. However, they have made something of a comeback and once again we can see the old furry rabbits on the butchers' marble slabs. Rabbit meat has plenty of flavour and is easily digested, even by invalids. Some prunes do not require soaking but you can, if you wish, soak the prunes for some time in the marinade.

Samuel Pepys, no mean gourmet and gourmand, liked rabbits tremendously and was fond of offering his guests 'fricassé rabbit', as well as 'rabbit hash' after a dish of oysters.

Combine all the marinade ingredients and mix well. Marinate the rabbit overnight.

Take the rabbit pieces from the marinade and wipe dry. Strain the marinade. Roll the rabbit in flour. Heat the oil, add the rabbit pieces and fry them all over until brown, turn them frequently to ensure even browning. Transfer the pieces of rabbit to a heavy pan, add the prunes, the red wine and enough of the marinade to cover the rabbit. Add salt, pepper and a dash of nutmeg, cover and cook gently for 1–1½ hours, or until the rabbit is very tender. Serve with a sharp jelly, such as redcurrant, rowan or cranberry, a green salad and French bread.

The French cook wild rabbit in a similar fashion but they add a few juniper berries, bayleaf, garlic and crushed cloves to the pan as well. When the rabbit is tender, take it from the pan, add the redcurrant jelly to the sauce and pour this sauce over the prunes and rabbit.

Left: pigeons in a chocolate sauce
right: rabbit with prunes, Flemish style

Hare in lemon with garlic

Lepre al limone e aglio
Italy

TO SERVE EIGHT

INGREDIENTS
1 2.7-kg (6-lb) hare, jointed
275 ml (½ pint) lemon juice
6–8 tablespoons oil
575 ml (1 pint) red wine
20–25 cloves garlic
1 medium-sized onion chopped
1 tablespoon finely chopped mixed herbs
salt and pepper
275 ml (½ pint) meat stock
beurre manié (*see page* 184)

This dish needs preparing two days in advance. Do not be put off by the large number of garlic cloves; curiously the result is not terribly garlicky and the quantity of lemon juice, although it seems rather a lot, gives a most unusual flavour to the hare. Rabbit may be cooked in the same manner.

Put the hare into a shallow bowl and pour over it the lemon juice and half the oil. Leave covered for 24–36 hours. Peel the garlic cloves, but leave them whole. When ready to cook drain the pieces of hare from the marinade and dry thoroughly. Heat the rest of the oil in a large pan, add the hare pieces and brown all over. Add the wine, garlic, onion, herbs and seasoning.

Cover the pan and cook gently for about 3 hours or until the hare is very tender. While the hare is cooking make the *beurre manié*. Take the pan from the direct heat, add the *beurre manié* stirring all the time, until the sauce is thickened. If available also add the blood from the hare, but when adding it do not let the sauce boil or it will curdle. Turn into a hot serving dish. Serve with large croûtons rubbed with garlic.

Spiced hare

Hazepeper
Holland

TO SERVE SIX

INGREDIENTS
1 2.7-kg (6-lb) hare
275 ml (½ pint) red wine vinegar
575 ml (1 pint) vinegar
1 bayleaf
12 peppercorns, crushed
100 g (4 oz) butter
about 350 g (12 oz) onions, sliced
4–5 tablespoons flour
2 teaspoons brown sugar
4 cloves
2 tablespoons soya sauce or Worcestershire sauce

The Dutch are particularly fond of hares and rabbits and have a vast selection of recipes for them. The large hares on the Dutch heathland are eagerly hunted by sportsmen for their well-flavoured flesh, which comes from their diet of heather. Start preparations on this dish at least 24 hours before it is to be served.

Chop the hare into 12 pieces. Combine the vinegar, wine, bayleaf and peppercorns in a large bowl, add the hare with its blood, cover the bowl and leave in a cool place for

24 hours. Take out the pieces of hare and wipe dry. Strain the marinade. Heat 75 g (3 oz) of butter in a large pan, add the hare pieces and fry quickly for about 15 minutes. In another pan heat the remaining butter, add the onions and fry until this is soft and a golden brown. Add the flour, stir well, then gradually pour in the marinade, stirring all the time. Turn this into the pan with the hare, add the sugar, cloves and soya sauce and cook gently for 2½–3 hours until the hare is very tender. Serve with mashed potatoes and red cabbage.

Left: hare in lemon with garlic; *right:* spiced hare

Casserole of venison

Britain

TO SERVE SIX

INGREDIENTS
1.5 kg (3 lb) venison
flour for coating
225 g (8 oz) fat bacon in
  1 piece
350 g (12 oz) onions, thinly
  sliced
350 g (12 oz) carrots, sliced
  thickly
4 cloves garlic
salt and pepper
275 ml (½ pint) red or port
  wine
275 ml (½ pint) meat stock

Game marinade
3 level tablespoons olive
  oil
425 ml (¾ pint) red wine
12 white peppercorns,
  crushed
2 bayleaves
100 g (4 oz) onions, sliced
2–3 cloves (optional)
6 juniper berries, crushed
  (optional)

Cut the venison into stew-size pieces and marinate overnight. The next day preheat the oven to 180°C, 350°F, Gas Mark 4. Drain the pieces of meat, wipe dry, and then roll in flour, shaking off any surplus. Dice the bacon and fry in a pan until the fat runs freely and the bacon is crisp. Take out the bacon with a spatula and drop into a large casserole. Add the venison pieces to the bacon fat and fry all over until brown. Take out with the spatula and add to the bacon. In the same fat lightly fry the onions (if necessary add a little more fat). Add these to the casserole together with the carrots, garlic, salt and pepper. Pour in the wine and stock and cover the casserole. Cook in the oven for 3 hours or, if preferred, on top of the stove over a low heat. Strain the marinade, add to the casserole and bring gently to the boil.

Serve with boiled potatoes and with either a redcurrant or grape jelly, or of course rowanberry or cranberry jelly. No further vegetables are necessary.

As a variation, about 225 g (8 oz) of cleaned, whole or thickly sliced mushrooms also may be added to the casserole, and 6–8 pickled walnuts may be added at the same time as the carrots.

Game marinade

The object of marinating poultry and game is to render their flesh tender and juicy. The word marinade derives from the Spanish *marinada*, which is from *marinar* 'to pickle'. Therefore, a marinade is a kind of pickle in which meats are steeped before being cooked. There are various types of marinades but there must always be enough liquid to cover the meat, otherwise the exposed portion will be in danger of decomposing. Turn the meat frequently to ensure the marinade thoroughly penetrates it. Mix the ingredients together. Do not add salt as it draws out too much of the juices from the meat. If preferred, you can use only 1 cup of red wine, making up the liquid with 1 cup of water and 4 tablespoons of wine vinegar; but make sure that there is enough liquid to cover.

Vegetables
and salads

Vegetables

The term vegetable covers a wide range of edible roots, plants and even herbs. Some are eaten raw, others cooked, while some can be served either way. Often it is difficult for the layman to distinguish between fruit and vegetables. For example, tomatoes, vegetable marrows, beans, peas and aubergines are all vegetables to the average housewife and probably to her greengrocer, but to the botanist they are fruits. For most of us vegetables are those foods which we cook in a savoury manner, fruits we cook with sugar.

The sixteenth century could be called 'the century of the vegetable' because it was then that many unknown vegetables were brought back to Europe from newly discovered lands. It was then also that Sir Arthur Ashley, a keen gardener from Dorset, introduced several new varieties of cabbage to England, bringing them from Holland. And in turn Cromwell's men later introduced them to Scotland. Again in the sixteenth century, broccoli, a variety of cauliflower, was introduced into Britain from Italy; cauliflower came later from Cyprus, at the turn of the seventeenth century. During the reign of Henry VIII we find globe artichokes becoming popular, having arrived from Peru via Spain and Italy, and in the same period Jerusalem artichokes appeared. In 1565 Sir John Hawkins is reputed to have brought potatoes to England and Sir Walter Raleigh introduced them to the Irish about twenty years later.

Although turnips are regarded with mixed feeling by some and considered very much a country vegetable, they were not widely grown in early days. The monks grew them in monastery gardens, but that was about all. But in the eighteenth century the second Viscount Townshend grew them extensively on his lands in Norfolk and conducted such a campaign to grow more and more turnips that he became affectionately known as 'Turnip Townshend'!

The cooking and serving of vegetables varies from country to country. In Britain they are generally regarded as something to accompany meat or fish dishes, but in Mediterranean countries it is customary to serve them as a separate course. Such dishes can be simple, for example, a dish of beans sprinkled with cheeses. In the Middle East, vegetables hold an important place but are usually combined with rice, meat or fish to make a substantial main course. Further afield to India, land of curries, there is no doubt that the best of these are made with vegetables. China produces hearty and rich vegetable dishes while those of Japan have a more delicate touch and are as lovely to look at as to eat. But it is Thailand that combines vegetables with fruit and flowers and all the roots of the earth and the results are almost intoxicating.

The popularity of vegetables in Britain has been something of a see-saw. At one time we had all kinds of 'foreign' vegetables growing in glass houses and on south facing walls, but then their popularity declined. People began to lose interest in vegetables and stuck to a few favourites, such as cabbage, cauliflower and Brussels sprouts, although the latter did not come into Britain from Belgium until the nineteenth century. There were general complaints of the boring and often disastrous manner in which the British cooked vegetables, swimming in water. But in more recent times this has all changed, bringing about a veritable revolution. This revolution is the result of increased travel abroad as well as an influx of foreigners into the country who introduced many unusual vegetables and their own ways of cooking them. The British gardener with his vegetable garden or allotment is not only growing his carrots, turnips, peas and beans: but attempting sweet peppers, aubergines and even okra, vegetable 'spaghetti' and *cho-cho,* a gourd which is grown on vines. Therefore, we can safely say that today vegetable cooking is becoming exciting, and a main dish of vegetables served once or twice or even thrice a week should be something to which we can look forward with joy.

Asparagus

Asperges à la flamande
Belgium

TO SERVE FOUR

INGREDIENTS
900 g (2 lb) fresh asparagus
4 hard-boiled eggs
50 g (2 oz) unsalted butter
salt and white pepper

The Belgians have excellent vegetables: splendid chicory, Brussels sprouts, which Belgian market gardeners developed, and asparagus, which is the third favourite vegetable in this small country of epicures and trenchermen.

Cut off the tough ends of the asparagus and discard; wash and tie the rest neatly into four bundles. Put these into a tall pan (special asparagus pans do exist), pour in boiling water to come just up to their tips, but do not let the water actually touch the tips as these must literally steam, they are so delicate. Cover the pan and boil for 20 minutes, or until the tips are tender. Drain,

untie and put a bundle of asparagus on to each plate. While the asparagus is cooking, shell the eggs, cut into halves and scoop out the yolks. Mash these to a paste. Melt the butter in a small pan, add the mashed egg yolks, a little salt and pepper and stir gently over a moderate heat to make a dressing. Pour some of the dressing on to each bundle of asparagus and serve at once.

As a variation serve the asparagus, as it often is in Belgium, with a shelled soft-boiled egg served in a glass with each portion. A bowl of melted butter is placed on the table with salt and pepper, and each person makes his own sauce in the small bowl with the egg.

Aubergine musaka

Musaca cu patlagele
Rumania

TO SERVE EIGHT

INGREDIENTS
butter for greasing and breadcrumbs
900 g (2 lb) aubergines
salt and pepper
flour
oil for frying
50 g (2 oz) butter
275 ml (½ pint) milk, scalded
2 eggs
100 g (4 oz) onions, finely chopped
450 g (1 lb) minced meat, preferably lamb or mutton
a few sprigs of parsley, finely chopped
150 ml (¼ pint) dry white wine
450 g (1 lb) tomatoes
75 g (3 oz) sharp cheese, grated

The Greeks have an almost identical dish.

Rub the bottom and sides of a deep casserole with butter and sprinkle with breadcrumbs. Peel the aubergines, cut into medium-thick slices and sprinkle with salt. Place on a large plate, which is tilted at a slight angle, cover and put a weight on top and leave for about 45 minutes to force the slightly bitter juices to ooze out. Rinse off all the salt and dry carefully. Preheat the oven to 180°C, 350°F, Gas Mark 4. Roll the aubergine slices in flour but shake off any surplus. Heat a fair quantity of oil in a frying pan until hot, add the aubergine slices and fry until they are brown on both sides, and, if necessary, add more oil as you cook. Drain well on absorbent paper. Heat half the butter in a saucepan, add 25 g (1 oz) of flour and stir it well into the butter. Gradually add the milk, stirring all the

time. Add salt to taste and continue cooking gently for 5 minutes. Take the pan from the stove, add 1 egg yolk, beating well all the time. Heat the remaining butter with 2–3 tablespoons of oil in another pan and fry the onion until soft but do not let it change colour. Add the meat, salt, pepper and parsley. When the meat is browned, add the wine and cook until the wine has evaporated. Meanwhile chop the tomatoes and rub through a sieve. Place a layer of aubergine at the bottom of the casserole, add a layer of white sauce, a layer of tomatoes, a layer of the cheese, another of aubergines and continue in this manner until all the ingredients are used up. Beat the remaining egg with the leftover egg white and spread this over the top of the *musaca*. Put into the oven and bake for about 30 minutes, or until the top is brown.

French beans in tomato sauce

Judias verdes con salsa de tomate
Spain

TO SERVE FOUR

INGREDIENTS
900 g (2 lb) French beans
450 g (1 lb) tomatoes
1 tablespoon olive oil
50 g (2 oz) finely chopped onions
1 clove garlic, finely chopped
100 g (4 oz) ham, finely chopped (optional)
1 tablespoon finely chopped parsley
1 teaspoon sugar
salt and pepper

This recipe, although credited to Spain, could just as easily be called Portuguese or Italian. It is enough for a main dish, but it could be served also with grilled chops, sausages, or with boiled potatoes. Runner beans may be used instead of French beans.

Trim the beans and break into 5-cm (2-in) lengths. Cook over a good heat in boiling salted water until the beans are barely tender. Drain and put aside. Blanch the tomatoes, peel, discard the seeds and chop finely. Heat the oil, add the onion and garlic and cook until the onion is soft, but do not let it brown. Add the ham (or bacon if preferred) and cook over a moderate heat for 5 minutes, then add the tomatoes, beans, parsley, sugar, salt and pepper. Continue to cook over a moderate heat for 15–20 minutes until the beans are quite tender and the mixture is very thick. Serve piping hot.

Top: French beans in tomato sauce
bottom: French beans Lyons style

French beans Lyons style

Haricots verts à la lyonnaise
France

TO SERVE TWO—THREE

INGREDIENTS
450 g (1 lb) French beans
50 g (2 oz) butter
1 tablespoon finely chopped onion
salt and pepper
2–3 tablespoons dry white wine or wine vinegar
finely chopped parsley to taste

This dish should be made with French beans but young and rather smallish runner beans cut into 5-cm (2-in) lengths may be used instead. French beans are best left whole, after snipping off the tips, unless they are particularly long, in which case break into halves. Strained lemon juice may be used instead of the dry white wine or wine vinegar.

Cook the beans until just tender in boiling, salted water over a good heat. Drain well and pat dry. Heat the butter in the same pan, add the onion and lightly fry until the onion is soft but not brown. Add salt, pepper and the beans and continue cooking over a moderate heat until the beans begin to brown. Add the wine, parsley (not too much of this), simmer for 2–3 minutes, then serve hot.

A pinch of freshly grated nutmeg may be added to the beans at the same time as the salt and pepper.

Boston baked beans

USA

TO SERVE SIX–EIGHT

INGREDIENTS

675 g (1½ lb) white beans
450 g (1 lb) piece of salt pork
175 g (6 oz) onions, peeled
1 heaped teaspoon prepared mustard
½ cup molasses or black treacle
1 teaspoon pepper
1 tablespoon salt

Boston brown bread

75 g (3 oz) rye flour
75 g (3 oz) yellow cornmeal (maize flour)
wholemeal flour
½ teaspoon bicarbonate of soda
1 teaspoon salt
160 g (5½ oz) black treacle
350 ml (12 fl oz) buttermilk
40 g (1½ oz) raisins (optional)

We usually think of Boston in connection with baked beans, but other parts of the United States also produce a similar dish. Perhaps the nicest dish of baked beans I ever had was in Beirut when an American gave a party on her roof to watch the spectacle of falling stars. She served a late-night buffet supper and, being a 'proper' Bostonian, took this opportunity to serve a bean pot full of this succulent and filling dish. It is still a typical Saturday night supper in Boston. It was a favourite dish of the Puritans who would prepare and cook it on Saturday for eating the following day, the Sabbath, with only the minimum of cooking.

Most Bostonians would insist that this dish owes its succulence not only to the way in which the beans are cooked (and no doubt every Bostonian has his or her own particular recipe and trick) but to the earthenware bean pot in which they are cooked. This has a bulging belly and a narrow neck. Such vessels, often called Dutch pots, are not in the least difficult to find today. Failing such a pot, any deep casserole can be used, provided it has a well-fitting lid.

Soak the beans in unsalted water overnight. Preheat the oven to 140°C, 290°F, Gas Mark 2. Early next day drain and put into a large pan, cover with water, bring

to the boil or cook until a white scum appears on the surface, and then drain. Slash the salt pork through the rind at intervals and put this at the bottom of a large bean pot together with the onion. Add the beans, mustard, molasses and pepper, and boiling water to cover. Put into the oven. After 2 hours' cooking, add salt and, if required, a little more boiling water, always keeping the surface of the water level with the beans. Continue cooking for 5–6 hours, checking from time to time to see if more boiling water is needed. About an hour before the beans are ready, uncover the pot, dig out the piece of pork and place this on top of the beans. Do not add any more water; continue cooking with the pot uncovered for another hour. By this time the pork will be crisp and brown and the top layer of the beans slighted crusted. When serving the beans, take out the pork and discard.

The two tricks of cooking this dish are, according to my Bostonian friends, the adding of boiling water up to that final hour of cooking so that the beans never have a chance to become dry, and the final hour of cooking with the pork on top and the pot left uncovered.

Boston brown bread

Boston brown bread is always served with the beans, a moist bread steamed in American baking-powder tins, but 450-g (1-lb) loaf tins obviously can be used instead. This quantity will make three loaves. Cornmeal is a variety of flour made from maize, either yellow or white, and is used in Italian polenta. Black treacle or molasses is a dark syrup produced during the manufacture of sugar and comes in three grades. It was once widely used in the United States as a household sweetener. It is still used in the flavourings of puddings, confectionery and general cooking. The various flours can usually be found in health-food shops.

Sift the dry ingredients together, make a well in the centre, add the treacle and buttermilk, and raisins if desired. Stir well. Place a circle of greased paper at the bottom of three 450-g (1-lb) tins and fill each tin three-quarters full. The tins must be lightly covered so that the bread does not force itself out as it rises. Place the tins in boiling water, enough to reach half-way up their sides, and steam for 3 hours, keeping the water always boiling and always at the half-way mark. Remove the tins from the pan, turn out the bread immediately and serve at once, cut into thick slices with plenty of butter and the baked beans.

Broccoli cooked in white wine

Broccolo al vino bianco
Italy

TO SERVE THREE–FOUR

INGREDIENTS
900 g (2 lb) broccoli
pinch of salt
olive oil
1 clove garlic, lightly
  bruised
275 ml (½ pint) white wine
salt and pepper

Botanically broccoli and cauliflower are varieties of the same species and this causes some confusion of terminology. The popular name broccoli is derived from the Italian *brocco* meaning 'sprout' or 'shoot'.

For this dish, very fresh thick purple or green broccoli is needed, with plenty of head. If not available, white winter cauliflower can be used instead. The stalks, buds and most of the leaves are edible.

Wash the broccoli and cook in just enough water until almost tender, adding salt to taste. Drain and divide into flowerets. Heat 1–2 tablespoons of olive oil, add the garlic, fry it until brown and discard. Add the broccoli and simmer until this browns, then add the wine and continue to cook until the broccoli is very tender. Sprinkle lightly with salt and pepper and serve the broccoli in its liquid. This dish can also be served as a separate course.

Stuffed cabbage leaves

Sarma od kiselog
Yugoslavia

TO SERVE SIX

INGREDIENTS
225 g (8 oz) pork
225 g (8 oz) beef
175 g (6 oz) onions
100 g (4 oz) rice, cooked
  weight, made from 50 g
  (2 oz) uncooked rice
½ teaspoon paprika pepper
1 firm cabbage, 900 g (2 lb)
100 g (4 oz) fat bacon
  rashers
225 g (8 oz) smoked pork,
  cubed
salt and pepper
900 g (2 lb) sauerkraut
yogurt or soured cream as
  a sauce

Before the Second World War we lived in Budapest and for reasons of work my husband often had to go to Yugoslavia, in particular Belgrade. Naturally I went with him as often as I could and, apart from the horror of the approaching war, these years were among the happiest of our lives. After the war we drove to India by car and passed through Yugoslavia and stopped to lunch on our first day in this country in Ljubljana and parked the car in a market square where peasant women were selling cherries, curds and local cheeses. Instantly the years dropped away, we were back amid the delights – and indeed aromas – of Balkan cooking and, by following our noses we came upon a typical local restaurant serving one of our old favourites, *sarma*. This is considered a winter dish in many districts, not only in Yugoslavia but throughout the Balkans.

Mince the pork (not the smoked), beef and onions. Mix with the cooked rice and flavour with paprika pepper; this makes the stuffing. Carefully strip off the leaves from the cabbage and select the finest of them. Drop these quickly into boiling water to make them pliable. If the centre vein is very thick, cut this out and carefully fold the leaf over in the middle to avoid an opening. In the centre of each leaf place a portion of the stuffing (how much you use depends on the size of the leaves and how many cabbage leaves you have). Wrap the leaf carefully round the stuffing and tie with cotton. Do not knot the cotton as this must be removed before serving. Put half the bacon in the bottom of a large saucepan, add the stuffed cabbage leaves, the smoked pork, salt and pepper and top with the remaining bacon and sauerkraut. Cover the pan and cook over a low heat for 3 hours.

To serve, put the *sarma* with all the ingredients on to a hot dish, remove the cotton, and serve separately a jug of yogurt or soured cream (the latter is more authentic). You can add a little dry wine to the pan just before serving. And, if you have an attractive oven-to-table casserole, use this for both cooking and serving.

Red cabbage

Rotkohl
Germany

TO SERVE FOUR–SIX

INGREDIENTS
900 g (2 lb) red cabbage
450 g (1 lb) medium-sized
  cooking apples
50 g (2 oz) lard, pork or
  other fat
1 large onion, 175 g (6 oz),
  finely chopped
1 tablespoon brown sugar
salt and pepper
150 ml (¼ pint) red wine or
  wine vinegar
4 cloves

This member of the cabbage family is treated royally in many European countries, especially in Germany and Scandinavia. It makes a splendid accompaniment to game dishes, in particular hare, duck and goose as well as boiled ham or bacon and pork in any form.

Trim the cabbage, discarding any bruised leaves, and drop into acidulated salted water. Cut into four and cut out the hard stalk. Drop the cabbage into boiling water and cook for 10 minutes. Drain, rinse in cold water, then drain again and shred. Peel and coarsely chop the apples. Melt the fat in a large pan. Add a layer of cabbage, then one of apples and onion and sprinkle with sugar, salt, pepper and wine.

Add 1–2 cloves. Repeat this until all the ingredients are used up. Cover and cook over a low heat until the cabbage is quite tender, between 1½ and 2 hours, stirring well from time to time.

The cabbage may be served on the day it is cooked but it is infinitely better if left and reheated the following day.

Top left to right: broccoli in white wine; stuffed cabbage leaves; *centre:* red cabbage; *bottom:* carrots Flemish style

Carrots Flemish style

Belgium

TO SERVE FOUR

INGREDIENTS
450 g (1 lb) young carrots
50 g (2 oz) butter
salt and pepper
½ teaspoon sugar
1 egg yolk
1–2 tablespoons cream
finely chopped parsley

Although young carrots are specified for this recipe, older and larger ones may be used but should be cut into rings. They can be served alone as a main dish, or with bacon and cutlets.

Wash the carrots and cut into chunks (or if they are very small, leave whole) and drop into salted boiling water. Leave for 5 minutes. Drain well. Melt the butter in a pan, add the carrots and just enough boiling water to cover. Add salt, pepper and sugar and cook the carrots until they are very tender, stirring them from time to time. Lightly beat the egg yolk with the cream and add to the pan, 'holding the pan just off the fire with the left hand while you stir with the right' instructs my

Belgian cook book. When mixed, turn out into a hot dish and sprinkle with parsley.

A variation, also from Belgium, that makes a main course in its own right, is as follows. Prepare the carrots as above, preferably in a shallow wide pan, but when in the pot with the melted butter add 275 ml (½ pint) of white stock (i.e. chicken or veal), sprinkle with nutmeg and cook gently until the carrots are tender and most of the liquid has evaporated. Break in 4 eggs, taking care that they fall well apart from one another. Let them cook until they are almost set, not completely as they continue to cook in the hot sauce when taken from the stove, and serve at once. Take carefully from the pan with a spatula or the eggs will break.

137

Cassoulet

France

TO SERVE SIX

INGREDIENTS
450 g (1 lb) dried white
  beans
2 cloves garlic
150 g (5 oz) fat smoked
  bacon
1 garlic sausage
225 g (8 oz) each pork and
  mutton
100 g (4 oz) onions
1 each carrot, leek, celery
  stalk
50 g (2 oz) pork dripping
  or other fat
1 bayleaf
1–2 sprigs parsley,
  coarsely chopped
1 small tin tomato
  concentrate
fine breadcrumbs
salt, pepper and thyme to
  taste
slivers of butter

Probably this is one of the most famous dishes of southern France but one over which the towns of Castelnaudary, Toulouse and Carcassonne quarrel, the argument concerning the creation of this magnificent dish of meat and beans. The word cassoulet embraces both the food and the dish in which it is cooked. The name is thought to have derived from the terracotta *cassole* in which it is baked, called always *cassole d'Iselle,* which became corrupted to cassoulet, but where or who was Iselle no one seems to know. Every French housewife in the region has her own version, and some add all kinds of delicacies which for most people outside the region are impossible to obtain without a bottomless purse. Garlic sausages for boiling are available in delicatessens; the bacon should be in one piece and rather fat.

Soak the beans overnight in plenty of cold water. Put with the water into a pan together with the garlic, bacon (in one piece) and the sausage. Bring all this gently to the boil. Cut the pork and mutton into small cubes. Slice the onions finely; clean and chop the remaining vegetables. Heat the fat, add the meat, the onions, vegetables, bayleaf and parsley. Fry until they are all brown and then turn them into the beans, fat as well. Add the tomato concentrate, stir well and bring it all to the boil. Heat the oven to moderate (180°C, 350°F, Gas Mark 4). Take the bacon and sausages from the pan, cut into smallish pieces and return to the beans. Turn the mixture into an ovenproof casserole and sprinkle with a fine layer of breadcrumbs, salt, pepper, thyme and slivers of butter. Bake for 10 minutes in the oven, then stir well so that the breadcrumbs sink into the cassoulet. Again sprinkle finely with breadcrumbs and slivers of butter and bake for a further 10 minutes. Stir well and for the third and last time repeat this performance, baking this time for a further 10–15 minutes. Serve in the same casserole.

Cauliflower musaka

Musaka od karciola
Yugoslavia

TO SERVE FOUR–SIX

INGREDIENTS
900 g (2 lb) white
  cauliflower
3–4 slices fat bacon
225 g (8 oz) onions, finely
  chopped
450 g (1 lb) minced pork or
  veal
100 g (4 oz) cooked rice
salt and pepper to taste

The *musaka* best known in Britain, in particular in Greek restaurants, is made with aubergine. The result is that many people are convinced that a *musaka* minus this vegetable is not a *musaka*. This is not so. The name usually implies a casserole-baked vegetable dish, but there are also stewed *musakas*.

Preheat the oven to 180°C, 350°F, Gas Mark 4. Wash the cauliflower well, discard the really tough stalks and cook whole in boiling salted water until tender. Drain, retaining the liquid; cool and break the cauliflower into fairly large flowerets. Fry the bacon until the fat runs freely, add the onions and cook until they begin to brown, then add the meat and simmer for about 15 minutes, stirring lightly from time to time. Arrange half the cauliflower at the bottom of a shallow baking dish or casserole. Cover with all the meat, rice and onions and spread with the remaining cauliflower. Sprinkle lightly with salt, generously with pepper and add enough of the cauliflower liquid to moisten the *musaka*. Bake in the oven for 45 minutes. Serve with a plain pilau (*see page 51*).

Chicory

Chicorée
Belgium

TO SERVE FOUR–SIX

INGREDIENTS
450 g (1 lb) chicory
juice of 1 small lemon
2 lumps sugar

Chicory is a clump of white fleshy leaves tightly clamped together, the tips faintly yellow. Generally available all the year round, it has the advantage of not being a wasteful vegetable for almost all of it is edible.

Cut off a thin slice from the base of the chicory heads and put them under quickly running water. If necessary, remove any bruised outer leaves. Put into a pan with salted boiling water flavoured with half the lemon juice and cook for 10 minutes. Take from the pan, drain, discarding the liquid, and put into another pan of boiling salted water flavoured with the rest of the lemon juice and the sugar and continue to cook until the chicory is tender, a further 10–15 minutes. Serve with roast veal or other roast meats.

As a variation, cook them *à la béguine*. Cook, drain and cut the chicory into medium-sized slices. Chop some chives, as many as you like. Heat enough cream just to cover the chicory, add the chives, salt and pepper and gently cook until the cream is heated – do not let it boil. Arrange the chicory on a hot serving plate together with its sauce and garnish with chopped hard-boiled eggs, using both the yolks and the whites.

Cucumbers in cream

Concombres à la crème
France

TO SERVE FOUR

INGREDIENTS
750 g (1¾ lb) cucumbers
a pinch of salt
100 g (4 oz) butter
150 ml (¼ pint) single
  cream

In Britain cucumbers usually are thought of in terms of salads but elsewhere they are cooked in a variety of ways. They are an ancient vegetable known in biblical times and are mentioned in the Book of Isaiah, but through the centuries their form has changed. George Stephenson, of 'Puffing Billy' fame, grew cucumbers, forcing them to grow straight by the use of specially made glass tubes of his own design, through which the embryo cucumbers were guided. Since then gardeners have cultivated cucumbers in this form. In the seventeenth and eighteenth centuries cucumbers were known as cowcumbers. Many people consider them indigestible but in 1655 Dr Thomas Muffet wrote: 'Cucumbers cooked engender good humours and settle a very cold and weak stomach as by practice and long experience I have proved on divers persons.' Finally, if you see cucumbers in a dream, it denotes that you will speedily fall in love, or, curiously, if you are not in love, that you will marry the object of your affections. Which does seem contradictory. Preferably use fairly young, small cucumbers in this recipe, those that have not had time to develop many seeds.

Peel the cucumbers and shape into balls or, if it is easier, cut into rounds, not too thin. Put about 1 litre (1¾ pints) of water into a pan, add a little salt and bring to the boil. Add the cucumbers and cook them for no longer than 5 minutes. Drain well. Heat the butter in a deep frying pan or shallow casserole. Add the drained cucumbers, sprinkle lightly with salt and cook over a low heat for about 20 minutes. Add the cream, stir well but gently, cover the pan and cook until the sauce thickens.

Serve as a separate dish or as an accompaniment to cold meats.

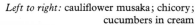

Left to right: cauliflower musaka; chicory; cucumbers in cream

Casserole of mushrooms

Ciuperci mode Cernăuţi
Rumania

TO SERVE FOUR

INGREDIENTS
450 g (1 lb) large
  mushrooms
3 tablespoons oil
225 g (8 oz) onions, finely
  chopped
1½ tablespoons flour
150 ml (¼ pint) milk
275 ml (½ pint) soured
  cream or yogurt
salt and pepper
1 tablespoon finely
  chopped parsley
freshly milled nutmeg to
  taste
about 4 tablespoons grated
  hard cheese
15 g (½ oz) butter

Any type of large mushroom may be used in this recipe, either field or cultivated ones. In Rumania mushrooms are collected in the woods and fields by everyone and there are many recipes for their preparation. Almost any hard cheese may be used provided it has a strong flavour. Fresh cream can be used instead of soured cream or yogurt.

Preheat the oven to 180°C, 350°F, Gas Mark 4. Wash the mushrooms, drain, pat dry and slice as thinly as possible, both caps and stems. Heat the oil and lightly fry the onions until they are soft but not brown. Add the mushrooms and cook over a low heat for about 15 minutes. Sprinkle in the flour, stir gently all the while but carefully and continue cooking until the flour has thickened the moisture from the mushrooms and onions. Combine the milk and soured cream and, stirring all the time, gradually add to the pan to make a sauce. Add salt, pepper, parsley and nutmeg and cook for about 5 minutes. Pour the mushrooms with their sauce into a shallow oval oven-to-table baking dish, 27 × 20 cm (10½ × 8 in). Sprinkle the cheese over the top, add the butter cut into slivers and bake in the oven until the top is brown, for 20–30 minutes.

Top: casserole of mushrooms
bottom: onion tart

Onion tart

Gâteau aux oignons
Switzerland

TO SERVE SIX

INGREDIENTS
4 tablespoons oil or fat for
  frying
450 g (1 lb) onions, thinly
  sliced
350 g (12 oz) flaky pastry
salt and pepper
3 eggs
275 ml (½ pint) single
  cream

This is a speciality from Schaffhausen where the tourists go to gaze at the Rhine falls, and then to eat the local onion tart.

Preheat the oven to 180°C, 350°F, Gas Mark 4. Heat the oil, add the onions and fry these until soft and transparent. Roll out the pastry and line a 23-cm (9-in) flan tin. Fill this with the onions and sprinkle with salt and pepper. Lightly beat the eggs, whisk into the cream and pour this over the top of the onions. Bake in the oven for about 40 minutes, or until the pastry is cooked and the filling set.

Instead of single cream, a thin *béchamel sauce* may be used and 1 extra yolk. Some Swiss cooks also add diced bacon to the onions when frying.

140

Stuffed sweet peppers

Punjene paprike

Yugoslavia

TO SERVE SIX

INGREDIENTS

450 g (1 lb) lean pork
2–3 rashers bacon
225 g (8 oz) onions
6 well-shaped peppers,
 each 225 g (8 oz)
900 g (2 lb) tomatoes
50 g (2 oz) rice
oil or butter for frying
salt and pepper to taste
1 teaspoon sugar

Courgettes, aubergines and tomatoes, with their centres scooped out and added to the stuffing, are all cooked in the same manner.

Preheat the oven to 200°C, 400°F, Gas Mark 6. Chop and coarsely mince the pork. Dice the bacon and finely chop the onions. Cut off a slice from the stem end of each pepper, retaining these as lids. Cut out the cores and seeds and any thick pith. Peel and chop the tomatoes. Wash, parboil and drain the rice, do not let it completely cook – 5 minutes should be sufficient time. Heat the oil. Lightly fry half the onions until a golden brown, add all the pork and bacon, let this begin to change colour, then add the rice. Cook over a low heat for 10 minutes.

Meanwhile put the prepared tomatoes and the remainder of the onions into a small pan and cook until the tomatoes are very soft. If the tomatoes are not juicy, add a few tablespoons of water. Add salt, pepper and sugar and rub through a sieve. Arrange the peppers in a shallow baking dish or casserole. Fill each with pork and rice stuffing, cover with their sliced-off tops. Pour the sieved tomatoes over the peppers and bake in the oven for about 45 minutes, or until the peppers are soft but still firm. If the peppers begin to show signs of browning too early, cover them with foil for the last period of their baking time.

Left: stuffed sweet peppers
right: Calabrian sweet peppers

Calabrian sweet peppers

Peperoni in padella alla calabrese

Italy

TO SERVE FOUR

INGREDIENTS

4 large peppers, 900 g (2 lb)
2 teaspoons capers
a little oil
1 heaped tablespoon
 fresh breadcrumbs
2 tablespoons grated cheese
pinch dried oregano or
 marjoram
salt and pepper

Although red and yellow peppers are locally preferred for this dish, if only green are available use these. The type of cheese called for is Pecorino or sheep's cheese, and there are many varieties of this rather strongly flavoured type. Substitute with any dry fine-grained strong cheese.

Wipe the peppers with a damp cloth, then roast over a high flame until they literally blacken. When the peppers are black, scrape off the skin (if preferred) and cut each into four. Put aside. Wash the salt off the capers in cold water. Heat the oil in a frying pan, add the strips of peppers and fry until they brown. Drain on absorbent paper. Very lightly rub a shallow casserole

with oil (preferably terracotta or flame-proof earthenware), add the peppers in one layer, then sprinkle with breadcrumbs, cheese, capers, oregano, salt and pepper. Put over a low flame and cook for about 10 minutes, stirring carefully from time to time. This dish can be served hot or warm, as a salad, or with meat, or simply as a vegetable dish in its own right.

141

Swiss fried potatoes

Rösti
Switzerland

TO SERVE THREE–FOUR

INGREDIENTS
900 g (2 lb) potatoes
75 g (3 oz) butter or lard
salt and pepper
1 medium-sized onion,
    finely chopped (optional)

This, one of the most typical of Swiss dishes, is served in all cantons, either as an accompaniment to meat dishes, or as a dish on its own.

Boil the potatoes in their jackets until tender. Peel them as soon as they are cool enough to be handled; either thinly slice them or put them through a ricer. Heat the fat in a frying pan, add the onions and potatoes, sprinkle with salt and pepper and fry over a good heat, turning the potatoes all the time until they are golden brown. Lower the heat, press the potatoes well down and continue to cook slowly for a few minutes until a crust forms underneath. Turn out to serve on a warmed plate, so that the brown crust is on top.

Jansson's temptation

Janssons frestelse
Sweden

TO SERVE FOUR–SIX

INGREDIENTS
675 g (1½ lb) potatoes
350 g (12 oz) large onions,
    sliced
40 g (1½ oz) butter
16 anchovy fillets, drained,
    reserving the liquid
    (*see recipe*)
275 ml (½ pint) single
    cream
vegetable oil or liquid from
    the anchovy fillets

I first learned of this recipe not in Sweden but in India, from a Swedish friend who served it with other *smörgåsbord* dishes. She explained that in Sweden it is normally served at the end of an evening, just before the party breaks up, as a *nattmat* (literally 'night food'), with a glass of schnapps. The guests go home with something warm, strong and good in their stomachs. The reason for the amusing name of this dish comes from a story that Janson, a nineteenth-century religious zealot who preached abstinence in food and drink, could never resist this particular dish of anchovy-flavoured potatoes and was seen by one of his disciples gorging himself. Sadly this was his downfall. However, like all legends, the story perhaps is not true since the names of the dish and the zealot are differently spelled.

Preheat the oven to 180°C, 350°F, Gas Mark 4. Peel the potatoes and cut into thin strips; keep them covered while you deal with the onions. Thinly slice the onions. Arrange half the potatoes at the bottom of a well-buttered baking dish, preferably a round one, spread the anchovies and the onions over the top, then cover with the rest of the potatoes. Dot with slivers of butter. Put into the preheated oven and bake for 10 minutes. Pour half the cream over the top. Sprinkle either with vegetable oil or the oil from the anchovies and continue baking for a further 20 minutes. Add the rest of the cream and continue cooking for a further 40–45 minutes, or until all the cream has been absorbed and the potatoes are tender. Serve the dish piping hot.

Gratin potatoes
recipe 1

Le gratin dauphinois
France

TO SERVE FOUR

INGREDIENTS
900 g (2 lb) potatoes
1 clove garlic
50 g (2 oz) butter
salt and white pepper
freshly ground nutmeg
2 eggs
425 ml (¾ pint) milk
2–3 tablespoons single or
    double cream (optional)

This dish of sliced and baked potatoes, typical of the mountainous regions of southern France, is well known and additions often made to the recipe cause certain local indignation.

Preheat the oven to 160°C, 325°F, Gas Mark 3. Peel and very thinly slice the potatoes: this can be done with a mandolin or in an electric slicer. Wash and pat the slices dry. Crush the garlic and rub it round a deep baking dish; rub the same dish with one-third of the butter and arrange the sliced potatoes in layers in the dish, sprinkling each layer with salt, pepper and nutmeg. Beat the eggs in a mixing bowl; warm the milk and pour it over the beaten eggs, stirring all the time. Pour this mixture in at the side of the dish, dot with slivers of the remaining butter and pour the cream over the top. Bake for 1½ hours. When the gratin is ready the potatoes will have absorbed all the liquid. Test with a fork, which should penetrate the gratin easily. Serve hot.

Gratin potatoes
recipe 2
Le gratin savoyard
France

TO SERVE FOUR

INGREDIENTS
225 g (8 oz) Beaufort
   cheese
900 g (2 lb) potatoes
75 g (3 oz) butter
salt and white pepper
plenty of freshly grated
   nutmeg (*see recipe*)
150 ml (¼ pint) clear stock

My recipe, which originates from the Savoy, calls for 1 whole nutmeg freshly grated; this may be too much for some tastes and this quantity can be modified. Any well-flavoured, firm cheese may be used as a substitute for Beaufort, which is a rich buttery cheese similar to Gruyère.

Preheat the oven to 180°C, 350°F, Gas Mark 4. Grate the cheese into thin strips. Wash, peel and thinly slice the potatoes (*see* Gratin potatoes *facing page*). Rub a baking dish with one-third of the butter. Arrange the potato slices in layers, sprinkling each layer with salt, pepper, nutmeg

and cheese. The top layer must be of cheese. Dot with the remaining butter cut into slivers, add the stock and bake in the oven until tender, about 1½ hours. When the gratin is ready the potatoes will have absorbed all the liquid. Test with a fork which should penetrate the gratin easily. Serve hot in the same dish.

Potatoes with onions
Pommes de terre à la Guignol
France

TO SERVE FOUR–SIX

INGREDIENTS
900 g (2 lb) potatoes
450 g (1 lb) onions, finely
   chopped
100 g (4 oz) butter
salt and pepper
1 tablespoon finely
   chopped parsley

This is more usually called *Pommes de terre à la lyonnaise*; the Guignol after which it is named is the local mascot, a cheeky puppet fashioned to look like the shrewd but witty silk weavers of Lyons. If possible choose firm, not floury, potatoes for this dish which is usually served with very spicy hot sausages, a speciality of Lyons. However, crisply fried bacon or other types of fried sausages can be served with the potatoes.

Wash the potatoes and cook in their skins in boiling, salted water until tender. Peel and finely chop the onions. Heat one-third of the butter in a frying pan and start to fry the onions just before the potatoes are ready. They often take quite a while to

cook until soft; do not let them brown too much. As soon as the potatoes are ready, take them from the pan and drop into cold water. When they are cold, drain well and peel, then slice fairly thickly. Heat the remainder of the butter in a deep frying pan, add the potatoes and sauté until they begin to brown all round the edges. Add the fried onions, mix well but carefully, otherwise the mixture will become a mash. Sprinkle with salt and pepper and pile pyramid fashion on to a hot serving plate. Sprinkle with parsley and serve either as a main dish, or as an accompaniment to meat.

Left top to bottom: Swiss fried potatoes; Gratin potatoes (recipe 1); *centre:* Jansson's temptation; *right top to bottom:* Gratin potatoes (recipe 2); potatoes with onions

Spiced potatoes

Dam alu
Kashmir

TO SERVE THREE–FOUR

INGREDIENTS
900 g (2 lb) small potatoes
 (*see recipe*)
oil for deep frying
40 g (1½ oz) ghee or
 vegetable fat
pinch salt
½ teaspoon chilli powder
2½ teaspoons ground
 coriander seeds
½ teaspoon ground ginger
1 teaspoon *garam masala*
 (*see page* 186)

The potatoes can be old or new but must all be of equal size in order to cook in the same time. Kashmiris use ground ginger when cooking with starchy ingredients as they consider it is good for the digestion.

Preheat the oven to 220°C, 425°F, Gas Mark 7. Wash the potatoes and cook in their skins until half tender. Take from the pan, drain and peel. Prick each potato through and through with a fine knitting needle or skewer without breaking it. Heat the oil, add the potatoes and fry them until they are light brown. Take out and drain. In a separate pan heat the ghee until it is smoking. Add the potatoes, salt, chilli, coriander and ginger, turning the potatoes over and over for a minute or two. Add

about ½ cupful of water and the *garam masala*, again turn the potatoes until well coated with the spices. Put the pan into the oven and continue cooking until the potatoes are tender but not soft or broken.

Serve as a separate dish or with a Nepalese egg salad (*see page* 155).

Potato cake

Torta di patate

Italy

TO SERVE FOUR–SIX

INGREDIENTS

600 g (1 lb 5 oz) potatoes
75 g (3 oz) butter
grated rind of 1 lemon
2 eggs, lightly beaten
3 tablespoons fine
  breadcrumbs
100 g (4 oz) Mortadella
75 g (3 oz) Fontina cheese
  (*see recipe*)

If Fontina is not available, use a soft white cheese such as Bel Paese. Instead of Mortadella, minced or diced cold meat may be used.

Preheat the oven to 220°C, 425°F, Gas Mark 7. Wash the potatoes and cook without peeling until very soft. Drain, peel as soon as possible and rub through a coarse sieve or ricer. Mix the potato in a bowl, add 50 g (2 oz) of the butter and the lemon rind and beat with a wooden spoon until the mixture is smooth and the butter melted. Add the eggs and lightly beat into the mashed potatoes. Rub a round baking dish – a cake tin or soufflé dish, 20 cm (8 in) in diameter, would be suitable – lightly with some of the remaining butter and sprinkle all over with about a tablespoon of breadcrumbs. Add half the mashed potatoes, then the Mortadella, the cheese and the rest of the potato. Sprinkle with the remaining breadcrumbs, top with slivers of butter and bake in the oven for 30 minutes. Turn out to serve, cut in wedges like a cake.

This dish requires no accompaniment except perhaps a mixed salad.

Potato cakes

Latkes

Israel

TO SERVE SIX

INGREDIENTS

1000 g (2 lb) potatoes
50 g (2 oz) self-raising
  flour
175 g (6 oz) onions, finely
  chopped
2 eggs
pinch ginger or nutmeg
  (optional)
salt and pepper to taste
deep fat or oil for frying

Apple sauce
450 g (1 lb) cooking apples
1 tablespoon lemon juice
1 thin strip lemon rind
1 dessertspoon sugar
15 g ($\frac{1}{2}$ oz) butter

This Jewish dish is served during the period of feasting to celebrate the victory of the Maccabees, led by Judas Maccabaeus, in 165 BC when the Temple in Jerusalem was saved from defilement by Antiochus of Syria. It recalls the cleansing after this attempt at defilement and re-dedication of the Temple. One drop of oil only was found with which to rekindle the Eternal Light, and this lasted a full eight days until more could be obtained. This miraculous preservation symbolizes the survival of the Jewish nation through overwhelming persecution. In Jewish homes during this time a large branched candlestick with eight candles stands on the sideboard, lit one each night for eight nights until the eight are lit, to signify the eight days during which the tiny cruse of oil burned for the Maccabees.

Although there are specific dishes for this period, it is customary to serve fritters and pancakes, since their method of preparation recalls the oil found in the Temple. Potato *latkes* are typical of Jewish cooking.

Peel the potatoes, grate and drop into iced water. Leave for 30 minutes to drain off their starch. Take them carefully from the bowl with a perforated spoon to leave all the starch on the bottom. Squeeze as dry as possible in a cloth. Put into a mixing bowl, add the flour, onion, eggs and seasonings and mix thoroughly. Heat the fat in a deep frying pan and drop tablespoonfuls of the mixture into the pan and fry until they become a golden-brown. Turn them carefully once. Drain well on absorbent paper. Serve very hot with cold apple sauce, or with a vegetable.

If instead of onions, 3 tablespoons of castor sugar are added, plus cinnamon and nutmeg, the *latkes* are then a sweet dish.

Apple sauce
Wash the apples, coarsely chop and put with lemon juice and rind and $\frac{1}{4}$ cup of water into a pan, cover tightly and cook over a gentle heat until a pulp, about 15 minutes. Rub through a sieve, add the sugar and butter and beat well. Cool, then chill.

Sweet-sour spinach

Spinaci agrodolce

Italy

TO SERVE THREE–FOUR

INGREDIENTS

1000 g (2 lb) spinach
50 g (2 oz) pork fat or
  butter
3 tablespoons sharp
  vinegar
salt, pepper and freshly
  ground nutmeg to taste
1 tablespoon brown sugar

The type of spinach most usually found in the Italian markets has a thick, almost curly leaf with very little wastage.

Pick over the spinach, discarding any brown or spoiled leaves. Wash in several changes of water until free from dirt. Drain lightly. Melt the fat in a large saucepan, add the vinegar, stir well, then add the spinach without any other liquid, stir again and cook over a moderate heat until the spinach is quite tender. Add salt, freshly ground pepper and nutmeg to taste and finally the sugar. Stir well until the sugar has dissolved and serve hot.

Stuffed tomatoes

Domates dolmasi
Turkey

TO SERVE SIX

INGREDIENTS
6 large firm tomatoes, each
  weighing 225 g (8 oz)
salt and pepper
1 teaspoon sugar
150 ml (¼ pint) olive oil
200 g (7 oz) onions, finely
  chopped
2 tablespoons finely
  chopped fresh mint
2 tablespoons finely
  chopped fresh parsley
25 g (1 oz) currants
25 g (1 oz) pine nuts
175 g (6 oz) rice
fine fresh breadcrumbs for
  sprinkling

Both for the sake of appearance and cooking the tomatoes should be of equal size. Olive oil is called for; however, if the tomatoes are to be served hot, a good quality vegetable oil may be used. If to be served cold, olive oil is important as it does not congeal.

Preheat the oven to 180°C, 350°F, Gas Mark 4. Slice off the stem end of each tomato and put aside to use as a lid. Scoop out the pulp, cores and seeds, finely chop the pulp and discard the cores and seeds. Sprinkle the inside of the tomatoes lightly with salt and sugar. Put aside until required. Heat the oil and fry the onions until a golden brown. Stir in the tomato pulp, mint, parsley, salt, pepper, currants and pine nuts. Simmer for a few minutes, then add the rice and 275 ml (½ pint) of warm water. Cook until the rice begins to

soften. When the rice is almost cooked take from the pan. Stir well and fill the empty tomato shells with this mixture. Remember the rice will continue to swell as it continues to cook. Arrange the tomatoes in a shallow baking tin, cover each with its appropriate 'lid', brush with oil, sprinkle with breadcrumbs and pour enough oil into the tin to prevent sticking or burning (water, stock or thin tomato juice may be used instead). Bake in the oven for about 45 minutes. Serve hot or cold – although in Turkey it is more usual to serve stuffed dishes cold.

Sardine-stuffed tomatoes

Tomates farcies aux royans
France

TO SERVE SIX

INGREDIENTS
6 large, firm tomatoes, each
  weighing 225 g (8 oz)
salt and pepper
butter or oil for greasing
6 large fresh sardines
2 large shallots
1 medium-sized onion,
  chopped
6 sprigs parsley
75 g (3 oz) butter

Nowadays fresh sardines are usually sold frozen by most fishmongers. The *royans* of this recipe are the large sardines found in the Bay of Biscay, which the French call the Golfe de Gascogne, a region famed not only for The Three Musketeers but also for the voracious appetites of the locals and the quality of their food.

Preheat the oven to 180°C, 350°F, Gas Mark 4. Wash the tomatoes, cutting off their tops to make lids for later use. Scoop out the seeds, cores and pulp. Discard the seeds and cores, crush the pulp, mix with salt and pepper and put aside. Rub a baking sheet with butter, place the tomatoes on this and bake in the oven for 20 minutes. Meanwhile wipe the fish clean and open them up flat. Grill on both sides until just

brown. Cut off their heads and put these aside. Remove and discard the centre bone from each sardine. Coarsely chop the sardines but do not mash them. Finely chop the shallots and parsley. Soften the butter on a plate with a fork, then add the chopped onion, parsley and the reserved tomato pulp. When well mixed, add the sardines. Put this mixture into the tomato shells, cover with the lids and bake in a very hot oven (230°C, 450°F, Gas Mark 8) for 5–10 minutes. Serve hot, each tomato garnished with one sardine head.

Left: stuffed tomatoes
right: sardine-stuffed tomatoes

Vegetable stew

Ratatouille

France

TO SERVE SIX

INGREDIENTS

900 g (2 lb) aubergines
450 g (1 lb) courgettes
450 g (1 lb) onions
900 g (2 lb) sweet peppers
450 g (1 lb) tomatoes
150 ml (¼ pint) olive oil
salt and black pepper
3 cloves garlic, finely
    chopped

I feel it is wrong to describe this dish as a vegetable stew, even though one or two of my old dictionaries describe it as 'a poor stew, bad stuff, mess, cagmag'. I had to look up cagmag: it means 'a tough old goose, unwholesome meat, offal'. Things have changed since then, *c.* 1771. Today this dish, an aromatic mixture of sun-warmed vegetables, is one of which Provence is rightly proud. The quantity of oil should be no more than will just cover the bottom of your pan, and please do not even think of adding any other liquid. The point of *ratatouille* is that it simmers for as long as it takes for the vegetables to soften, preferably 2–3 hours.

Peel the aubergines, courgettes and onions, coarsely chop but keep separate. Cut off the stem end of the peppers, discard the cores, seeds and thick pith and cut the flesh into strips, or halves, or thirds, according to the size of the peppers. Blanch, peel and chop the tomatoes. Heat the oil in a casserole, add the vegetables in layers in the pan, starting with the onions and finishing with the tomatoes, sprinkle each layer with salt, pepper and chopped garlic. Cook very slowly over a moderate heat, stirring from time to time to mix the vegetables and prevent them from sticking to the bottom of the pan.

Ratatouille is designed as a main dish but it can be served with roast or boiled meats, or topped with boiled or poached eggs. It is served either hot or cold. Adding beaten eggs to the *ratatouille* and scrambling them makes it a Basque *pipérade*.

Vegetable curry

Sabzi ki kari

India

TO SERVE FOUR–SIX

INGREDIENTS

900 g (2 lb) mixed
    vegetables (*see recipe*)
350 g (12 oz) tomatoes
175 g (6 oz) onions
5 chillies
2–4 cloves garlic
½ teaspoon cumin seeds
½ teaspoon coriander seeds
½ teaspoon ground
    turmeric
4 tablespoons vegetable oil
½ teaspoon sugar
½ teaspoon salt

For the uninitiated, this is a fairly hot curry. Reducing the amount of chillies will make it milder.

Among the mixed vegetables you may include potatoes, turnips, carrots, beans, peas, sweet peppers and courgettes; these should all be washed, trimmed or peeled as required and cut into reasonably small cubes. The tomatoes must be peeled and coarsely chopped, the onions diced; the chillies chopped and their seeds removed. Chop the garlic and pound together with the cumin seeds, then mix with the remaining spices with very little water, enough to make a paste. Heat the oil, add the curry paste and fry this for 5 minutes. Add the diced onions and the chillies, stir well, then add the tomatoes, stir again and cook for 3 minutes. Add the remaining vegetables and sugar, gently stir (rough handling will make the vegetables mushy). Add salt and just enough water to cover. Cook over a moderate heat until the vegetables are tender but not mushy.

It is usual to serve this curry with rice, lentils and *chapatis*, a variety of flat Indian unleavened bread. Where this is not available, use large pappadums (*see page* 187), which are easily available.

Left: vegetable stew
right: vegetable curry

Salads

Salads are no new invention but have long been popular in Europe. In the first century BC Cato gave as a recipe for salad the following: 'Select white, black and mottled olives and stone them. Mix and cut them up. Add a dressing of oil, vinegar, coriander, cumin, fennel, rue and mint. Mix well in an earthenware dish and serve with oil.' The Italians, who have an enormous variety of vegetables to choose from, continue to make salads in much the same manner today.

Possibly the first notice of the use of salads in England was made in the fifteenth century by the writer Gilbert Kymer when he noted that some vegetables in spring and summer were eaten raw, together with olive oil and spices, but he doubted the propriety of such a custom. Probably the first book written on salads in Britain was by the seventeenth-century English diarist and horticulturist John Evelyn. His recipe given for a green salad is no different from the classic recipe we know today. He advised that all ingredients should be chosen carefully, that the greens be washed and placed in a strainer and 'swinged and shaken gently', and then 'all should fall into their place like the notes in music in which there should be nothing harsh or grating'. For the dressing Evelyn favoured a mixture of oil and vinegar, warning against using too much oil.

Old cookery books list several kinds of salads, with fascinating mixtures which were not just to eat on ordinary days but also to be served on special occasions, such as 'a brave warming salad for winter', which included as many herbs as green leaves and onions. Cowslips and violets were included in a Grand Salad for spring. Lettuce salads were advised for those dying of unrequited love and Galen, the great Greek physician, declared that lettuce repressed the vapours, mitigated pain and had a wholesome effect upon the morals.

Salad dressing

FOR ONE LARGE LETTUCE

INGREDIENTS
3–4 tablespoons olive or walnut oil
1 tablespoon vinegar or lemon juice
salt and freshly ground black pepper to taste

It is almost impossible both to give the exact quantity of ingredients in the mixing of this type of salad dressing since it depends on the quantity of lettuce or other green vegetables, or what else you have in your salad bowl, and to take account of varying tastes. The ability to mix a salad dressing founded the fortune of a Frenchman called d'Albignac. One evening in the early nineteenth century he was dining alone in a smart London tavern when he was asked by the host at a neighbouring table whether, as he was a Frenchman, he would dress their salad for them. This he did to such good conclusion that he was subsequently invited to dress salads at the finest houses in London. His dressing became fashionable and he designed a special conveyance to get himself with his servant and his salad-making equipment around the town, appearing at all fashionable dinners, routs and suppers, finally retiring to France a rich man.

No two salad dressers agree with the proportions of oil to vinegar, from 3–1 or 6–1. Equally, experts quarrel as to whether to use a mild fine wine vinegar (never malt, this is death to a dressing) or lemon juice. In the Caribbean a mild lime juice is preferred. Again, great French cooks disagree as to whether the oil should be mixed first with the seasonings, and then the vinegar, or the reverse. Yet again, some say plenty of salt and only a suspicion of pepper. Never use metal spoons when mixing. Hilaire Belloc insisted on horn spoons but most people are happy to use wooden ones.

Mix the vinegar with salt and pepper, add the oil and stir until cloudy.

Waldorf salad

USA

TO SERVE FOUR

INGREDIENTS

225 g (8 oz) celery
  lettuce
225 g (8 oz) apples
juice of ½ a lemon
salt and pepper
3 tablespoons mayonnaise
50 g (2 oz) broken walnut
  pieces, or blanched
  almonds

This salad takes the name of a famous New York hotel, the Waldorf Astoria, and usually is served as an hors d'oeuvre. In the United States pecan nuts are often used instead of walnuts, and not all cooks blanch the celery before dicing it; in Canada they have an almost identical salad which they call apple salad. This is also served on lettuce leaves.

Dice and drop the celery into boiling water and leave for 3–4 minutes, drain well and put under cold running water, shaking well. Line a bowl with freshly washed lettuce leaves. Peel and dice the apple – the dice should be the same size as the celery dice – and put together with the celery into a second bowl, adding at once the lemon juice and a little salt and pepper. Cover and leave to rest for 15 minutes. Meanwhile make the mayonnaise, add this to the apple and celery, then add three-quarters of the nuts and stir well but not vigorously. Add the remainder of the nuts immediately before serving and place on the lettuce leaves. Do not let the salad stand before serving as the nuts will discolour the apple.

Russian salad

Vinyegryet

Russia

INGREDIENTS

cold cooked carrots,
  potatoes, beetroots and
  peas
oil and vinegar for
  marinade (*see recipe*)
chopped pickled herring
  fillets
chopped anchovy fillets
finely chopped fresh dill
  and parsley

There are no exact quantities given for this salad, of Imperial Russian origin. Cooks were able to list as many as 36 kinds of *vinyegryet*, which doubtless accounts for the astonishing diversity of the salad internationally known as Russian salad. Instead of herring, cooked shrimps may be used.

Slice the carrots, potatoes and beetroots into *julienne* strips and leave them with the peas in a mixture of two-thirds oil and one-third vinegar almost to cover. Leave for about 1 hour, drain, mix with the herrings and anchovies and enough of the oil and vinegar marinade to hold the salad together. Put into a salad bowl. Sprinkle with dill and parsley.

Another version is as follows: the thinly sliced remains of cold, cooked meats are cut into thin strips and mixed with thin strips of cooked carrots, potatoes, salted or fresh cucumbers or gherkins, chopped hard-boiled eggs, stoned and chopped olives, a salad dressing and cooked or tinned chopped shellfish. Mayonnaise may be used instead of a dressing.

Left: Waldorf salad
right: Russian salad

Vegetable salad with a peanut sauce

Gado-gado
Indonesia

TO SERVE SIX

INGREDIENTS
225 g (8 oz) white cabbage
225 g (8 oz) green or
  French beans
225 g (8 oz) spinach
handful of bean sprouts
450 g (1 lb) potatoes
350 g (12 oz) sliced onions
prawn crackers
1–2 hard-boiled eggs
Peanut sauce
2 tablespoons oil
1 small onion, 100 g (4 oz),
  finely chopped
2 cloves garlic, crushed
2 red chillies, chopped
salt to taste
½ cup peanut butter
1 cup coconut milk (*see
  page* 185)
1 tablespoon lemon juice
1 tablespoon sugar

This salad or vegetable dish is a great favourite with connoisseurs of Indonesian food. It can be served with rice, but it is usual to serve it alone as a cold salad. The sauce is poured over the top while it is still warm, although there are some people who add the sauce when it is cool or even cold. All the vegetables must be cooked separately.

Wash, shred and cook the cabbage until just tender. Trim and break the beans into 3-cm (1-in) pieces and cook until tender. Wash the spinach, cook until tender, drain and then chop finely. Blanch the bean sprouts for 1 minute in boiling water. Drain. Peel the potatoes and cook whole until tender. Cool and slice into medium-thick slices. Separately fry the onions until dark brown and the prawn crackers until they fluff out and are crisp.

Make the sauce; heat the oil and fry the onion, garlic and chillies until the onion begins to soften and change colour, then add the salt, peanut butter and coconut milk. Bring this to the boil, add the lemon juice and sugar. If the sauce seems a little thick, add more coconut milk. Failing coconut milk, use a mixture of water and fresh milk.

When all the vegetables are ready, arrange them in layers in a large deep dish or large wide shallow bowl in the order given above. Add the sliced eggs and crisply fried onions; or the onions can be served separately. Sometimes fresh shredded coconut also is added to the *gado-gado*. Serve the prawn crackers separately.

Tomato savoury jellied mould

USA

TO SERVE SIX

INGREDIENTS
600-g (1-lb 5-oz) tin peeled tomatoes
1–2 strips lemon rind
1 teaspoon sugar
salt and pepper to taste
1 teaspoon tomato purée
1–2 bayleaves
1–2 cloves garlic, crushed
40 g (1½ oz) gelatine
water or dry white wine for topping up

This recipe of American origin makes a useful starter to a meal. The mould can be filled with almost any type of cold creamed savoury mixture and garnished with cold cooked vegetables, in particular either peas or broad beans, asparagus or cooked chopped baby carrots. It should be served with a dressing separately and again this is a matter of choice: simple mayonnaise, one flavoured with garlic, or a salad dressing. An alternative, popular in the United States, is a dressing made from cottage cheese mixed with cream, or the top of the milk, and, of course, natural yogurt goes splendidly with the mould.

Put the tomatoes together with their juice into a pan, add the lemon rind, sugar, salt, pepper, tomato purée, bayleaf and garlic, bring gently to the boil, stir well, lower the heat and cook for 5 minutes. Rub through a very fine sieve. While the tomatoes are cooking, soak the gelatine in water, about 150 ml (¼ pint), stir well and leave until dissolved, 3–4 minutes. Stir the gelatine and water into the hot tomato purée and let it completely dissolve. Measure, and if there are not quite 1.2 litres (2 pints), add water or dry white wine to bring it up to this quantity. Pour into a rinsed ring mould of 1.2 litres' (2 pints') capacity, cool and then leave in the refrigerator to set firmly. Unmould to serve on a round dish and garnish with the chosen filling, vegetable and dressing.

Top: tomato savoury jellied mould
bottom: tomato, pepper and anchovy salad

Tomato, pepper and anchovy salad

Salade niçoise
France

TO SERVE FOUR–SIX

INGREDIENTS
1 lettuce
675 g (1½ lb) firm ripe tomatoes
salt
1 tin anchovy fillets
1 green pepper
12 black olives
hard-boiled eggs, sliced (as many as you wish)
salad dressing (*see page* 148)

This salad is Ligurian in origin and in some of my early books on Provençal cooking it is not listed at all. The Ligurians, who occupied the south of France for a century or so under the Kings of Sardinia, brought this extremely simple country salad with them and, although I have given exact quantities in this recipe, usually it is a matter of mixing the ingredients according to taste. Olive oil should be used in the dressing if possible.

Wash and dry the lettuce and separate the leaves. Thinly slice the tomatoes, removing the seeds. Sprinkle lightly with salt, also with sugar if liked. Line a large, round dish with lettuce leaves and place the sliced tomatoes over them. Drain the oil from the anchovies and arrange the fish over the tomatoes. Cut the pepper into thin rounds, discarding core and seeds. Scatter the rounds over the tomatoes. Garnish with olives and sliced hard-boiled eggs. Make a dressing and sprinkle this over the salad.

Finely chopped fresh basil also may be added to the dressing.

151

Orange and onion salad

Munkaczina
Middle East

TO SERVE FOUR–SIX

INGREDIENTS
4 thin-skinned sweet
  oranges
350 g (12 oz) mild or sweet
  Spanish onions
12 black olives, stoned
lemon juice
olive oil

Over the years this recipe has become somewhat legendary; no one knows much about its origin except that Anatole France, a late nineteenth-century writer, brought it from the Middle East to France. There are stories about it being compared to the splendid jewels of Aladdin's cave, and its beauty being equal to the Emir's pearls.

Wash and thinly slice the oranges; you can dispense with the peel or leave it on, as you wish. Peel and thinly slice the onions. Arrange the oranges in a shallow bowl with the onion on top, garnish with the olives and sprinkle lightly with lemon juice and olive oil.

Spiced onion salad

Cachoombar
India

TO SERVE THREE–FOUR

INGREDIENTS
225 g (8 oz) mild white
  onions
450 g (1 lb) firm ripe
  tomatoes, blanched
225 g (8 oz) cucumber
4 small green chillies
2 sprigs fresh coriander or
  parsley
1 teaspoon salt
150 ml ($\frac{1}{4}$ pint) malt
  vinegar

As mild white onions are not always available, large spring onions would be a good substitute. If neither fresh coriander nor parsley is available, then they must be omitted, as the dried variety would not give the right effect.
   Green chillies are hot so it is important to remove their seeds. Failing green chillies – which, however, are usually available these days – use red ones or $\frac{1}{2}$ teaspoon of either chilli or cayenne pepper, or less if this should seem too pungent. A light malt vinegar is the natural choice for this salad but other vinegars, except wine vinegar may be substituted.

Peel and chop the onions, tomatoes and cucumber into very small cubes of an equal size. Finely chop the chillies and the coriander. Combine all these ingredients, put into a shallow bowl, sprinkle with salt, add the vinegar and leave for 30 minutes before serving.

Banana salad

Canada

TO SERVE FOUR

INGREDIENTS
1 lettuce
1–2 bananas
1–2 tablespoons salad
  dressing (*see page* 148)
1–2 tablespoons finely
  chopped nuts

Any kind of nuts may be used in this recipe, except perhaps almonds.

Pull off the lettuce leaves and wash in cold water. Drain and dry. Arrange the leaves in a flat salad dish or plate. Peel and slice the bananas thinly and spread over the lettuce leaves. Add the salad dressing and sprinkle with the nuts. Serve at once, otherwise the bananas might discolour.

Left top to bottom: orange and onion salad; spiced
onion salad; banana salad
right top to bottom: aubergine salad; German
potato salad

Aubergine salad

Baba ghanouge
The Middle East

TO SERVE FOUR–SIX

INGREDIENTS
675 g (1½ lb) aubergines
3 cloves garlic
1–2 teaspoons salt
juice of 1 lemon
3 tablespoons sesame sauce
  (*see recipe*)
pomegranate seeds
  (optional)
finely chopped fresh mint
paprika pepper
olive oil

To the people of the Middle East the purple aubergine is what the potato is to the Irish, the cabbage to the British and the tomato to the Italian. Everyone eats aubergine, rich and poor alike, and many are the recipes that have evolved for its use. This recipe is said to have been created by a Circassian slave in the harem of one of the Ottoman Emperors. Sesame sauce, or *tahina*, is available in Greek stores, as well as in many health-food stores.

Spear the aubergines on a toasting fork and grill over a gas or other open flame until the skin burns black and is broken. Put the aubergines into a paper bag, close it tightly and leave for 15 minutes. After this they should be easy to peel. Cut the flesh into small pieces and either pound or mash to a purée. Pound the garlic with salt to a pulp, add the lemon juice and, when blended, add the sesame sauce (*tahina*). Beat this mixture into the aubergine purée. Arrange the salad in a shallow bowl, usually of pottery, garnish with pomegranate seeds (if using), sprinkle with mint, paprika pepper and very lightly with olive or vegetable oil. Chill before serving.

Instead of pounding the chopped aubergines together with the garlic, salt, lemon juice and sesame, the flesh can be whirled in a liquidizer.

German potato salad

Kartoffelsalat
Germany

TO SERVE SIX

INGREDIENTS
900 g (2 lb) potatoes
4 spring onions
1 teaspoon capers
salt and good pinch
  cayenne pepper
1 teaspoon sugar
2 egg yolks
4 tablespoons olive oil
150 ml (¼ pint) red wine
4 tablespoons meat stock
1 teaspoon Continental
  mustard
1 tablespoon tarragon
  vinegar

Germans usually make their potato salads with boiled potatoes that are still hot. This particular salad has a piquant sauce.

Cook the potatoes in their skins in boiling, salted water. Meanwhile finely chop the white part of the spring onions, chop the capers and combine these two ingredients. Add the salt, pepper and sugar. Mash the egg yolks and beat with the oil until the mixture is thick. Add the wine, meat stock, mustard and vinegar. When well mixed, combine with the spring onions and capers. Peel the potatoes as soon as possible, cut into cubes, put into a deep bowl and mix the dressing into them while still hot. Serve warm.

153

Cucumber salad with crabmeat

Sunomono

Japan

TO SERVE FOUR–SIX

INGREDIENTS
1 large cucumber
  (*see recipe*)
salt
meat from 1 medium-sized
  crab
white wine vinegar

This is a cool summer salad. The Japanese prefer to use 3–4 small, fat, rather sweet cucumbers for this salad in preference to our larger, slightly bitter variety of cucumber, and they also add thin strips of bamboo shoots, which have been marinated in a dressing for about 1 hour.

Thinly peel the cucumber in ribs, leaving thin strips of peel on the cucumber. Rub with salt and leave for 30 minutes. Meanwhile mash the crabmeat and mix it with a little vinegar and salt, just to moisten the meat. Wash off the salt from the cucumber and cut into halves. Scoop out the seed and some of the centre and fill the cavity with the crabmeat. Now cut the cucumber into 1-cm ($\frac{1}{4}$-in) slices and serve with mayonnaise, salad dressing or soya sauce.

Mushroom salad

Borani garch

Iran

TO SERVE FOUR–SIX

INGREDIENTS
450 g (1 lb) mushrooms
2–3 tablespoons olive oil
175 g (6 oz) onions, finely
  chopped
salt and pepper
150 ml ($\frac{1}{4}$ pint) natural
  yogurt
dried mint, crushed

Cultivated or field mushrooms may be used in this recipe. Iranians use quite a lot of dried mint in their cooking, crushed to a fine powder. Use just enough yogurt to cover the remaining ingredients.

Wash the mushrooms, separate the caps from the stems – the latter can be used to flavour a soup. Pat the mushroom caps dry and cut into thick slices. Heat the oil and fry the onion until it changes colour, add the mushrooms and fry for exactly 5 minutes. Remove both the onions and the mushrooms from the pan and place in a porcelain salad bowl. Leave until cold. Add salt and pepper, cover with yogurt and gently mix. Chill, and sprinkle the crushed mint over the top just before serving.

Left: Iranian mushroom salad
right: Rumanian mushroom salad

Mushroom salad

Ciuperci cu vin

Rumania

TO SERVE FOUR

INGREDIENTS
450 g (1 lb) large
  mushrooms
juice of 1 lemon
3 tablespoons olive oil
225 g (8 oz) onions, finely
  chopped
150 ml ($\frac{1}{4}$ pint) red wine
salt, pepper and finely
  chopped parsley to taste

This salad can be used as a starter, together with other salads, and I have used it to accompany grilled and devilled chicken. It is usual to garnish it with black olives and watercress. It is important, however, to use olive oil in its preparation since the mushrooms are served and eaten cold.

Wash the mushrooms, drain and pat dry. Slice thinly, caps and stems together, drop into a bowl and sprinkle with lemon juice.

Gently toss the mushrooms round and round to make sure that the juice coats all of them. Leave for 15 minutes. Heat the oil in a deep frying pan, add the mushrooms and cook over a moderate heat for 15 minutes. Add the onions and cook gently until these are soft, but they must not be overcooked. Add the wine, salt, pepper and parsley, stir and cook for another 5 minutes. Turn out into a dish and leave until quite cold. Lightly garnish.

Tunisian salad

Grande salade tunisienne
Tunisia

TO SERVE FOUR

INGREDIENTS
450 g (1 lb) potatoes
175 g (6 oz) carrots
100 g (4 oz) shelled peas
100 g (4 oz) firm cheese
Salt and pepper
Juice of 1 lemon
150 ml (¼ pint) olive oil
8 artichoke hearts
8 each black and green
  olives, stoned
1 tablespoon chopped
  capers
1 tablespoon finely
  chopped parsley

Artichoke hearts are available from delicatessen and grocery shops, both in jars and tins. The salad can be served cold but it is generally served warm. Instead of parsley, finely chopped mint is often used.

Wash but do not peel the potatoes and boil; scrape the carrots and cook separately in boiling salted water until tender. Cook the peas (separately), unless using tinned ones. Drain the potatoes, peel and cut into small cubes; drain and cut the carrots into rounds of the same size; drain the peas. Put these 3 ingredients into a porcelain salad bowl. Cut the cheese into small cubes, add to the bowl and sprinkle generously with salt and pepper. Mix the lemon juice with oil and beat well; pour this dressing over the still warm vegetables. Cut the artichoke hearts into thick slices or cubes, and add to the salad. Add the remaining ingredients and stir with great care. The salad may be garnished with slices of hard-boiled eggs.

Egg salad

Phool ka achar
Nepal

TO SERVE SIX

INGREDIENTS
12 eggs, hard-boiled
25 g (1 oz) butter
1 teaspoon chilli pepper
1 teaspoon cumin seeds,
  well pounded
¼ teaspoon cardamom
2 cups thick curd or
  natural yogurt
3 tablespoons finely
  chopped coriander or
  parsley
1 small lime or lemon,
  finely chopped with the
  peel

This dish is called a chutney in Nepal but I feel that anyone trying it for the first time would find this title somewhat misleading. It makes an interesting start to a meal and can be served with a green salad or spiced potatoes (*see page* 144), or with chopped tomatoes, the red of the tomatoes and the white of the egg complementing each other. This recipe came from a Nepalese princess and was given to me well over 30 years ago in the 1940s when I was in Katmandu, which was still in those days a rather unknown but fascinating city.

Shell and halve the eggs. Heat the butter, add the spices and lightly fry, stirring them well as they burn easily. The frying is to help rid the spices of their raw flavour and also to develop the basic spice flavour. Beat the curd, add the fresh coriander or parsley, lemon juice and rind and finally the fried spices. If using parsley, try to use the straight-leaved variety which has more flavour. Mix all this together, then add the eggs. Combine gently so that the eggs do not break and, equally carefully, turn out into a shallow dish. Serve cold.

Puddings, cakes
and pastries

Puddings

The serving of sweet puddings in Britain as 'afters' comes from the English adoption of an eighteenth-century French custom in the arrangement of table courses. It began with the wealthy classes and was quickly taken up by the tavern keepers who, by the end of the century, were terminating their meals with a sweet pudding, a tart or pie. Gradually the custom percolated throughout the country. Previously it had been the custom to serve a sweet dish at the beginning of a meal, and at formal dinners between the courses sweet water-ices or sorbets. This custom dated back to the earliest days. Generally speaking, in the West today sweet puddings are served at the end of a meal.

Puddings in the earliest days were rather sloppy and made with grain, swollen in water until almost bursting, far more like a dish of porridge than what we today recognize as a pudding. But with time and the coming of sugar, spices, dried fruit and flour these concoctions were made firmer until by the seventeenth century puddings in Britain had reached the height of their popularity. It must be admitted that the British were by no means the inventors of sweet dishes, indeed, they came later than most people to liking such a taste.

Many are the ancient Greek and Latin recipes which read like our puddings of today. Ices and sherbets were known to the Persians and Arabs who buried ice and snow in pits to keep their food cold. We are told Marco Polo brought back a recipe for milk ice-cream from his Chinese voyage and ices were served by French royalty in the sixteenth century.

That not all puddings stem from British kitchens is clearly shown by the following recipes, also that not all dishes labelled 'puddings' are puddings in the strict sense of the word. We are apt to refer to a dish of stewed apples as a pudding, as well as other sweet concoctions. Some may call them all desserts which, strictly speaking, they are not since a dessert should really mean the final course of a meal after the table has been cleared and the nuts, dried fruits and chocolate truffles or *dragées* are served. The word dessert is derived from the French *desservir,* to clear the table, and was first used in England in the seventeenth century. A sweet dish, whether it is large or small, does give a finishing touch to a meal but it must create a stir of interest, it could well be dramatic, and it should have glamour.

Salzburg dumplings

Salzburger Nockerln
Austria

TO SERVE THREE

INGREDIENTS
25 g (1 oz) unsalted butter
4 egg whites
3 tablespoons castor sugar
1 teaspoon vanilla sugar
3 egg yolks
25 g (1 oz) flour

These baked dumplings are the culinary pride of Salzburg. The Salzburgers say those who do not like them have no taste, adding that Austrian women who cannot make them have no talent as cooks. The dumplings were first made at the beginning of the seventeenth century under the instruction of one Ägide Dietrich von Raitenau, Archbishop of Salzburg, who loved power, pomp and puddings. Salzburg dumplings are mainly made of air, eggs and the smallest quantity of flour. If not correctly handled they collapse. If the right heat is not applied, or there is a trace of draught, they flop. However, despite this solemn Austrian warning, I do not consider they are any more difficult to make than a soufflé.

Butter a shallow 25 × 15-cm (10 × 6-in) baking dish before preparing the dumplings so that there is no delay between the final mixing of the egg whites and adding them to the pan. Preheat the oven to 220°C, 425°F, Gas Mark 7. Beat the egg whites until stiff, add the sugar and vanilla sugar and continue beating to a stiff meringue consistency. Take out 3 tablespoons of the beaten egg whites, beat this into the egg yolks, then fold the mixture back into the egg whites. Sift the flour over the top of the mixture and carefully fold in. This quantity makes three dumplings. Scoop out one-third with a large metal spoon, place carefully in the prepared baking dish and add the rest in the same manner, the three portions close together. Put the dish into the oven and bake for 8–10 minutes. Take the dumplings from the oven, bring to the table to serve in the dish in which they were cooked. Make sure there is no draught *en route* and that there is no great difference in temperature between the kitchen and the dining room.

Carrot halva

Gajjar halva
Pakistan

TO SERVE SIX–EIGHT

INGREDIENTS

750 g (1½ lb) large carrots
2.3 litres (4 pints) milk
good pinch saffron, soaked
  in milk for 30 minutes
  (optional)
350 g (12 oz) granulated
  sugar
sultanas (optional)
50–75 g (2–3 oz) unsalted
  butter
2–3 sheets silver leaf (*see
  page* 189)
blanched almonds or
  cashew nuts to taste
2 cardamom seeds, crushed

The usual carrot for this pudding is a translucent orange-red type indigenous to the Indian subcontinent. However, more important is the shredding of the carrots, for the shreds should be as long as possible. It is usual to make fairly large batches of *halva* which will keep for at least a week in a refrigerator, its flavour improving all the while. In Piedmont I have found carrots weighing as much as 750 g (1¾ lb), sweet and tender right through. I use them to make *halva* with great success.

Scrape the carrots and shred them into long strips. Bring the milk to the boil in a large pan, add the carrot and saffron and cook over a simmering heat until the carrots are thick and soft and all the milk has been absorbed, between 3 and 4 hours. Stir from time to time; the more you stir the better. Add the sugar, sultanas and butter. Stir well and pour this mixture into another hot but dry pan and boil, stirring constantly until the mixture begins to solidify and change to a deep red colour. Turn it out on to a dish and garnish with silver leaf as well as blanched almonds and cardamom seeds.

Carrot *halva* is served both hot and cold and reheats easily.

Layered pancakes

Palacsinta torta
Hungary

TO SERVE SIX–EIGHT

INGREDIENTS
12 very thin pancakes,
  15 cm (6 in) in diameter
175 g (6 oz) apricot or
  damson jam
75 g (3 oz) grated
  chocolate
100 ml (4 fl oz) double or
  single cream
75 g (3 oz) ground walnuts
  or hazelnuts
50 g (2 oz) raisins
3 egg whites
175 g (6 oz) castor sugar

This dish of pancakes was considered, and probably still is, as one to give to a 'magnate'. The Hungarians have a large repertoire of pancake dishes, not all as rich as this and not all sweet – in fact, the majority are savoury. It is extremely important that the pancakes are thin and all of the same size. This pudding is cut like a cake.

Preheat the oven to 200°C, 400°F, Gas Mark 6. Make the pancakes using 100 g (4 oz) of flour, 1 egg and 275 ml (½ pint) milk. As you make them, place them on a warm plate, one on top of the other. When all are ready, take one pancake and place this on a round ovenproof plate. Spread this lightly with jam. Cover with a second pancake and spread this with the grated chocolate and a little cream. Add a third pancake and spread this with the ground

nuts and a few of the raisins, plus a little cream. Add a fourth pancake and spread with chocolate and cream. Continue in this fashion until all the ingredients are used up, leaving the top pancake uncovered. Put this pile into the oven while you prepare the meringue topping. Make a meringue topping using the eggs and sugar. Take the pancakes from the oven, raise the heat to 220°C, 425°F, Gas Mark 7 and spread the meringue over the pancakes, covering the top quickly, and all round the sides. Return to the oven and bake until the meringue topping is tipped with brown specks. Serve warm, cut into slices like a cake. It can be lightly sprinkled with vanilla sugar before serving, or served accompanied by a chocolate sauce.

Left: layered pancakes
right: coconut bread pudding

Coconut bread pudding

Pudim de pão com côco
Brazil

TO SERVE SIX–EIGHT

INGREDIENTS
butter for greasing
4 thick slices white bread,
  crustless
575 ml (1 pint) milk
100 g (4 oz) sugar
½ cup coconut milk (*see
  page* 185)
15 g (½ oz) butter, melted
100 g (4 oz) shredded
  coconut
6 egg yolks, slightly
  beaten
½ teaspoon vanilla essence
3 egg whites, stiffly beaten

If you have any unfortunate childhood memories of bread pudding, do not let them put you off this excellent Brazilian version. If it is possible, use fresh coconut, grated or shredded, but desiccated coconut of the best quality can be used as a substitute.

Preheat the oven to 180°C, 350°F, Gas Mark 4. Rub a baking dish, 25 × 15 cm (10 × 6 in) and 8 cm (3 in) deep, generously with butter. Soak the bread in the milk until very soft, then rub through a wire sieve into a mixing bowl. Add the

sugar, coconut milk, melted butter, shredded coconut, egg yolks, vanilla and mix well. Fold in the egg whites: they must be really stiff, enough to form peaks. Pour into the baking dish and put into a pan containing enough water to reach halfway up the sides of the dish. Bake in the oven for 45–50 minutes. The pudding is turned out for serving, either hot or cold. If serving hot, let it settle a little before turning it out. Serve with a sweet sauce; in Brazil the pudding is served with a caramelized custard sauce.

Almond chocolate foam

USA

TO SERVE EIGHT

225 g (8 oz) sweet cooking
  chocolate
50 g (2 oz) slivered
  almonds
8 eggs, separated
½ teaspoon salt
275 ml (½ pint) double
  cream
almond essence
bitter chocolate to garnish

This recipe was presented to me by an American who claimed it to be 'the richest sweet dish in the world'. Perhaps an exaggeration but it certainly is rich and a joy for those who love chocolate.

Break the sweet chocolate into small bits and put together with the almonds into the top of a double boiler and cook over hot water until the chocolate has melted. Beat the yolks until thick and lemon coloured. Pour the melted chocolate and nuts into the yolks, stirring all the while, and mix thoroughly. Beat the egg whites, adding the salt, until stiff but not dry and fold them with a metal spoon into the chocolate mixture and blend well without beating. Pour this into a medium-shallow, large crystal bowl and chill for at least 4 hours before serving. When ready to serve, whip the cream until thick, adding just a few drops of almond essence, and spread this lightly over the top of the chocolate. Add the bitter chocolate, shaving with a fine grater over the top of the cream. Serve with wine biscuits, cat's tongues, or similar dessert biscuits, which are not too sweet.

Left: cream of paradise
right: almond chocolate foam

Cream of paradise

Yakh dar behisht

Iran

TO SERVE SIX

INGREDIENTS
100 g (4 oz) unsalted butter
3 eggs, separated
pinch of salt
275 ml (½ pint) double
  cream
75 g (3 oz) sugar
50 g (2 oz) praline (*see
  recipe*)

This is a very rich pudding but, provided you have an electric beater or a strong arm, not in the least difficult to make. Instead of praline, coarsely ground nuts may be used. If using praline, this must be pounded to a fine powder.

Soften the butter, do not on any account melt it, then beat until it is creamy and very light (if using the strong arm instead of the beater it takes 30 minutes according to the Iranians). Whisk the egg yolks until fluffy, the egg whites with the salt until peaks form, and the cream until stiff. Mix the butter with the egg yolks and beat again well until this mixture becomes spongy. Add the sugar, beat again, then add the pounded praline or ground nuts; finally fold in the egg whites and the cream. Pour this mixture into a mould and chill. Turn out to serve. A variation of this is to line the mould with cat's tongues, or Savoy biscuits. This ensures that the mould turns out easily and looks very attractive.

Banana frost and fire

Bahamas

TO SERVE FOUR

INGREDIENTS
3 large egg whites
50 g (2 oz) castor sugar
4 large bananas
450 g (1 lb) block ice
   cream, well frozen
2 tablespoons rum

This could be called the West Indian version of the Baked Alaska. Preferably coffee ice cream, frozen very hard, should be used in this dish but vanilla will do as well.

Preheat the oven to 230°C, 450°F, Gas Mark 8. Beat the egg whites until they begin to stiffen, then gradually add the sugar and continue beating until the mixture is stiff and forms into peaks. Peel and slice the bananas into halves lengthwise and cut each half into 3 lengths. Arrange half the bananas in a 25-cm (10-in) ovenproof baking dish; they should form a base just a little longer and wider than the ice cream block. Place the ice cream on top of the bananas, cover with the remaining bananas, then spread quickly with the meringue, like icing a cake so that the bananas and ice cream are completely covered and sealed. Bake in the oven for 4 minutes or until the meringue topping is tipped with brown – no longer or the ice cream will melt. Meanwhile warm the rum. As soon as the 'frost' is ready, take from the oven, pour the warmed rum 'fire' over the top, ignite and serve flaming at table.

Calvados omelette

Omelette normande
France

TO SERVE TWO

INGREDIENTS
225 g (8 oz) cooking apples
50 g (2 oz) unsalted butter
3 tablespoons Calvados
4 eggs (size 2)
1 tablespoon milk
pinch of salt
castor sugar
ground cinnamon

Norman cooking means a prodigious use of cream, cider, butter and apples. From their apples the Normans make a strong apple brandy, Calvados, which lends character to this simple but excellent pudding. Calvados, named after the town in Normandy, a region rich in apple orchards, is kept in casks and the best is matured for six years. The Americans have an equivalent, applejack, but this is marketed much younger than the Norman Calvados. Failing Calvados, rum or brandy can be used.

Peel and slice the apples. Melt 40 g ($1\frac{1}{2}$ oz) of the butter in a saucepan, add the apples and 1 tablespoon of Calvados, cover the pan and cook until the apples are soft. Take from the heat but keep hot. While the apples are cooking, beat the eggs with the milk and salt. Heat the remaining butter in an omelette pan (or heavy frying pan) and when it is nut-brown pour in half of the beaten eggs, let these cook for 2 minutes, then gently spread the apples over the top and cover with the rest of the eggs. Continue cooking over a moderate heat until the eggs have set. Turn out on to a hot plate and sprinkle with sugar and cinnamon. Put under a hot grill to glaze the top, pour the remaining Calvados over the top, ignite and serve the omelette flaming.

Top: banana frost and fire
Bottom: Calvados omelette

162

Baked meringue apples

Manzanas asadas
Spain

TO SERVE FOUR

INGREDIENTS
4 large equal-sized cooking
   apples
100 g (4 oz) castor sugar
25 g (1 oz) unsalted butter
150 ml ($\frac{1}{4}$ pint) sweet
   white wine
3 egg whites (size 2)
few drops anise (*see
   page* 184)
apricot jam

This recipe comes from Asturia where, it is claimed, Spain's finest apples are found. It is also the cider region of the country. If anise is not available, simply forget it; or if you have any Kümmel or Pernod in the cupboard, then a few drops of either would be useful.

Preheat the oven to 190°C, 375°F, Gas Mark 5. Wipe the apples, twist off their stems, scoop out the cores, slit round the skin half-way down the sides of the apples, put into a large shallow ovenproof baking dish, 25 × 20 cm (10 × 8 in), and sprinkle each lightly with sugar, using about a quarter of it, and top with a small nut of butter. Add the wine. Bake in the oven for 30–40 minutes, or until tender when pierced with a skewer. Meanwhile whisk the egg whites until stiff, and halfway through whisking fold in the rest of the sugar. Add a few drops of anise and continue whisking until the whites form stiff peaks. Take the apples from the oven. On to each apple drop a spoonful or so of apricot jam and spread each apple equally with beaten egg white. Return to the oven to continue cooking until the apples are tender and the meringue golden.

Cherries in kirsch

Cerises en kirsch
France

TO SERVE FOUR

INGREDIENTS
1 tin or bottle of black
 cherries in syrup
75 ml (3 fl oz) kirsch
sugar to taste (optional)
1 teaspoon cornflour
1 tablespoon water

Drain the cherries from their juice, making sure all the juice has been drained off. Put the juice aside. Stone the fruit and marinate it for 2–3 hours in the kirsch. Turn the cherries fairly often. When ready to serve, boil the cherry juice in a small pan and let it reduce to about one-third of its original quantity. Add sugar if a really sweet dish is liked but check before adding it; better still is a squeeze of lemon juice. When the juice has reduced and come to a gentle boil, mix the cornflour with the water to a thin paste and stir this into the juice. Continue cooking until the sauce is thick. Strain the cherries from the kirsch and blend them into the sauce, stirring well but carefully. Slightly warm the kirsch, add to the pan, ignite and serve hot, still flaming.

Easter pudding

Pashka
USSR

TO SERVE SIX–EIGHT

INGREDIENTS
3-cm (1-in) piece vanilla
 pod
2 egg yolks
100 g (4 oz) castor sugar
50 g (2 oz) butter
450 g (1 lb) dry curd
 cheese, such as Ricotta
50 g (2 oz) almonds,
 blanched and chopped
275 ml (½ pint) double
 cream
1 egg white

To the Russians and the Poles this pudding is considered as an Easter dish to set before their family and guests, but it can be served throughout the year. It is easy to make and happily requires no cooking. Russians shape it in a traditional mould rather like a flower pot in form. It is a four-sided pyramid mould embossed on the sides with the Christian symbols of the Orthodox Cross and the letters XB, for *Khristos Voskryesye*, 'Christ is Risen'. Failing the wooden mould, use an ordinary clean terracotta flower pot, 13 cm (5 in) across and 12 cm (4¾ in) high, and line it with fine white muslin.

Slit the vanilla pod down the centre, take out the seeds and chop the pod. Beat the yolks with half the sugar. Add the chopped vanilla pod and seeds and leave to stand for 20–30 minutes to absorb the flavour of the vanilla (or a good-quality vanilla extract could be used). Remove the vanilla pod and cream the remaining sugar with the butter until it is pale, almost white, and the

sugar completely dissolved. Beat this mixture into the egg yolks. Rub the cheese through a coarse wire sieve directly into a large mixing bowl. Add the eggs and butter mixture and mix well. Add the almonds. Beat the cream until thick, stir this into the cheese. Whisk the egg white until stiff and fold into the cheese mixture. Line the flower pot with the muslin, add the cheese mixture and pack down smoothly. Wrap the ends of the muslin over the top, place a saucer with a weight on top and leave in the refrigerator for several hours, or better still overnight. Excess whey will drip out through the hole in the bottom of the pot. Unmould to serve and cut as for a cake.

The pudding can be served as it is without garnishing, although traditionally *kulich*, a type of dry fruit cake, is served with it. Some people add raisins to the cheese, also sultanas, glacé cherries, chopped candied peel, angelica or even extra slivers of almonds. Where there is no refrigerator, leave the *pashka* in a cold place to settle and omit the cream.

Pavlova cake
New Zealand

TO SERVE FOUR

INGREDIENTS
6 egg whites
150 g (6 oz) castor sugar
1 teaspoon light malt
  vinegar
$\frac{1}{4}$ teaspoon vanilla extract

Both New Zealand and Australia claim credit for having created this cake in honour of the Russian ballerina Pavlova. However, although a favourite in both countries, probably New Zealand has the stronger claim and it is from that country my recipe comes. As with all famous recipes, it has its variations. One, for example, is to make a meringue shell and fill it with cream and fruit. Although described as a cake, a Pavlova is served usually as a pudding.

First prepare a paper casing. Draw a circle 20 cm (8 in) in diameter on heavy, non-stick paper (silicone) or foil and lay this on a flat baking sheet. Then make the side of the casing by folding the paper or foil in a 10-cm (4-in) high ring placing it round the circle. (You now have what looks like a round cake tin.) Preheat the oven to 140°C, 275°F, Gas Mark 1. Whisk the egg whites until stiff, then add half the sugar, whisk again vigorously, then add the remaining sugar and continue whisking, at the same time adding the vinegar and vanilla extract, drop by drop. When the meringue mixture is smooth, pour it into the paper case and bake in the centre of the oven for about 1½ hours or until the meringue is firm and only just coloured to an ivory shade. Let the cake cool in the oven with the door open and the heat off. When the cake is cold, remove the casing and ease the cake on to a round, flat dish.

Serve topped with whipped cream and decorated with fresh raspberries. If raspberries are not available, other sweet, decorative fruits such as strawberries, drained tinned lichees or well-drained fruit salad may be used.

Caramel custards

Leche

Spain

TO SERVE FOUR

INGREDIENTS

575 ml (1 pint) milk

150 g (5 oz) sugar

3 eggs, plus 2 egg yolks

¼ teaspoon vanilla essence

100 g (4 oz) sugar to make
the caramel (*see recipe*)

This is Spain's favourite sweet dish, or so it would seem, for not only do the Spaniards serve it everywhere and every day in restaurants and homes, they even took the recipe with them when they went to South America, for I was served it again and again when travelling in those parts where its usual name was flan.

Preheat the oven to 180°C, 350°F, Gas Mark 4. Put the milk and the first quantity of sugar into a saucepan and cook gently until the sugar is dissolved. Take from the heat. Thoroughly beat the eggs and the yolks together, then add the vanilla essence. Pour the beaten eggs gently over the milk, which by now will be slightly cooled, and mix well with a fork or a wire whisk. Make the caramel. Put the second quantity of sugar into a small saucepan and cook over

a moderate heat, stirring all the time with a small wooden spoon until the sugar turns a golden brown and melts – this is a matter of minutes. Take it from the heat and at once add 2 tablespoons of water. Take care when doing this as the mixture will bubble up, so do not peer too closely into the pan. Return the pan to the stove and continue cooking and stirring until a smooth syrup is formed. Rinse one large or four small moulds with cold water. Pour the caramel into these, then add the custard. Put into a bain-marie, or a pan with cold water (the water should come half-way up the sides of the pan) and bake in the oven for 30–40 minutes. Before taking the custards from the pan, insert a knife into them, if it comes out clean, the custards, which should be fairly firm, are ready. Cool, then chill and turn out to serve.

166

Mont Blanc

Monte Bianco

Italy

TO SERVE SIX–EIGHT

INGREDIENTS

900 g (2 lb) chestnuts
1.2 litres (2 pints) milk
1 small piece vanilla pod
225 g (8 oz) sugar
150 ml (¼ pint) water
3 tablespoons Strega
  liqueur or brandy
275 ml (½ pint) double
  cream
1 tablespoon castor sugar

This is a popular recipe in most chestnut-growing countries and as usual there are variations on the basic recipe. I first met it when living in Budapest. It was made for me by a Jewish fruit-stall vendor from whom I bought my peaches and apricots in summer, but chestnuts in the winter. We became good friends and one day she invited me to her home and served me, among several other Hungarian specialities, this sweet dish of puréed chestnuts and cream. I still remember her with affection, also sadness, for she disappeared during the Second World War.

Cut a cross on the flat side of the chestnuts with a sharp knife, then cook in boiling water for about 20 minutes or until the skins peel off easily. Discard the skins while the chestnuts are still hot, then put the nuts into a pan together with the milk and vanilla and cook gently until they are very soft, about 20 minutes – the exact time depends on the type of chestnuts used. Meanwhile put the sugar into a pan with

the water and cook over a moderate heat until the sugar is dissolved. Raise the heat and, without stirring, cook the syrup until it reaches the soft boiling stage and thickness. This will take 6–10 minutes. When the chestnuts are very soft, drain (take out the vanilla) and rub the chestnuts through a sieve. Take the syrup from the stove and mix into the purée, add the Strega and beat the mixture until smooth. Press the purée through a potato ricer and let it fall lightly into a heap on to a flat dish on which you are to serve the 'mountain'. Whip the cream until stiff, add the castor sugar and beat again until the cream is really very stiff. Drop this gently on top of the puréed chestnuts and let it spread, some of it down the sides of the 'mountain'. It should cover the peak but leave the base clear.

There are variations to this recipe. Some cooks like to put it on to a base of liqueur-soaked spongecake, which is very good; some make a round of chocolate and use this as a base; and others grate bitter chocolate over the top.

Egg brocade

Nishiki-tamago

Japan

TO SERVE TWELVE

INGREDIENTS

12 eggs, hard-boiled
6 tablespoons castor sugar
pinch of salt

This is a strange little egg dish but surprisingly good and certainly one to offer your guests after lunch or dinner with coffee. It looks a bit like coconut candy for the bottom half of it is white and the top a bright yellow.

Separate the egg whites from the yolks. Rub the whites through a fine sieve – they rub through easily. Mix the whites with half the sugar and a tiny pinch of salt. Put this mixture into an oblong mould (I use an ice tray as I do not have the correct Japanese mould) and press it down smoothly but with a light touch. This

quantity fills about three-quarters of an average-sized ice tray. Now rub the yolks through the sieve and mix with the remaining sugar. Spread this mixture on top of the egg whites. Put the mould in a shallow pan, or baking dish, with enough water to come half-way up the container. Cover and steam for 10–15 minutes. Take the tray from the pan of water, let the mixture cool, put into the refrigerator and, when it is quite cold, remove the egg from the container and cut into small pieces, roughly 2 cm (¾ in) thick.

Top to bottom: rosewater pudding; syllabub; spiced curd pudding

Spiced curd pudding

Shrikund

Nepal

TO SERVE SIX

INGREDIENTS

¼ teaspoon saffron
1 teaspoon rosewater
900 g (2 lb) curd cheese
275 g (10 oz) sugar
1 teaspoon mixed ground
   cloves, cinnamon,
   cardamom seeds and
   black pepper

This recipe was given to me by the Princess Princip Shah of Nepal in 1954 when she served it to me at a festive dinner one lovely evening in Katmandu. In those days Nepal was hardly on the international map, with but one hotel and few tourists.

Soak the saffron in the rosewater for about 10 minutes. Rub the curd through a wire sieve into a mixing bowl. Add the rosewater-saffron and beat. Add the remaining ingredients and thoroughly blend. Turn into a glass dish and chill.

Although it is not optional, saffron can be omitted if liked. It gives the pudding a pale yellow colour but does not add greatly to its flavour, which is predominantly spicy.

Rosewater pudding
Mahallebi
Turkey

TO SERVE FOUR

INGREDIENTS
3 tablespoons cornflour
1 litre (1¾ pints) milk
4 tablespoons rosewater,
    plus a little extra
100 g (4 oz) castor sugar
ground pistachio nuts or
    almonds as a garnish

If this combination sounds strange, let me say that once tried it will never seem odd again. The pudding, which is refreshing, light and very digestible, must be served chilled.

Mix the cornflour to a thin paste with a little of the milk and 4 tablespoons of the rosewater. Bring the rest of the milk to the boil in a saucepan, add the sugar and the cornflour paste and cook until the mixture thickens, stirring all the time. Continue stirring and cooking for at least 5 minutes. Take the pan from the stove and beat the mixture until it is cool. Rinse a glass dish with rosewater, pour the cornflour mixture into the dish, cover and cool, then chill in the refrigerator. Just before serving, sprinkle with ground nuts; it is difficult to give an exact quantity of nuts, but 3–4 tablespoons should be ample. If preferred, the pudding can be poured into 4 individual bowls, each rinsed with rosewater.

In Morocco, where a similar pudding is made, orange-flower water is used instead of rosewater, or often a mixture of both. Or some cooks make a honey syrup and thin it down with a little water or orange-flower water. Again, instead of a garnish of ground nuts, I have met *mahallebi* decorated with crystallized rose petals and violets, but never in Turkey. A further variation is to mix about 100 g (4 oz) of finely ground blanched almonds into the pudding after it has thickened and then continue as above. Finally, instead of only cornflour, use half cornflour and half ground rice.

Syllabub
England

TO SERVE FOUR

INGREDIENTS
1 large lemon
275 ml (½ pint) white wine
3 tablespoons lemon juice
50 g (2 oz) castor sugar
275 ml (½ pint) double
    cream

This ancient English pudding requires no cooking but its preparation must start the day before it is to be served. One of the oldest of English sweet dishes, it was reputed to be the favourite of the ill-fated queen, Anne Boleyn, although in her day it was considered more as a drink than as something to serve after a meal. There were sundry recipes, for the basis could be ale, cider or white wine, but the one feature in which all those old recipes agreed was that the milk should be added, not simply from a jug or a bowl, but straight from the cow. The basic mixture was taken to the cow and the milk squeezed into the bowl, producing a wonderful thick froth which was not to be disturbed. Up to 160 years ago or so cooperative cows were taken to the London parks to be thus milked by vendors who sold syllabub from stalls. This recipe does not require such a delightful personal touch but nevertheless produces a cool and pleasant dish.

Wipe the lemon with a damp cloth and peel as thinly as possible, removing all the pith. Put the wine into a small bowl, add the lemon rind and juice, stir well, cover and leave overnight. Next day strain the wine and lemon mixture, add the sugar and stir until this has dissolved. Whip the cream until it is stiff and stands in peaks. Fold into the wine and lemon mixture and beat again until thick. Pour the syllabub into glasses, piling it well above the rim and chill. Serve with wine biscuits.

Banana cream
Fiji and South Sea Islands

TO SERVE FOUR–SIX

INGREDIENTS
6 very ripe unbruised
    bananas
275 ml (½ pint) thick
    coconut milk (*see page*
    185)
juice of 1 lime or lemon

A simple little dish rather like a fool. It must be served iced and preferably, if you have them, in the empty halves of brown coconut shells.

Peel the bananas and mash them until smooth and completely without lumps. Rub through a sieve into a bowl. Gradually stir in the coconut milk and the lemon juice until the mixture is thick and like a fool. Pile into sundae glasses or the coconut shells and chill before serving.

Red-berry pudding

Rødgrød med fløde
Denmark

TO SERVE FOUR–SIX

INGREDIENTS
675 g (1½ lb) redcurrants
675 g (1½ lb) raspberries
1.7 litres (3 pints) water
castor sugar to taste
2 tablespoons potato flour
  or cornflour
½ teaspoon vanilla essence
slivered almonds as garnish
double or single cream as a
  garnish

I almost hesitate to include this delightfully cooling summer pudding from Denmark for it is one that should only be made with fresh fruits during those two magic months when redcurrants and raspberries are both available. However, frozen fruits may be used in the same manner, also gooseberries and blackberries. The name of this dish is a terrible tongue-twister and one which no foreigner, unless a student of Danish, can possibly pronounce and it amuses the Danes when any of us try. An identical Swedish recipe is called *bärkräm* or 'berry cream'.

Wash the fruits, put into a pan with the water and bring to the boil. Cook until the berries are very soft. Force the berries through an extra fine sieve and return the sieved fruit to the pan, add sugar to taste but do not make it too sweet. Mix the potato flour with enough cold water to make a thin paste.

Bring the sieved fruit to the boil, take the pan from the stove and slowly add the potato flour, stirring briskly all the time to avoid lumps forming. Return to the stove and, stirring all the time, bring gently just to the boil. Take from the stove, add the vanilla essence and, while still hot, pour into a glass bowl. Cover and let the mixture cool. When it begins to thicken, garnish with slivers of blanched almonds. Serve the cream in a separate bowl or jug.

Semolina and wine pudding

Dolce di semolina al vino
Italy

TO SERVE FOUR–SIX

INGREDIENTS
225 ml (8 fl oz) water
275 ml (½ pint) dry white
  wine
150 g (5 oz) fine semolina
1 tablespoon almond oil
50 g (2 oz) castor sugar
2 egg whites
225 g (8 oz) raspberries
100 g (4 oz) icing sugar

This typical Italian pudding has a delicate flavour and a light spongy texture which comes from using wine instead of the more conventional milk. If almond oil cannot be found, use another oil but not a strong olive oil, to which not more than 2–3 drops of a fine quality almond essence may be added. Instead of raspberries, other fruits may be used, strawberries, blackberries or, when available, black cherries preserved in brandy. But whatever sauce you make, let the colour be very strong to contrast with the white of the pudding.

Mix the water and wine and put into a pan and bring almost to the boil over a medium-high heat. Pour in the semolina 'like rain', stirring continuously with a wooden spoon until the semolina is thick and comes away from the sides easily – about 8 minutes, but much depends on the quality of the semolina. Take the pan from the heat and beat the mixture thoroughly: the more you beat the lighter will be the pudding. Let this become quite cold, but do not refrigerate. Rub a mould with almond oil or another substitute. I use a square mould, 20 cm (8 in) in diameter and 8 cm (3 in) deep, sloping towards the bottom. When the semolina is quite cold, beat in the sugar. Beat the egg whites until stiff and in peaks. Fold these into the semolina and pour the mixture into the oiled mould. Put into the refrigerator and leave for at least 1 hour, but an hour or two longer is of no consequence. While the pudding is being chilled, make the raspberry sauce. Rub the raspberries through a fine sieve and then mix them with the icing sugar, more or less, depending on the raspberries, to make the sauce reasonably thick. Turn out the pudding to serve with the raspberry sauce poured over the top.

Hungarian rice

Riz hongroise
Hungary

TO SERVE SIX

INGREDIENTS
175 g (6 oz) Carolina rice
575 ml (1 pint) milk
75 g (3 oz) sugar
a few drops of vanilla
  essence
75 g (3 oz) glacé fruits
3–4 tablespoons kirsch
275 ml (½ pint) double
  cream

This Hungarian method of serving rice brings back to me poignant memories of Budapest. Before the last war in the Hungarian capital we had a favourite restaurant to which we took our daughter on her fifth birthday. When it came to the pudding, the waiter, an old friend, proposed *riz hongroise*, and on the house. And what a dish of rice it was, splendid is hardly the way to describe it. I can still visualize and taste it. As kirsch is so important to this dish, I do recommend getting one of those miniature bottles if you have none in the house. However, another liqueur or brandy could be used instead.

Put the rice into a pan with cold water, bring to the boil and boil for 3 minutes.

Drain, return to the pan, add the milk, sugar and vanilla and cook in the milk over a moderate heat until the milk has been almost absorbed and the rice is soft, about 20 minutes. Meanwhile chop the fruit and steep in the kirsch. When the rice is soft, let it cool. Beat the cream until stiff. Stir half the cream into the rice, add half the fruit with all the kirsch. Do this carefully to avoid mushing the rice. Pile the rice into stemmed individual glasses and chill. When ready to serve, top with the remaining cream and garnish with the rest of the glacé fruits.

Left to right: red-berry pudding; semolina and wine pudding; Hungarian rice

Sweet potato and pineapple pudding

Camote y piña
Mexico

TO SERVE FOUR–SIX

INGREDIENTS
450 g (1 lb) sweet potatoes
675 g (1½ lb) fresh
  pineapple
100 g (4 oz) sugar
2 egg yolks, well beaten
shelled and halved walnuts
  for garnish

Sweet potatoes, of which there are many many varieties, grow in most warm countries and are tubers of a creeping vine, belonging to the convolvulus family. They are often confused with yams, which belong to another family. When they were introduced into Britain some 300 years ago, they became quite popular but later interest in them was lost. In the United States, where they are very popular, they can be bought tinned or dried, as well as fresh. They can be boiled, like ordinary potatoes, peeled, sliced and mashed and used both in savoury and sweet dishes. They are available also in Britain, especially in areas where West Indians live. If fresh pineapple is not available, tinned may be used, but drain the pieces thoroughly.

Wash and peel the sweet potatoes and cook in boiling, lightly salted water until soft.

While still hot, drain and rub through a potato ricer or mash thoroughly. Chop the pineapple into small pieces. Mix with the sweet potatoes, add the sugar, put into a saucepan and cook over a low heat for about 15 minutes, stirring all the time. The mixture should thicken; if it doesn't, then continue cooking and stirring for 2–3 minutes more, or until it does. Beat the egg yolks until fluffy. Stir a little of the hot potato mixture into the eggs, then stir back into the pan. Continue cooking for a further 5 minutes, stirring all the time so that the mixture does not curdle. Turn into a flat dish or tin and spread to about 4 cm (1½ in) thick, smoothing down the top. Garnish with walnut halves or, if preferred, with toasted almonds: the quantity you use depends entirely on taste. Cut into diamond shapes and leave until cold. Serve after a meal with the coffee. The mixture is rather like a soft candy or fudge.

Veiled farm lasses

Tilslørete bondepiker
Norway

TO SERVE SIX

INGREDIENTS
1.5 kg (3 lb) cooking apples
225 g (8 oz) brown sugar
100 g (4 oz) butter
100 g (4 oz) fresh
  breadcrumbs
275 ml (½ pint) double
  cream

This recipe comes from a Norwegian friend but it appears also as a Danish speciality with slight variations. This pudding is 'scrumptiously crunchy', and very much a party dish. Danish recipes call for rye or pumpernickel crumbs, others simply for white or brown bread – if the latter it must be at least 3–4 days old. There are also 'veiled farm lasses' made with large ripe plums.

Peel and core the apples and chop coarsely. Put into a pan with very little water, just enough to prevent burning, add 75 g (3 oz) of the sugar and cook over a moderate heat until the apples are pulped. Beat until smooth. Melt the butter in a heavy frying pan and when the foam subsides, add the breadcrumbs, stir well with a wooden

spoon, then add the rest of the sugar, stirring all the time. Lower the heat and continue stirring and frying until the sugar and crumbs are completely blended, dry and crisp, a matter of a minute or so. When the crumb mixture is cold it has a praline texture. Whisk half of the cream until thick. Put a layer of apple in the bottom of a 23-cm (9-in) glass bowl, add a layer of crumbs and a thin layer of cream. Add another layer of apple and crumbs and put into the refrigerator until ready to serve and the pudding is quite cold. Lightly whisk the rest of the cream again then spread it over the top of the crumbs. The Danes add a sprinkling of finely grated chocolate over the cream immediately before serving.

Rhubarb cream

Rabarberkräm
Sweden

TO SERVE FOUR

INGREDIENTS
900 g (2 lb) rhubarb
100 g (4 oz) sugar
3 tablespoons potato flour
  or cornflour

It is best to make this cream early in the season when rhubarb is young and tender. However, it can be made with mature or tinned rhubarb but this, after cooking, will require to be forced through a coarse sieve before the potato-flour paste is added.

Wash the rhubarb and chop it into small pieces. Put into a pan with just enough water to cover. Add the sugar and cook gently until the rhubarb is mushy.

Meanwhile mix the potato flour with enough cold water to make a paste. When the rhubarb is ready and still boiling, take the pan from the stove, stir in the potato-flour paste, return to the stove and, stirring all the time, bring just to the boil. Take at once from the stove, stir well and while still hot pour into a glass dish, cover and cool. Serve with a jug of cream. Sugar can be sprinkled over the top, if liked.

Top: rhubarb cream
bottom: veiled farm lasses

Cakes and pastries

Both cakes and pastries have played an important part in the history of food throughout the world. The ancient Egyptians had such a penchant for honey cakes they considered them worthy to be offered to the gods and the Greeks and the Romans all made honey cakes of varying shapes and sizes. Apicius, the famous Roman cookery-book writer, talks of wine cakes soaked in milk, then baked in honey.

Both the pagan and the Christian year was based upon a cycle of religious festivals which were always celebrated with special dishes, which were often cakes served with ceremonial rites. For example, when we make our Yule cake, how many of us remember its origin? It can be traced directly to ancient Scandinavia where extravagant feasts were prepared in honour of the god Thor to herald in the long winter solstice. This was the longest night of the year and the pagan worshippers celebrated it as a commemoration of the Creation and called it 'Mother Night'. The Festival was dominated by Yule, or Yeol, and among the offerings dedicated to Thor were cakes of fine flour sweetened with honey. Thus today we have our Yule cake, for those pagans, while content to give up their pagan worship, were not so happy to lose their joyous festivals. The Church compromised and the festival was given over to the Nativity of Christ and the cakes continued to be made.

Wedding cakes derive from both Greek and Roman tradition. In Rome only the highest ranking families were allowed to have a wedding cake at their marriage ceremonies, while in Greece the bride and her friends spent days sifting, cleaning and grinding the wheat for the wedding cake.

The English celebrate Twelfth Night with cakes, a night which King Alfred the Great, who allegedly burnt the cakes while ruminating on his war strategy, declared as a night for feasting and celebrations. Fewer people celebrate Twelfth Night nowadays but there remains one outpost, Drury Lane Theatre, in London, where the actors gather together to eat cake and drink a toast in honour of Richard Baddeley, a baker-turned-actor who left in his will the sum of £100 to be used to provide a Twelfth Night supper in his memory.

There is almost no end to the fascinating history attached to cakes. They are important the world over, from the rich heavy black cakes of Britain to the ethereal, colourful cakes of Japan, and the creamy offerings of the Americans.

Clove buds

Apple dumplings
Britain

TO SERVE FOUR

INGREDIENTS
Pastry
150 g (5 oz) flour
pinch of salt
75 g (3 oz) butter
cold water (*see recipe*)
1 egg, well beaten
castor sugar
Filling
4 medium-sized apples
mixed dried fruit to taste
grated lemon rind to taste
75 g (3 oz) brown sugar

Mrs Beeton called these dumplings 'a plain family dish', which indeed they are but they can be served formally as well. She suggests piling them up on a hot dish, like a pyramid, to serve and, if a richer dumpling is called for, using puff pastry instead of short. Apple dumplings have long been a favourite of country people. In the eighteenth century they reached a peak of popularity, probably because King George III, known as 'Farmer George', had a particular predilection for them.

Instead of using only water to mix the flour and butter, try instead a mixture of dry sherry or brandy, or even whisky with water to produce an even lighter pastry.

Preheat the oven to 230°C, 450°F, Gas Mark 8. Sift the flour with the salt in a cool bowl. Cut in the butter, then rub it in until the mixture resembles breadcrumbs. Add gradually enough liquid to make a stiff dough – it is not possible to say exactly how much since flour varies considerably, but 4–5 tablespoons should be enough. Mix the dough to a smooth round, cut into four pieces, roll each piece gently into a round, then roll out into rounds large enough completely to cover one apple each.

Peel and core the apples. Place one on each round of dough and fill the cavities with mixed dried fruit, lemon rind and brown sugar, pressing the mixture well down. Dampen the edges of the dough with water and gather up round the apples, pressing the joins firmly. Put the apples on to a baking tin with the joins underneath; brush with beaten egg and dust with sugar (or you can brush with water if preferred). Bake in the oven for about 30 minutes, or until the apples are cooked.

Serve hot or cold with double cream, vanilla sauce or custard.

Apple and Ricotta cake

Melarancia

Italy

TO SERVE FOUR–SIX

INGREDIENTS

butter for greasing the tin
very fine bread or biscuit
   crumbs for coating
2 eggs (size 2), separated
75 g (3 oz) castor sugar
225 g (8 oz) Ricotta cheese
a little vanilla sugar or
   essence
2 tablespoons orange or
   similar liqueur
50 g (2 oz) fine semolina
pinch of salt
4 tablespoons strained fresh
   orange juice
50 g (2 oz) sultanas
1 tablespoon olive oil
15 g (generous ½ oz) baking
   powder
350 g (12 oz) cooking
   apples, peeled and thinly
   sliced
1–2 tablespoons icing
   sugar

This recipe comes from Liguria. If unable to find Ricotta, use another dry white cheese. Vanilla sugar is better than essence.

Preheat the oven to 200°C, 400°F, Gas Mark 6. Grease a round 23-cm (9-in) cake tin with butter and sprinkle with crumbs, shaking off any surplus. Beat the egg yolks and sugar together in a large bowl until thick. Rub the Ricotta through a fine sieve into the bowl. (This is simpler than it sounds.) Mix with the yolk and sugar mixture, then add the vanilla sugar or essence, liqueur, semolina, salt, orange juice, sultanas and oil and sift in the baking powder, as it is often lumpy, and finally add the apples. Beat the egg whites until stiff and carefully fold these into the mixture. Pour into the greased tin, sieve the icing sugar over the top and bake in the oven for about 40 minutes. When the top of the cheesecake is brown, turn off the heat, open the oven door, but not widely, and leave the cheesecake to cool in the oven: this prevents it from sagging in the middle. When cool, turn out to serve: it will be quite firm yet light. Serve cold, but not refrigerated, either plain or with whipped cream.

A variation is to substitute peaches for apples, brandy for orange liqueur, and lemon juice for orange juice.

Top: apple and Ricotta cake
bottom: apple dumplings

Apple sauce cake
USA

TO SERVE SIX–EIGHT

INGREDIENTS
100 g (4 oz) sultanas
450 g (1 lb) cooking apples,
    peeled, cored and
    coarsely chopped
100 g (4 oz) unsalted butter
3 eggs (size 2)
175 g (6 oz) soft brown
    sugar
275 g (10 oz) plain flour
2 teaspoons ground
    cinnamon
½ teaspoon grated nutmeg
2 teaspoons baking
    powder
pinch of salt
100 g (4 oz) blanched
    chopped walnuts, shelled
    weight

This cake should be cooked in a ring mould, approximately 20 cm (8 in) in diameter, well rubbed with butter or oil.

Soak the sultanas in tepid water for about 1 hour or until they are swollen. Cook the apples in a small quantity of water over a low heat until they are very soft – the quantity of water should be just enough to cover the bottom of the pan. Cream the butter in a warm bowl, add the eggs one at a time, beating vigorously after each addition. Preheat the oven to 190°C, 375°F, Gas Mark 5. When the butter and eggs are completely blended, gradually add the sugar, beating all the time. Mix the flour, spices, baking powder and salt together and sift into the bowl. Stir well. By this time the apples should be quite soft. Rub through a coarse wire sieve and beat until cool. Drain the sultanas and pat dry. Add the apple purée to the batter, stir well, then add the sultanas and the walnuts. Pour the mixture into the mould and bake in the oven for about 1 hour, or until a fine skewer inserted into the cake comes out clean. Turn off the heat but leave the cake in the oven with the door closed for 15–20 minutes to cool and settle before being taken out. Serve hot or cold with cream or a custard sauce.

Sacher cake
Sachertorte
Austria

TO SERVE SIX

INGREDIENTS
butter for greasing
150 g (5 oz) bitter
    chocolate
150 g (5 oz) unsalted butter
5 eggs, separated
150 g (5 oz) sugar
100 g (4 oz) flour
apricot jam
Chocolate icing
150 g (5 oz) chocolate
4 tablespoons sugar

This is Vienna's most famous cake and the subject of considerable culinary dispute as to which is the authentic recipe. Franz Sacher was the chef of the diplomat and politician Metternich who thought as much about his kitchen as he did about his devious politics. During the Congress of Vienna in 1815 Sacher was asked for something different (probably to compete with Talleyrand who had delighted the Congress with the introduction of Brie) and so he produced this cake, saying rather loftily at the time: 'I just flung together a few ingredients, and there you are.' Surely he could not have known what a success story he was going to produce, for *Sachertorten* are still sold all over Vienna and packed for tourists to take home with them.

Rub a 23-cm (9-in) cake tin with butter. Preheat the oven to 180°C, 350°F, Gas Mark 4. Melt the chocolate and beat it while still warm into the butter. Continue beating until the mixture is fluffy. Add the egg yolks, one by one, beating steadily all the time and alternating with all but 4 tablespoons of sugar. Beat the egg whites until stiff, add the remaining sugar and continue beating until the mixture is of a meringue consistency and stands up in peaks. Fold this into the chocolate mixture. Sift the flour and add this to the batter. Pour the batter into the prepared cake tin and bake for 45–60 minutes.

Make the chocolate icing. Break the chocolate into small pieces and melt in the top of a double boiler over hot water. Meanwhile dissolve the sugar in 2 tablespoons of warm water and cook in a small pan to the thread stage (to test, cool slightly, dip in the index finger, press against the

Top: apple sauce cake
bottom: Sacher cake

thumb and a thread should form when finger and thumb are separated), or until the syrup is just beginning to thicken. Take the syrup from the stove and cool. Stir in the melted chocolate and continue stirring over the top of the stove until the mixture thickens.

Take the cake from the oven and leave until cold before turning it out (Austrian cooks differ on this point, some preferring to take it out while hot). When quite cold,

spread it with the warmed apricot jam, covering top and sides, or cut into halves and spread the bottom half with apricot jam. Spread the chocolate icing over the cake, both top and sides. It is important that the thickness of the jam and icing should be equal.

It has become fashionable to serve a bowl of whipped cream separately with the Sacher cake; although this is not traditional it is extremely good.

Plum tart

Zwetschgenkuchen
Germany

TO SERVE SIX–EIGHT

INGREDIENTS
15 g (½ oz) dried yeast
150 ml (¼ pint) milk, warmed
pinch of sugar
450 g (1 lb) flour
75 g (3 oz) butter
pinch of salt
1 teaspoon grated lemon rind
1 egg (size 2), beaten
900 g (2 lb) ripe plums or damsons
ground cinnamon

Open tarts are extremely popular in Germany and are made with a variety of fruits but probably plums and apples are the two favourites. *Zwetschgen* are actually fresh prunes rather than plums, but these are less readily available in Britain than either plums or damsons. Thinly sliced apples may be used in precisely the same manner.

Dissolve the yeast in half the milk. Add a pinch of sugar. Sift the flour into a warm bowl, make a hollow in the centre, add the yeast, sprinkle over it a little of the flour in the bowl, cover with a cloth and leave in a warm place until it rises, about 30 minutes. Soften the butter, mix with 25 g (1 oz) of sugar, a pinch of salt, lemon rind, the egg and the remainder of the milk. Add this to the risen pastry. Knead well until the dough comes away from the sides of the

bowl and is a shining smooth mass. Dust with flour, cover and leave once more to rise to double its bulk. Preheat the oven to 220°C, 425°F, Gas Mark 7. Roll out the dough very thinly and spread on a flat greased baking sheet. Dredge with sugar or, if preferred, with fine breadcrumbs. This is to prevent the juice from the fruit soaking into the dough. Stone the fruit and cut into halves. Make an incision on each half so that it will flatten down neatly. Lay them in neat rows, closely side by side (they should overlap slightly). Sprinkle with sugar and ground cinnamon and leave the dough to rise again, about 15 minutes. Bake in the oven for 25–30 minutes.

If using apples, peel and thinly slice them. You may lightly brush the fruit with a fruit cordial, or sugar syrup, before baking to give them a glaze.

Sugar tart

Zuckerwähe
Switzerland

TO SERVE FOUR–SIX

INGREDIENTS
225 g (8 oz) rich short pastry
4 eggs
100 g (4 oz) sugar
50 g (2 oz) butter
½ teaspoon ground cinnamon

A very sweet speciality of Zürich.

Preheat the oven to 180°C, 350°F, Gas Mark 4. Roll out the pastry and line a flan tin. Beat the eggs lightly with 1 tablespoon of sugar, pour into the pastry case and dot with half the butter. Bake until the custard

has set firm and the pastry is a golden brown. Just before serving, blend in the remaining butter with the rest of the sugar and cinnamon to make a butter-sugar crumble. Sprinkle this over the top of the custard. Return the tart to the oven to let the topping just melt.

Top: plum tart
bottom: sugar tart

Poppy-seed cake

Tort Makowy

Poland

TO SERVE SIX

INGREDIENTS

butter or oil for greasing
flour for dusting
25 g (1 oz) unsalted butter
100 g (4 oz) sugar
6 egg yolks
100 g (4 oz) poppy seeds
50 g (2 oz) unblanched but shelled almonds
1 teaspoon mixed ground cinnamon and cloves
1 tablespoon grated orange rind
3 egg whites

Poppy seeds are taken from a large type of poppy grown in Holland. They are used extensively in European and Oriental cooking. They can be either black or grey in colour and have no fragrance but a distinctive flavour. It takes about 900,000 seeds to make 450 g (1 lb).

Rub an 18-cm (7-in) cake tin lightly with melted butter or cooking oil. Sprinkle lightly with flour, shaking off any surplus. Preheat the oven to 180°C, 350°F, Gas Mark 4. Cream the butter, add the sugar and egg yolks and beat until the mixture is light and almost fluffy. Blanch the poppy seeds and then either pound thoroughly or grind in a liquidizer. Add to the egg mixture. Grind and add the almonds to the batter with the spices and orange rind.

Beat the egg whites until just stiff and fold into the mixture. Pour this into the prepared tin and bake in the oven for 30–45 minutes, or until a knife inserted into the cake comes out clean.

When cold the cake can be served as it is or, as is so often done, spread with a chocolate or rum-flavoured icing, or with whipped cream. Instead of fresh orange peel, finely chopped candied lemon or orange peel may be used. Czechoslovakia has a similar cake which is split into half and the lower half spread with jam and sandwiched together again.

Banana loaf

Zimbabwe

TO SERVE FOUR–SIX

INGREDIENTS

4 ripe bananas
1 teaspoon lemon juice
100 g (4 oz) butter, plus a little for greasing
100 g (4 oz) soft brown sugar
2 eggs (size 2), well beaten
225 g (8 oz) flour
1 teaspoon baking powder
¼ teaspoon bicarbonate of soda
pinch of salt
2 tablespoons soured milk, yogurt or buttermilk
100 g (4 oz) finely chopped mixed nuts

Preheat the oven to 180°C, 350°F, Gas Mark 4. Rub a 900-g (2-lb) loaf tin generously with butter. Peel and mash the bananas and add the lemon juice and rub if necessary through a sieve. Cream the butter and gradually add the sugar. Add the eggs, adding 1 tablespoon flour with each egg. Mix with the bananas. Sift the remaining flour with the baking powder,

bicarbonate of soda and salt and quickly stir into the mashed bananas. Add the soured milk and the nuts. Pour into the prepared tin and bake in the oven for 1 hour, or until a knife inserted into the loaf comes out clean. Turn out and slice when cool. Spread with butter.

Top: poppy-seed cake
bottom: banana loaf

Sweet 'salami'

Ovocný salám
Czechoslovakia

TO MAKE TWO–THREE
'SALAMI'

INGREDIENTS
50 g (2 oz) almonds,
  shelled weight
50 g (2 oz) walnuts,
  shelled weight
225 g (8 oz) stoned dried
  dates or figs
candied or fresh lemon
  peel, about 25 g (1 oz)
100 g (4 oz) bitter
  chocolate
100 g (4 oz) sugar
1 egg, well beaten
icing sugar to taste

This is a sweet dish made in Czechoslovakia for festive occasions and in particular at Christmas time. Its only relationship to a real salami is that when cut in slanting slices it has a dark, marbled salami effect. It is extremely useful for serving as an after-dinner sweet, or with morning coffee. It will also keep for several weeks in a cool place, not necessarily the refrigerator. The Yugoslavs have a similar recipe.

Finely chop the nuts, peel and fruit. Melt the chocolate over hot water in a double boiler, or over a very low heat on a direct flame, stirring all the time. Still stirring, add the sugar and continue stirring until this is dissolved. Add the chopped nuts, peel and fruit. Gently heat until a very thick paste is formed. Add the egg and mix it well into the paste. Take the pan from the heat, turn the mixture out into a mixing bowl and beat until it is cool. Sift plenty of icing sugar on to a large dish or tray and at the same time rub the palms of your hands in icing sugar. Divide the mixture into two or three. Roll the paste into two or three 4 cm (1½ in) thick sausage-shaped rolls, i.e. 'salami', shake off any surplus sugar and wrap the 'salami' in foil or greaseproof paper. Leave in a cool place, but not the refrigerator, for 24 hours and bring to room temperature before serving in slices.

Zwieback

Lomnicky suchar
Czechoslovakia

TO MAKE THIRTY–FORTY

INGREDIENTS
25 g (1 oz) dried yeast
275 ml (½ pint) warm milk
450 g (1 lb) flour
1 teaspoon salt
100 g (4 oz) butter
1 egg yolk, lightly beaten
fat for greasing
vanilla icing sugar

Zwiebacks are internationally famed. Whether they are actually of Czechoslovakian origin, I am not sure, but certainly this is a favourite Czech recipe. I have given here one of the simplest recipes.

Put the yeast into a bowl, add a little of the warm milk, cover and leave until the yeast rises. 1 teaspoon of sugar can be added to assist this process. Sieve the flour and salt into a mixing bowl. Cut in the butter and mix thoroughly, rubbing the butter in with the fingers. Mix the egg yolk with the milk and the yeast mixture, stir lightly, then pour this mixture into the flour and stir to a smooth dough. If necessary add a little more flour should the dough not be quite stiff enough: the quality of flour and the size of egg vary considerably. Knead the dough until it is quite smooth and pliable, then put into a warm dry bowl, cover with a cloth and leave until it doubles its bulk. Break into 2–3 pieces and shape into long sausages or, if you prefer, French loaves. Put these on to a greased baking sheet and cover. Leave until the dough has risen again. Preheat the oven to 180°C, 350°F, Gas Mark 4. When the dough has risen, bake the 'loaves' for 40–45 minutes until golden brown. Take from the oven, ease off the baking sheet and leave until the following day. Preheat the oven to fairly hot (200°C, 400°F, Gas Mark 6). Slice the loaves and arrange on a baking sheet. Bake in the oven until they are dry and a light golden brown. Take from the oven and, while still hot, sprinkle with vanilla-flavoured icing sugar.

Brownies

USA

MAKES ABOUT 45 SQUARES

INGREDIENTS
40 g (1½ oz) unsalted butter
2 eggs (size 3)
175 g (6 oz) castor sugar
50 g (2 oz) unsweetened
  chocolate
75 g (3 oz) flour
1 teaspoon vanilla essence
100 g (4 oz) broken
  walnuts, shelled weight

Brownies are a favourite American confection, rich and chewy. They are sometimes described as fudge but they are harder than the British-style fudge. Recipes vary slightly from cook to cook and, instead of using crushed walnuts, some cooks suggest coarsely grated fresh orange peel. They are served as mid-morning snacks with coffee, as an after-dinner dessert with a glass of brandy or port, or with afternoon tea. They are favourites for all festive occasions.

Preheat the oven to 180°C, 350°F, Gas Mark 4. Line a shallow baking tin approximately 20 × 30 cm (8 × 12 in) with foil or heavy greaseproof paper. Do not rub with grease. Let the butter soften at room temperature. Beat the eggs thoroughly. Sift the sugar over the butter. Mix well, and then add half the beaten eggs (this is to assist in beating the butter and sugar to a cream). When the mixture is smooth and creamy, add the remainder of the egg. Put aside. Break the chocolate into small pieces and melt in a small pan over a low heat, stirring continuously. Take from the heat and continue stirring until the chocolate is cool. Stir into the creamed butter and egg mixture and stir until completely combined. Sift in the flour and vanilla, add the nuts and stir well. When the mixture is blended, pour it into the baking tin. Bake in the oven for between 15 and 30 minutes. Take from the oven, let the mixture cool slightly, then cut into squares with a sharp knife while still in the baking tin, cutting right through the mixture. Serve cold. They can be stored in an airtight tin for several days without becoming soft.

Top to bottom: sweet 'salami'; zwieback; brownies

Malakoff cake

Malakofftorte
Austria

TO SERVE SIX–EIGHT

INGREDIENTS
100 g (4 oz) unsalted butter
100 g (4 oz) castor sugar
3 egg yolks
100 g (4 oz) ground
  almonds
1.2 litres (2 pints) double
  cream
30–40 sponge fingers
rum or brandy to taste

I do not pretend that this cake can be made every day, nor would most people want to eat such a rich cake so often. But for a special occasion it is another matter. It is not cooked but should be made in a 20-cm (8-in) spring-form cake tin and is served ice-cold with stiffly whipped cream.

Beat the butter until soft, add the sugar and continue beating until the mixture is creamy. Add the egg yolks, one by one, beating vigorously after each addition. Add the almonds and 275 ml ($\frac{1}{2}$ pint) of the cream. Beat the rest of the cream until stiff. Split the sponge fingers across into halves, reserving a few whole ones for decoration. Arrange a layer at the bottom of the pan. Sprinkle lightly with rum. Spread with the buttercream filling, then with a layer of whipped cream. Cover with another layer of sponge fingers, sprinkle with rum, spread with the butter-cream filling and whipped cream. Continue in this manner until all the ingredients are used up, with a top layer of sponge fingers. Press down lightly, cover and put into the refrigerator. When ready to serve, take the cake from the refrigerator, remove from the ring, place on a round plate and serve with whipped cream, either spread on the cake, or served separately.

Chocolate cake

Tort Generala Iwaszkiewicz
Poland

TO SERVE SIX

INGREDIENTS
225 g (8 oz) chocolate
175 g (6 oz) almonds
6 eggs, separated
175 g (6 oz) sugar
butter for greasing
grated chocolate or icing
  sugar to taste
Filling
100 g (4 oz) butter
100 g (4 oz) sugar
vanilla to taste
75 g (3 oz) chocolate
1 egg

General Iwaszkiewicz was of Russian–Polish parentage and became an officer in the Russian Imperial Army. Apart from being a fine soldier, he led a life of adventure and was described by a Polish officer as 'quite a guy'. The general was fighting with the Poles when they were striving for independence and, as can be imagined, chocolate layer cakes, whether simple or otherwise, were quite a luxury. But this general's known weakness for chocolate cake brought out the local women whenever he camped nearby; they had raided the entire neighbourhood in order to get the ingredients to prepare a cake for their beloved hero. Maybe they could not always get all the ingredients – here and there an egg was missing, or there was a shortage of chocolate but, as soon as it was known the general was in receiving distance out went those women with their chocolate cakes. It was a brave gesture for these women were themselves struggling hard to scrape together enough for their families to live on. The following recipe is typically Polish and produces a cake which the women would like always to offer their general; it is rich and quite delicious and certainly a 4-star cake for a 4-star general.

Bring out the champagne for the general.

Preheat the oven to 140°C, 275°F, Gas Mark 1. Gently melt the chocolate, put aside but keep warm. Grind the almonds without peeling them. Mix the egg yolks with the sugar and beat until the mixture is white. Add the chocolate to the sugar and egg mixture while still warm, beat until smooth, and then add the almonds. Beat the egg whites until stiff and gently fold into the mixture. Rub two 20-cm (8-in)

Top: Malakoff cake
bottom: chocolate cake

sandwich tins with butter, pour in the chocolate mixture and bake in the oven for about 55 minutes, or until a skewer inserted in the centre comes out clean. Take from the oven, cool slightly in the tins, then remove with the utmost care as the top of the cake is quite crisp; the base shrinks slightly but not the crisp top. Put the cakes aside while you make the filling.

Soften the butter to room temperature, then beat until it begins to cream, add the sugar and vanilla and beat well. Gently melt the chocolate, then beat it into the butter and sugar. When thoroughly blended, beat in the egg until the mixture is creamy. Let it cool but, while still soft, spread with care over the top of one of the cake's layers; cover with the second layer and sprinkle with icing sugar and with grated chocolate.

Glossary

Allspice

This is also known as Jamaican pepper and comes from a pimento tree, native to the West Indies, Central and South America. Allspice is not, as many people think, a combination of mixed spices; it is one spice, looking like large peppercorns and combining the flavours of cloves, cinnamon and nutmeg. It should be bought whole and ground when required. Allspice is used in sweet and savoury dishes, in rich fruit cakes, in Scandinavian fish marinades, and in many Middle Eastern dishes.

Anise

One of the most ancient and beautiful herb annuals. Its leaves are used for garnishing fruit and vegetable salads and its seeds to flavour savoury dishes such as curries, stews and casseroles, as well as in confectionery, cheese and breads.

Bouquet garni

The French name for a bundle of mixed herbs, a term more usual today than the old English name, a faggot of herbs. The herbs are tied together with thread or wrapped in a piece of muslin to facilitate removal from the pan when cooking is finished. The bunch usually consists of 3 stalks of parsley, 1 of thyme and 1 bayleaf, but there are variations. A Provençal bouquet garni includes a strip of dried orange peel and stalks of marjoram, winter savory or lemon thyme.

Butter

1. Clarified. Although one of the best of the frying mediums, it is also extravagant for from 225 g (8 oz) of butter, only 175 g (6 oz) remains when clarified. However, both the flavour and colour of food cooked in clarified butter is much improved. There are several ways in which butter may be clarified: here is one. Melt the butter in a pan together with about one-third of its volume in water. Bring to a gentle boil and cook for 2–3 minutes, stirring from time to time. Leave to cool, then to become cold and solidify. Carefully skim off the layer of pure fat that lies on the top of the water leaving impurities behind. Other fats can be clarified in the same manner.

2. Kneaded (*beurre manié*). This is important and used as a thickening (*liaison*) for many sauces, soups and stews. It is added to the pan shortly before serving, allowing just enough time to dissolve and blend into the sauce. The butter melts and draws the flour into the liquid which is to be thickened without forming lumps. It is used mainly when a quick thickening of liquid is required. To thicken 275 ml ($\frac{1}{2}$ pint) of liquid, you require 25 g (1 oz) of butter and 15 g ($\frac{1}{2}$ oz) of flour. Soften the butter on a plate with a fork and work in the flour to make a thick paste. Break into small pieces. The mixture may be used immediately, i.e. dropped into the pan in small pieces, or it can be chilled and left in the refrigerator for later use. When the *beurre manié* is in the pan do not stir but gently shake the pan. When the liquid is thickened and glossy it is ready.

3. *Maître d'hôtel*. This is a garnish used for fried fish, steaks and mixed grills, as well as vegetables, especially carrots. Soften 50 g (2 oz) of butter on a plate, add about 1 tablespoonful of finely chopped parsley, a few drops of lemon juice, also salt and pepper to taste. There should be only just enough lemon juice to moisten the butter. Chill and shape into small pats to serve.

Caraway

This ancient spice has taken something of a back seat in British cooking although in Tudor times it was much used; caraway seed cake was once famed and there was an old song, 'Can she make a seedy cake, my boy Johnny?', and if she couldn't, then as a wife she wasn't going to be much use. This once famous cake has now gone almost completely out of fashion. However, caraway is used a great deal in Austrian and Hungarian cooking: the Hungarians add it to their goulash. It is also used in sauerkraut, cabbage and potato dishes. An aromatic oil is obtained from caraway seeds and used by distillers to flavour Kümmel, anisette and some schnapps. It is also used medicinally.

Cardamom

In the East these aromatic seeds are called Seeds of Paradise, and in the days of the Romans were used as a perfume. The plant is a member of the ginger family and it is the dried pods that we use in our kitchens. The pods vary considerably in length and colour, from dead white to almost black. Inside the pods are the seeds. Their texture is hard and the flavour pungent, almost exotic. They have a reputation for being both stimulating and antiseptic. Cardamom seeds are used in Indian cooking, in particular curries; Kashmiris use them to flavour tea, and the Arabs their coffee. In Scandinavia, Germany and Russia liqueurs and cakes are flavoured with cardamom.

Cayenne pepper

A type of chilli pepper originally supposed to have come from Cayenne in French Guiana. It is used to give an extra fillip or strong flavour to hearty dishes and is ground finer than ordinary pepper.

Chick peas

These are small, hard, round, corn-coloured peas that come from a Mediterranean and Asiatic plant. Some of the best are said to come from Spain. In their countries of origin they are used both fresh and dried. We find them usually in Britain dried, hard and a deep corn colour; they require overnight soaking before being used. They lend themselves to many earthy dishes and can be made into soups and curries and they are always used in *couscous*. When correctly cooked until tender they make pleasant eating.

Chilli pepper

Chilli peppers are very pungent indeed, some excessively so to the Western palate. They are used both fresh and dried and can be bought in Oriental shops. Japanese chilli peppers are the least pungent, African the most; but always use with caution unless experienced in their use.

Chinese wine

This is not a true wine, rather more a liqueur. It is made from rice and comes in various strengths; some rice wines, like the Cantonese, are very strong, some are distinctly mild. Chinese wine is usually available in Oriental stores and other specialist shops. It should be served warm and not hot, as is so often done. Serving the wine hot was done to disguise bad quality wine and the habit spread to better-class wines.

Chorizo

A variety of Spanish sausage, coarsely textured, red and spicy. It is made from a mixture of pork meat, pork fat, paprika pepper and garlic, and is obtainable in delicatessens.

Cinnamon

Cinnamon and cassia have more or less the same flavour and in many countries these are treated as one article; in Britain only true cinnamon is allowed to be sold as such. Good cinnamon has a delicate flavour, whereas cassia is somewhat pungent. For cakes, ground cinnamon is used, and this should be bought in small quantities only, used quickly and kept in airtight containers. For savoury dishes or to flavour syrups, it should be used in its whole or quill form, obtainable in delicatessens.

A ginger plant

Coconut milk

This is not the watery liquid found in coconuts but is made by combining grated coconut flesh with water and squeezing it through muslin. Break a coconut in half or into large pieces, pick out the inside white flesh, scrape off the brown skin and either grate the flesh on a grater or whirl in a liquidizer. Steep the grated coconut in 275 ml ($\frac{1}{2}$ pint) of warm water and leave for 20 minutes. Strain through muslin and squeeze hard, very hard, to extract every drop of the liquid, which is now coconut milk. One coconut will make just over 2 cupfuls of thick milk. If a thin coconut milk is called for, the procedure is the same but the quantity of water doubled. To make coconut cream, use only half the quantity of water. If fresh coconut is not available, use a good quality desiccated coconut in the same quantities.

Coriander

A delicate lacy annual whose leaves and seeds are both used in the kitchen. It is extensively cultivated in the Mediterranean, India and along the northern coast of Africa but has also established itself in Britain as a wild plant. Its leaves can be used like parsley. The seeds are tiny and yellowish, very aromatic and when crushed emit a warm flavour that is a cross between sage and lemon peel. They are used in curries, pilaus, stews and other savoury dishes. Some Continental pastries are flavoured with coriander seeds, as are some gins and liqueurs. It is the seed that in days gone by was sugar coated and sold as comfits or Scottish candy. Wild game and sausages also are flavoured with it.

Fennel

This is a herb native to Europe, and of ancient lineage with bright green stalks and feathery leaves. The seeds are small, darkish yellow in colour and their flavour resembles aniseed. Both leaves and seeds can be used in cooking; the former makes a pretty garnish for many dishes. Although in Britain fennel is mainly matched with fish, it can also be used with pork and beef stews or casseroles, with fruit cakes and interestingly with apple dishes. The wise men of the East believed it to be one of the nine sacred herbs that could counteract nine causes of disease.

Fines herbes

A mixture of finely chopped parsley, chervil and often chives. In earlier times chopped mushrooms and truffles were added. In France the mixture is much used to flavour omelettes but can also be used to flavour grilled meats or a plain green salad.

Garam masala

This is a mixture of spices used in many curries. It can be kept in an airtight container for a considerable time without losing its pungency; 15 g ($\frac{1}{2}$ oz) ground cinnamon is also often added to the mixture given here.

100 g (4 oz) dark cardamom pods
25 g (1 oz) whole cloves
50 g (2 oz) black cumin seeds
$\frac{1}{4}$ teaspoon each grated nutmeg and mace.

Dry-fry the cardamom pods, cloves and cumin seeds in a heavy pan for a few minutes until they exude a pleasant aroma. Grind them finely and sift together twice through a fine sieve. Mix with nutmeg and mace, cinnamon if used, pack into an airtight jar, shake well and store.

Ghee

This is clarified buffalo butter, used in Indian and Pakistani cooking. It can be bought in Indian or Pakistani shops. Failing ghee, other cooking fats may be used: clarified butter for example, or other clarified vegetable fats.

A nineteenth-century market in Augsburg, Germany

Ginger

The root of a sweet and lovely plant, a member of the lily family. It grows in damp heights, such as amid the swirling clouds of the Jamaican Blue Mountains. The roots, which are dug up when the plant is about 1 year old, are washed and dried in the sun. Exposure to the sun bleaches the roots and brings out the typical pungent flavour of ginger. The roots look like a horny potato that has started to reproduce small potatoes on itself. The skin is light brown, and the flesh rather like old ivory, firm and pungent. It is much used in Oriental cooking, in pickles, preserves and marinades. It is available in Oriental shops as well as many health food stores.

Gold leaf: see Silver leaf.

Grinding mills

These are essential in any kitchen and there should not be one but several, all used for a particular purpose only. For example, a salt mill, one each for black and white pepper, another for allspice and one for nutmeg. A small electric grinder is useful when grinding spices for curries and similar dishes (once used for curries, the grinder can never be used for anything else as the curry flavour permeates the mill). Coffee lovers will, of course, have a coffee grinder. Also most electric liquidizers grind well.

Hamburg parsley

Botanically this is a true parsley although grown as a root vegetable. Its white fleshy taproot can be eaten uncooked, like a carrot. Its flavour is a cross between celeriac and parsnip. It is not well known in Britain but can often be found in quality cosmopolitan greengrocers.

Herbs and spices

In all cooking throughout the world both are of extreme importance and, therefore, it is important to attempt to build up a good range of both in the kitchen. It is wise to buy herbs and spices in small quantities since both – with one or two exceptions – lose their flavour and aroma quickly once the container has been opened. Although dried herbs are sold in packets and jars, they are at their best when fresh. Most herbs can be grown in British gardens, on window-sills and balconies. Herbs also freeze easily. They should be washed and dried, and then frozen whole without chopping. When required for use they can be broken or chopped while stiff and frozen. Many spice dealers offer their customers a chart explaining the uses of spices and herbs.

Mustard

This is a widely used condiment known from biblical times and much used by the Romans. The British type of mustard was 'invented' by an obscure old lady, Mrs Clements of Durham, who hit upon the idea of grinding mustard to make a fine powder. She managed to secure the patronage of King George I and no doubt founded a family fortune. English mustard today is a mixture of two kinds of mustard seeds, black and white, and when mixed produces a strong mustard, quite unlike that produced generally on the Continent. When a French, Italian, or a German recipe calls for mustard, it must be Continental mustard and preferably mustard from the same country as the dish.

Mustard seeds

These are used in Indian and other curries. Mustard seeds, which are small, and either black or a reddish yellow (called white), as such are not hot. The best come from Britain, France, the Netherlands and California.

Oils

These are many and varied. Olive oil is much used throughout the Mediterranean where olive trees flourish. It varies from region to region in strength and flavour, although neither is an indication of its quality. There are grades of olive oil, but the finest is the virgin oil or first pressing. Refined oil is the last pressing, refined in more senses than one. For dishes that are cooked in oil and meant to be served cold, olive oil is important since it does not congeal when cold, even chilled.

Other important oils, especially for salads, are walnut and almond. Peanut oil is excellent in cooking as it has no predominant flavour and is a favourite with the Chinese. Sesame oil has many adherents, especially in the Orient. In America corn oil, which is an extract of maize, is much used, and in the Indian subcontinent mustard-seed and sunflower-seed oils are both popular. In Africa palm-kernel (also known as palm butter) and coconut oils are basic cooking ingredients.

Dried orange and lemon peel

Strip off the pith from as much orange and/or lemon peels as required. Wipe the peels and put into a warm oven (or range them on top of a central heating radiator in winter) and leave until dry and hard. Store in airtight jars and use in soups, stews, stocks, casserole dishes (especially if cooking game) and similar dishes. The size of the peel is immaterial and it can be dropped into the dish it is to flavour without being softened. The peel stores well and will keep for two or three years without losing any of its flavour if correctly stored.

Pappadums

These are considered as a variety of Indian bread and served generally with curries, although the very small pappadums are often served with snacks and other small eats. They come in several sizes from about side-plate size to tiny cocktail chips or small shapes like conches. Some are plain, others coloured; some are spicy, often highly so, others peppery; some are without any flavouring at all. They are usually fried in deep, very hot oil. Frying time varies but usually a few seconds is sufficient to make them swell up and lightly brown. They must be taken out as soon as they are brown (use kitchen tongs for this) and drained on absorbent paper, when they will immediately become crisp. They can be fried some hours before being served, but will not keep overnight as a rule. If preferred, the large pappadums can be grilled or baked in the oven. They will swell and crisp in the same manner. When frying, use a large, deep pan.

Paprika pepper

This is a dark-red powder made from a particular variety of capsicum. It is not related to true pepper, although often wrongly called red pepper. There are several grades of paprika pepper, in the main divided into mild, sweet, semi-pungent, and very pungent. Although the type of capsicum used in the preparation of this pepper is not of true Hungarian origin, having been introduced by the Turks from the New World, today Hungarians cannot conceive that cooking ever existed without paprika pepper.

Pepper

This is produced from the berries of a climbing plant. The berries grow in strings. To produce black peppercorns the berries are picked when green and dried in the sun. There are several qualities of black peppercorns varying in size, colour and aroma. Good quality peppercorns should be even in size and free from leaves and stalks. They keep indefinitely if stored in a jar. White peppercorns are produced from the black berries after the outer husk has been removed, or the berries are left on the vines until they are completely ripe when they split and burst. To obtain the true flavour of pepper, it is important to grind the peppercorns only when pepper is needed. Ground pepper loses its flavour rapidly. Use black pepper for dark dishes, white for lighter ones.

A pepper plant

187

Pinenut kernels or pinoli

These are the kernels of pine cones used extensively in Turkish, Balkan and Italian cooking. They are fat, white and waxy in appearance. They are expensive but a few will give sufficient flavour and they can be stored in a jar for a considerable time.

Prawn crackers or puffs (*kropuk*)

These are shrimp or prawn crackers, crisp when fried, originally made in Indonesia from tapioca flour and dried shrimps. Today they are made by the Chinese and sold in Oriental shops and many delicatessens. They can be grilled but are usually fried (like pappadums) in deep hot fat, when they puff up swiftly, in a matter of seconds. It is important to watch them closely and to pick them out of the fat the moment they become swollen, using kitchen tongs. Drain on absorbent paper and they will instantly crispen. Apart from their use in Oriental dishes, they can be served with drinks. Before cooking they look like bone chips. They are usually all of the same size and rather small. They have a distinct flavour of prawns.

Rosewater

An extract of rose petals used in Balkan, Middle Eastern, Pakistani and Indian cooking, particularly in sweet dishes, creams and pastries. It is an acquired taste, perhaps, but for my taste one easy to acquire.

Roux

This is a *liaison* of flour and fat, usually butter, and is the basis of flour sauces, both sweet and savoury. The longer the mixture is cooked, the deeper will be its colour. A *roux* can be white with hardly any colour at all, or allowed to cook until dark for use in brown sauces. For most dishes the *roux* is used half-and-half.

Melt 25 g (1 oz) of butter slowly in a thick pan, add 25 g (1 oz) of flour when off the heat, stirring all the time, until there is a perfect blending of the two. Return the pan to the heat and, if a light *roux* is required, cook it for 3 minutes. For a darker hue, the *roux* can be cooked to a russet colour and an almost nutty aroma emerges. When adding liquid to a *roux*, if it is still hot, add the liquid cold; if the *roux* has been allowed to become cold, as it is for soufflés, then the liquid should be added hot.

Saffron

This expensive spice is made from the orange-coloured stigmas of a mauve crocus. It takes 200,000 of these to produce 450 g (1 lb) and all must be gathered by hand.

Fortunately, only a small quantity is needed in cookery. It is used to give certain dishes a pale yellow colour, in the French *bouillabaisse*, in *arroz con pollo*, and in *paella*. It also enhances sauces, breads, cakes such as Cornish saffron cakes, fish, chicken and rice. At one time, in the Middle Ages, it was widely cultivated in England and the town of Saffron Walden was an important producer of the flower; its town arms still have three saffron flowers pictured within turreted walls. There are several red spices sold as saffron that are not saffron at all. In some parts of the Far East turmeric is sold as saffron, rather from ignorance than from any attempt to cheat. The two spices give roughly the same colour to a dish but each has an entirely different flavour.

Salt

There is hardly a dish in the world not improved by a pinch of salt, including many sweet dishes. There are several varieties of salt. Bay or sea salt (*gros sel*) can be bought in varying degrees of fineness, and there is cooking salt, of which the best is block salt – this is less refined and can be used for general domestic purposes. Table salt is household salt finely ground and contains a proportion of magnesium carbonate and calcium phosphate to make it run more easily, also to keep it dry. Rock salt is a mineral deposit and commercial salt is obtained from it.

Sesame seeds

These come from a lovely aromatic herb, a native of India, and are important in Far Eastern cooking. The seeds, when dry and roasted, will emit something of the flavour of toasted almonds. They vary in colour from the so-called white to a greyish black, and there is one grade that is bright orange. Sesame seeds are used in the USA in cakes and pastries, and in Central Europe and the Balkans they are used in bread and rolls.

Shoyu sauce

This is the Japanese version of the Chinese soya sauce. It is salty and liquid and varies in colour and strength according to the method of production. It is made from soya beans, salt and barley and imparts to Japanese dishes their characteristic flavour and aroma. It should be used sparingly. It can be used to flavour Western savoury dishes. It is thought that shoyu was brought to Japan from China by a Buddhist monk in the sixth century and was at first used only by noble families; but six centuries later it had reached greater popularity among all classes.

Silver and gold leaf

Both are used in Indian and Pakistani cooking but mainly in Muslim cooking. The art of reducing gold and silver to thin leaves is an ancient one and Pliny the Elder observed that a small quantity of gold could be beaten into 750 leaves. Gold and silver beating has been known in the East for centuries and still in Far Eastern markets you can see and hear the artisans busy at their ancient craft. In the East the leaves are used mainly to garnish sweetmeats and sweet dishes, or pilaus. Gold in the Middle Ages was considered a universal cure for all illnesses and the key to a long life and gold dust was sprinkled on the food of the wealthy sick. Tiny specks of gold are still a feature of Danziger Goldwasser and of a similar liqueur called the Belgian Elixir d'Anvers.

Soured cream

This cream is widely used in Slav countries and often confused with yogurt, which it is not. Soured cream is simply what it calls itself, cream that has been soured – today deliberately but in early times by accident. Cream went sour quickly in the days of no refrigeration and Slav housewives instead of throwing it away, used it in their cooking. In time they became so accustomed to soured cream they preferred it this way. Many Slav cakes, pastries and savoury dishes owe their flavour to it. It is nowadays possible to buy soured cream in many shops but, failing this, a thick natural yogurt may be substituted but the flavour of the finished dish will not be quite the same: soured cream is sour-tasting, natural yogurt is not.

Soya-bean sauce

This is a popular Chinese sauce made from soya beans, salt and bruised wheat. It comes in several qualities, light and dark, mild and not so mild. It is used in almost all Chinese savoury dishes. It can be used effectively in Western dishes and a few drops in a soup adds considerably to its flavour. It also strengthens sauces and stews and can be used as you would Worcestershire Sauce.

Terracotta 'bricks'

These terracotta 'bricks' are in fact terracotta baking dishes and today they have become fashionable. Food cooked in them retains all its flavour. They are still in regular use in Tuscany, where they mostly originated, and in other parts of Italy. There are varying shapes and sizes, some for chicken, others for fish, and one for cooking steaks. Today they are also made in Britain.

Vanilla pods

Vanilla pod or bean

Vanilla is one of the best known of flavourings, used throughout the world. Much of what is called extract or essence of vanilla contains nothing of the true vanilla pod. The vanilla is the flower of a climbing plant, a member of the orchid family. The flowers are followed by a 15 cm (6 in) long, flat pod which, after it is dried for culinary purposes, is black and shiny. The aroma is sweet and permeating. A vanilla pod can be used several times in milk to flavour a custard, provided it is rinsed and well dried after each use.

Vanilla sugar

In many sweet dishes vanilla sugar can be used instead of either the bean or essence. It is simple to make. Fill a jar with white sugar, granulated or castor, or a jar of both; break a whole vanilla pod into two or three pieces and stick these well into the sugar. Close the jar tightly and leave for several weeks before using. As the sugar is used, replenish with more sugar as long as the aroma of the vanilla bean remains intact.

Vinegars

There are good and bad and coarse and mild vinegars. It is never wise to buy a cheap vinegar: like bad wine it will ruin any dish with which it is cooked. Generally, mild vinegars are used in cooking and in salads, the harsher ones for brines and pickles. There are malt and cider vinegars, herb and wine vinegars – all have their own uses and the interested cook will have several varieties in his or her larder.

Yogurt

Today everyone knows what yogurt is, a semi-solid creamy curd that does not readily separate. It has a pleasant acid rather than sour flavour and the plain natural type is used extensively in cooking – salads, sauces. Most yogurt in Britain is factory produced, although many health-food stores sell the farmhouse-produced variety and also starters if you want to make your own. Although the Balkan peoples claim to be the inventors of this enjoyable dish of curds, it is said that the Patriarch Abraham introduced it to the Middle East when an angel whispered the secret of souring milk to him. And who are we to doubt such an ancient legend?

Index

Achiote paste 118, 119
Achoori 46
Adobo 97
Agneshko v yaitse i limovox sos 90
Aïoli, Le grand 69
Alexander Dumas's sauce 71
Allspice 184
Almonds: almond chocolate foam 161; almond sauce 101; almond soup 28; Malakoff cake 182
Ameijõas na cataplana 73
AMERICAN RECIPES: 12, 13 (starters); 24, 25, 29, 36 (soups); 71, 72 (shellfish); 86 (chile con carne); 116, 117 (chicken); 120–1 (duck); 135 (vegetables); 149, 151 (salads); 161 (pudding); 176 (cake); 180 (brownies)
Anchovies: 'Caviar' niçoise 11; scrambled eggs with 46
Angels on horseback 16
ANGLO-INDIAN RECIPE: 28
Anise 184
Anitra alle olive 121
ANTIGUAN RECIPE: 27
Apples: apple and Ricotta cake 175; apple dumplings 174; apple sauce 145; apple sauce cake 176; baked meringue apples 163; Calvados omelette 162; veiled farm lasses 172
Apricot soup 24
ARGENTINIAN RECIPES: 85 (beef); 101 (ox tongue)
Ärter med fläsk 31
Asparagus (*Asperges à la flamande*) 133
Aubergines: musaka 133; salad 153
AUSTRIAN RECIPES: 79 (beef); 99 (*Schnitzel*); 117 (chicken); 158 (pudding); 176–7, 182 (cakes)
Avocado soup, iced 25

Baba ghanouge 153
Bacon: devils on horseback 16; quiche Lorraine 44
BAHAMAN RECIPE: 162
Baida mooli 47
Bananas: cream 169; frost and fire 162; loaf 179; salad 152
Barack leves 24
Beans: Boston baked 135; cassoulet 138; French, Lyons style 134; French, in tomato sauce 134
Beef: cooked in foil 83; goulash 82–3; stew with peaches and pears 85; Stroganov 82; tartare 21;

boiled 79; boiled, with vegetables 80; chile con carne 86; lobscouse 85; Lucca eyes 15; meatballs 86; meat loaf 102; pot roast 81; Spanish stew 84–5; spiced beef 80
See also Steaks
BELGIAN RECIPES: 37 (soup); 127 (rabbit); 133, 137, 139 (vegetables)
Bernese alderman's platter (*Berner Ratsherrenplatte*) 102
Beurre manié 184
Biryani 55
Bisque de crevettes 37
Blandad fruktsoppa 31
Bliny 18
Bobotee 95
Borani garch 154
Bortsch Ukrainian style 26
Boston baked beans 135
Boston brown bread 135
Bouillabaisse 65
Bouquet garni 184
BRAZILIAN RECIPES: 73 (prawn); 160 (pudding)
Bread, Boston brown 135
Bread pudding, coconut 160
BRITISH RECIPES: 10, 11, 12, 16 (starters); 30, 34 (soups); 43 (cheese); 54 (rice); 61, 63 (fish); 107 (chicken); 124 (guinea fowl); 129 (venison); 169, 174 (puddings)
Broccoli cooked in white wine (*Broccolo al vino bianco*) 136
Brownies 180
BULGARIAN RECIPES: 24 (soup); 90 (lamb)
Butter: clarified 184; kneaded 184; *maître d'hôtel* 184; smoked salmon 10
Byefstroganov 82

Cabbage: soup 26; red cabbage 136; stuffed cabbage leaves 136
Cachoombar 152
Cakes: apple and Ricotta 175; apple sauce 176; chocolate 182–3; Malakoff 182; Pavlova 165; poppy-seed 179; potato 145; Sacher 176–7
Calabrian sweet peppers 141
Calvados omelette 162
Camarões com vinho do porto 11
Camote y piña 172
CANADIAN RECIPES: 101 (veal and pork pie); 152 (salad)
Caramel custards 166
Caraway 184
Carbonada criolla 85
Cardamom 184

Carrots: Flemish style 137; *halva* 159
Cassoulet 138
Cauliflower musaka 138
'Caviar' niçoise 11
Cayenne pepper 185
Cerises en kirsch 164
Cerkes tavugu 118
Cheese: baked cheese dreams 42; fondue 41; garnished 42; Welsh rabbit or rarebit 43
Cherries in kirsch 164
Chestnuts: Mont Blanc 167
Chicken: à la King 116; casseroled 118; Circassian 118; Demidoff 114; fried (Mohammed Shah) 113; fried, with walnuts 116; fried (Viennese) 117; grilled, with peanut sauce 109; kebab 108; Kiev 115; Marengo 110; paprika 112; roast, with egg and parsley stuffing 107; spatchcock 107; *tanduri* 109; chicken, prawn, mushroom and quail's egg soup 35; coq au vin 110; Country Captain 117
Chick peas 185
Chicory (*Chicorée*) 139
Chile con carne 86
Chilli pepper 185
CHINESE RECIPES: 35 (soup); 45, 46 (egg); 57 (rice); 116 (chicken)
Chinese wine 185
Chocolate cakes 176–7, 182–3
Chorizo 185
Chowder, clam 36
Chow fan 57
Chutney: cucumber 94; mint 94; onion 94
Cinnamon 185
Circassian chicken 118
Ciuperci mode Cernăuţi 140
Ciuperci cu vin 154
Clams: chowder 36; steamed, with ham and sausages 73
Cocido 84–5
Cock-a-leekie 34
Coconut bread pudding 160
Coconut milk 185; fish in 68
Cod's roe salad, smoked 15
Cola de buey con salsa de almandras 101
Concombres à la crème 139
Consommé madrilène 32
Coq au vin, Alsace-style (*Coq sauté au riesling*) 110
Coquilles St Jacques 75
Coriander 185
Country Captain 117
Court-bouillon 61
Couscous 92
Cozumel 67

Crabs: black 72; devilled 72
Cream: banana 169; rhubarb 173; soured 189; cream of paradise 161
Csirke paprikàs 112
Cucumbers: chutney 94; in cream 139; salad with crabmeat 154
Curd pudding, spiced 168
Curries: egg 47; mutton 94; prawn 74; vegetable 147
Custard, savoury 45
CZECHOSLOVAKIAN RECIPES: 18

Dam alu 144
DANISH RECIPES: 85 (beef); 170 (pudding)
Devils on horseback 16
Dinde en daube 119
Djuvec 97
Dolce di semolina al vino 170
Domates dolmasi 146
Dried-fruit soup, mixed 31
Duck: roast 120–1; with olives 121; wild, roast 121
Dumplings: apple 174; Salzburg 158
DUTCH RECIPES: 56 (rice); 63 (fish); 80 (beef); 128 (hare)

Easter pudding 164
Eggs: baked 44; brocade 167; curry 47; ragoût 44; salad 155; scrambled 46; scrambled, with anchovies 46; savoury custard 45
Emperor Schnitzel 99
Escargots 17

Faisane normande 122
Faraona con i funghi 124
Får i kål 89
Fennel 185
FIJIAN RECIPES: 68 (fish); 169 (pudding)
Fines herbes 185
Fish (*see under* Trout, etc.): braised 65; in coconut milk 68; *Le grand aïoli* 69; pickled 67; soup 35 (Spanish); 37 (Belgian)
Fondue, cheese 41
Forshmak 21
FRENCH RECIPES: 11, 12, 17, 19 (starters); 24, 32, 34, 37 (soups); 44 (egg); 65, 66, 69 (fish); 71 (lobster); 75 (scallops); 87 (beef); 88 (lamb); 97 (pork); 110, 114 (chicken); 119 (turkey); 122 (pheasant); 134, 138, 139, 142, 143, 146, 147 (vegetables); 151 (salad); 162, 164 (puddings)
Ful Sudani 28

Gado-gado 150
Gajjar halva 159
Game marinade 129
Gâteau aux oignons 140
Gazpacho 23
Gehakte Leber 19
GERMAN RECIPES: 15, 21 (starters); 32 (soup); 80 (beef); 86 (meatballs); 125 (partridges); 136 (vegetables); 153 (salad); 178 (cake)
Geschnetzeltes Kalbfleisch 100
Ghee 186
Gigot d'agneau 88
Gingani yaki 83
Ginger 186
Gohst ki kari 94
Gold leaf 189
Goulash, beef 82–3
Gratin dauphinois 142
Gratin savoyard 143
GREEK RECIPE: 15
Grinding mills 186
Grouse, roast 123
Guinea fowl: with mushrooms 124; pie, with grapes 124
Gulai guisado 74
Gulyás 82–3

Halibut in a piquant sauce 67
Hamburg parsley 186
Hare: in lemon with garlic 128; spiced 128
Haricots verts à la lyonnaise 134
Haringsla 63
Harissa 92
Hazepeper 128
Herbs 186
He tao chi ting 116
Herrings: salad 63; meat, herring and potato pie 21
Hollandaise sauce 66
Holsteiner Schnitzel 99
HONG KONG RECIPE: 98
Huancaina sauce 87
Huîtres à la bordelaise 12
HUNGARIAN RECIPES: 24 (soup); 42 (cheese); 46 (egg); 82–3 (goulash); 112 (chicken); 160, 171 (puddings)
Hutspot 80

INDIAN RECIPES: 33 (soup); 46, 47 (egg); 47, 74, 94, 147 (curry); 109, 117 (chicken); 147 (vegetables); 152 (salad)
INDONESIAN RECIPES: 56 (rice); 109 (chicken); 150 (salad)
Ingelegde 67
IRANIAN RECIPES: 154 (salad); 161 (pudding)
Irish stew 90
ISRAELI RECIPES: 19 (starter); 102 (meat loaf); 145 (vegetables)
ITALIAN RECIPES: 51 (rice); 110 (chicken); 121 (duck); 124 (guinea fowl); 128 (hare);

136, 141, 145 (vegetables); 167, 170 (puddings); 175 (cake)

JAMAICAN RECIPE: 72
Jansson's temptation (*Jansson's frestelse*) 142
JAPANESE RECIPES: 14 (starter); 68 (fish); 83 (beef); 154 (salad); 167 (pudding)
JEWISH RECIPES see ISRAELI RECIPES
Jhinga ki kari 74
Jing daahn 45
Judias verdes con salsa de tomate 134

Kartoffelsalat 153
KASHMIRI RECIPE: 144
Kebabs: chicken 108; lamb 88
Kedgeree 54
Klops 102
Königsberg meatballs (*Königsberger Klopse*) 86
Kotlyety Po-Kiyevski 115
Kurczeta nadziewane 107

Labskovs 85
Lamb (*see also* Mutton): braised leg of 88; couscous 92; in egg and lemon sauce 90; on skewers 88; lamb and cabbage casserole 89; stew with prunes 91; meat loaf 102
Latkes 145
Leche 166
Lemon peel, dried 187
Lentil soup 30
Lepre al limone e aglio 128
Liptói körözött 42
Liver: grilled 102; minced 19
Lobscouse 85
Lobster mayonnaise 71
Lobster Newburg 71
Lomnicky suchar 180
Lomo huancaina 87
Lucca eyes (*Lucca-Augen*) 15

Mackerel with a gooseberry sauce 63
Mahallebi 169
Maître d'hôtel butter 184
Malakoff cake (*Malakofftorte*) 182
MALAYSIAN RECIPE: 109
Manzanas asadas 163
Meatballs, Königsberg 86
Meat casserole, baked curried 95
Meat, herring and potato pie 21
Meat loaf 102
Melarancia 175
Meringue apples, baked 163
MEXICAN RECIPES: 28 (soup); 67 (fish); 86 (chile con carne); 118–19 (chicken); 172 (pudding)
MIDDLE EASTERN RECIPES: 152, 153 (salad)

Milagu-tannir 33
Mint chutney 94
Mont Blanc (*Monte Bianco*) 167
MOROCCAN RECIPE: 91
Mulligatawney 33
Munkaczina 152
Murghi Pulao 113
Musakas: aubergine (*Musaca cu patlagele*) 133; cauliflower (*Musaka od karciola*) 138
Mushrooms: casserole 140; salads 154
Mustard 187
Mustard seeds 187
Mutton: curry 94; with rice 55; Irish stew 90

Nasi goreng 56
NEPALESE RECIPES: 155 (salad); 168 (pudding)
NEW ZEALAND RECIPES: 42 (cheese); 165 (cake)
Nishiki-tamago 167
Noisettes de porc aux pruneaux 97
NORTH AFRICAN RECIPE: 92
NORWEGIAN RECIPES: 62 (fish); 89 (lamb); 172 (pudding)

Ochsenschwanzsuppe 32
Oeufs ragoût 44
Oils 187
Omelette normande 162
Onions: chutney 94; salad 152; tart 140
Orange and onion salad 152
Orange peel, dried 187
Ovocný salám 180
Oxtail soup 32
Ox tongue with almond sauce 101
Oysters: angels on horseback 16; in champagne 12; on the half shell 12; Rockefeller 13; with sausages 12

Paella 52
PAKISTANI RECIPES: 55 (rice); 108, 109, 113 (chicken); 159 (pudding)
Palacsinta torta 160
Pancakes: layered 160; Russian 18
Pappadums 187
Paprika chicken 112
Paprika pepper 187
Pariser Schnitzel 99
Partridges with sauerkraut 125
Pashka 164
Pâté, pork and veal (*Pâté de veau et de porc*) 19
Pâté de Noël 101
Patties 20
Pavlova cake 165
Peanuts: peanut sauce 109, 150; peanut soup 28
Pecena divlja plovka 121
Peperoni in padella alla calabrese 141

Pepper 187
Peppers, sweet: Calabrian 141; stuffed 141
PERUVIAN RECIPE: 87
Pheasant Normandy style 122
PHILIPPINE RECIPES: 65 (fish); 97 (pork)
Phool ka achar 155
Pichones estofados 126
Pigeons in a chocolate sauce 126
Pilau 51
Pinenut kernels (*Pinoli*) 188
Pirozhki 20
Plum tart 178
POLISH RECIPES: 107 (chicken); 179, 182–3 (cakes)
Pollo Pibil 118–19
Pommes de terre à la Guignol 143
Poppy-seed cake 179
Pork: fillets with prunes 97; in a sour sauce 97; sweet and sour 98; pork and veal pâté 19; pork and vegetable stew 97
PORTUGUESE RECIPES: 11 (starter); 73 (clams)
Potatoes: fried 142; gratin 142, 143; spiced 144; Jansson's temptation 142; cakes 145; salad 153; with onions 143
Pot-au-feu 34
Pot roast 81
Poulet Demidoff 114
Prawns: bisque 37; crackers 188; curry 74; pie 73; in port 11; stew 74
Prunes: lamb stew with 91; pork with 97; rabbit with 127
Pudim de pão com côco 160
Pumpkin soup 27
Punjene paprike 141

Quarter-of-an-hour soup 35
Quebec veal and pork pie 101
Quiche Lorraine 44

Rabarberkräm 173
Rabbit with prunes, Flemish style 127
Ragoût, egg 44
Raie au beurre noir 65
Ratatouille 147
Rebhühner mit Sauerkraut 125
Red-berry pudding 170
Red pepper sauce 92
Rhubarb cream 173
Rice, types of 50
Rice dishes: fried 56 (Indonesian), 57 (Chinese); Hungarian 171; kedgeree 54; mutton with 55; paella 52; pilau 51; shellfish risotto 51
Risotto con frutti di mare 51
Risted ørret med kremsaus 62
Riz hongroise 171
Rødgrød med fløde 170
Rosewater 188; rosewater pudding 169

Rösti 142
Rotkohl 136
Roux 188
RUMANIAN RECIPES: 133, 140 (vegetables); 154 (salad)
RUSSIAN RECIPES: 18, 20, 21 (starters); 26 (soup); 44 (egg); 82 (beef); 115 (chicken); 149 (salad); 164 (pudding)

Sabzi ki kari 147
Sacher cake (*Sachertorte*) 176–7
Saffron 188
Salad dressing 148
Salade niçoise 151
Salads: aubergine 153; banana 152; cod's roe 15; cucumber, with crabmeat 154; egg 155; herring 63; mushroom 154; spiced onion 152; orange and onion 152; potato 153; Russian 149; tomato, pepper and anchovy 151; Tunisian 155; vegetable, with peanut sauce 150; Waldorf 149
Salmon: poached 61; smoked 10
Salt 188
Salzburg dumplings (*Salzburger Nockerln*) 158
Sardine-stuffed tomatoes 146
Sarma od kiselog 136
Sashimi 14
Sateh 109
Sauces: Alexander Dumas's 71; almond 101; apple 145; gooseberry 63; grape 63; *Hollandaise* 66; huancaina 87; peanut 109, 150; red pepper 92; shoyu 188; soya-bean 189; sweet and sour 98; Russian tomato 21
Sauerbraten 80
Savoury custard 45
Scallops au gratin 75

Schnitzel 99
Semolina and wine pudding 170
Sesame seeds 188
Shchi 26
Shellfish dishes 71–5; risotto 51
Shoyu sauce 188
Shrikund 168
Shrimps, potted 11
Silver leaf 189
Sis kebabi 88
Skate in black butter 65
Snails 17
Sole bonne femme 66
Sopa de cuarto de hore 35
Soups: almond 28; apricot 24; avocado 25; black-bean 29; Bortsch 26; cabbage 26; chicken, prawn, mushroom and quail's egg 35; clam chowder 36; cock-a-leekie 34; *consommé madrilène* 32; fish 35 (Spanish), 37 (Belgian); dried-fruit 31; *Gazpacho* 23; lentil 30; Mulligatawney 33; oxtail 32; peanut 28; *pot-au-feu* 34; prawn *bisque* 37; pumpkin 27; quarter-of-an-hour 35; Vichyssoise 24; walnut 28; yellow-pea 31; yogurt and cucumber 24
SOUTH AFRICAN RECIPES: 67 (fish); 95 (casserole)
SOUTH PACIFIC RECIPE: 74
Soya-bean sauce 189
SPANISH RECIPES: 23, 35 (soups); 52 (rice); 84–5 (stew); 126 (pigeons); 134 (vegetables); 163, 166 (puddings)
Spatchcock, chicken 107
Spices 186
Spinach, sweet-sour (*Spinaci agrodolce*) 145
Steaks: with huancaina sauce 87; Tournedos 87

Stews: beef, with peaches and pears 85; *bouillabaisse* 65; Irish 90; lamb, with prunes 91; pork and vegetable 97; prawn 74; Spanish 84–5
SUDANESE RECIPE: 28
Sugar tart 178
Sunomono 154
Sushi 14
SWEDISH RECIPES: 31 (soups); 142 (vegetables); 173 (pudding)
Sweet potato and pineapple pudding 172
Sweet 'salami' 180
SWISS RECIPES: 41 (cheese); 44 (egg); 100 (veal); 102 (liver etc.); 140, 142 (vegetables); 178 (tart)
Syllabub 169

Tafelspitz 79
Tagine 91
Tanduri chicken 109
Taramasalata 15
Tarator 24
Tarts: onion 140; plum 178; sugar 178
Tempura 68
Terracotta 'bricks' 189
Tilslørete bondepiker 172
Tim suen goo lo yuk 98
Tinolang bangus 65
Tojas szardellaval 46
Tomates farcies aux royans 146
Tomatoes: stuffed 146; sardine-stuffed 146; tomato, pepper and anchovy salad 151; sauce 21; savoury jellied mould 151
Torta de camarão 73
Torta di patate 145
Tort Generala Iwaszkiewicz 182–3
Tort Makowy 179
Tournedos 87
Tourtière 101

Trout in soured cream 62
Tuna fish: 'Caviar' niçoise 11
Tunisian salad 155
Turkey, casseroled 119
TURKISH RECIPES: 51 (rice); 88 (lamb); 118 (chicken); 146 (vegetables); 169 (pudding)

Vanilla pod or bean 189
Vanilla sugar 189
Veal: chopped 100; escalope 99; pork and veal pâté 19; veal and pork pie 101
Vegetables (*see under* Carrots, etc.): curry 147; *ratatouille* 147; salad, with peanut sauce 150
Veiled farm lasses 172
Venison, casserole of 129
Vichyssoise soup 24
Vinegars 189
Vinyegryet 149
VIRGIN ISLANDS RECIPE: 81
Vlaams konijn met pruimen 127

Waldorf salad 149
Walnut soup 28
Waterzooi 37
Welsh rabbit or rarebit 43
Wiener Backhendi 117
Wiener Schnitzel 99
Woon dow chow daahn 46

Yaitsa v chashkye 44
Yakh dar behisht 161
Yellow-pea soup 31
Yogurt 189; yogurt and cucumber soup 24
YUGOSLAVIAN RECIPES: 97 (pork); 121 (duck); 136, 138, 141 (vegetables)

ZIMBABWE RECIPE: 179
Zuckerwähe 178
Zürcher Leberspieseli 102
Zwetschgenkuchen 178
Zwieback 180

Acknowledgments

The producers of the book would like to thank the following for their help:
Carol Bowen and Debbie Clarke for preparing the recipes for photography; Vicki Robinson for proof reading and for the index; Martin Newton for additional design; the restaurant Ikeda, 30 Brook St, London W1 for allowing us to take the photographs on pages 14 and 68; Donald Sproat Ltd, 5 and 10 St John Street, London EC1 for supplying game for the photography; and the following companies for the kind loan of accessories for the photography:
The Craftsmen Potters, Marshall St, London W1
Harvey Nichols, Knightsbridge, London SW1
Inca, 45 Elizabeth St, London SW1
Mag Mell Gallery, 31 Paddington St, London W1
David Mellor, 4 Sloane Square, London SW1
Noritake, 105 Baker St, London W1
The Reject China Shop, Beauchamp Place, London SW3
The Swedish Table, 7 Paddington St, London W1

The Swiss Centre, 2 New Coventry St, London W1
The Storrington Gallery, 42 High St, Storrington, Sussex
The Warren, 48 High St, Storrington, Sussex

Colour illustration acknowledgments
Ardea London Ltd pages **104-5**
John Topham Picture Library (Photo: P. Charpentier) pages **156-7**
Mireille Vautier, Paris pages **48-9**
Zefa Picture Library UK Ltd pages **8-9** (Photo: Ray Halin), **38-9** (Photo: E. M. Bordis), **58-9** (Photo: F. A. H. Bloemendal), **76-7** (Photo: F. Walther), **130-1** (Photo: Dr G. Haasch)

Black and white illustration acknowledgments
Bildarchiv Preussischer Kulturbesitz, Berlin pages **22, 132, 158, 174, 185, 186, 187, 189**
The Fotomas Index pages **78, 158**, endpapers
Sonia Halliday page **50**